Advent,
after Christmas and
Ordinary
after the Epiphany
Sermons

Advent, after Christmas and Ordinary after the Epiphany Sermons

From the Untrained Mind

Robert Tippett

Copyright © 2020

All rights reserved. Produced in the United States of America. No part of this publication may be reproduced, or transmitted, in any form or by any means electronic, mechanical, photocopying, recording, or otherwise, without the prior written permission of the author.

ISBN 978-1-952076-09-1 Paperback
ISBN 978-1-952076-11-4 Epub

Published by Katrina Pearls, LLC

Dedication

This book is dedicated to the memory of my loving wife, who passed away in late 2019. Joycelyn Tippett was a fellow Apostle; my partner in service to God. She was the editor of my books and everything I have written since we married in 2006. She is greatly missed by a world that needs more like her. I am comforted by her continued spiritual presence with me and the insight to this series of books I owe to that presence.

Table of Contents

From the Untrained Mind 9
Seasons Named Advent,
   Christmas and Epiphany 21

Year A
  Advent   53
    First Sunday of Advent 55
    Second Sunday of Advent 63
    Third Sunday of Advent 73
    Fourth Sunday of Advent 81
  Christmas   89
    First Sunday after Christmas 91
    Second Sunday after Christmas 99
  Epiphany   109
    First Sunday after the Epiphany 111
    Second Sunday after the Epiphany 119
    Third Sunday after the Epiphany.................. 127
    Fourth Sunday after the Epiphany 137
    Fifth Sunday after the Epiphany................... 147
    Sixth Sunday after the Epiphany 155
    Seventh Sunday after the Epiphany.............. 165
    Last Sunday after the Epiphany.................... 175

Year B
  Advent   187
    First Sunday of Advent 189
    Second Sunday of Advent 199
    Third Sunday of Advent 207
    Fourth Sunday of Advent 217
  Christmas   227
    First Sunday after Christmas 229

Second Sunday after Christmas	237
Epiphany	251
First Sunday after the Epiphany	253
Second Sunday after the Epiphany	265
Third Sunday after the Epiphany	275
Fourth Sunday after the Epiphany	287
Fifth Sunday after the Epiphany	295
Last Sunday after the Epiphany	307

Year C

Advent	317
First Sunday of Advent	319
Second Sunday of Advent	327
Third Sunday of Advent	337
Fourth Sunday of Advent	349
Christmas	357
First Sunday after Christmas	359
Second Sunday after Christmas	371
Epiphany	387
First Sunday after the Epiphany	389
Second Sunday after the Epiphany	403
Third Sunday after the Epiphany	415
Fourth Sunday after the Epiphany	427
Last Sunday after the Epiphany	437

From the Untrained Mind

The sermons contained in this book are a collection of those offered up on my WordPress blog, entitled "Bus Stop Sermons." This collection of Advent, after Christmas, and after the Epiphany sermons totals thirty-six that have been recreated here, from over one hundred seventy posts there.

I have written all of the posts. The totality of those posts cover every Sunday over a three-year span of time, with the motivation being the schedule of readings from the Holy Bible, as posted by the Episcopal Church's lectionary. Included in that schedule are the four Sundays in the season of Advent, with two Sundays after Christmas and between five and eight Sundays in the after the Epiphany, an Ordinary season. One Sunday after the Epiphany is deemed The Presentation of our Lord or The Presentation of Jesus in the Temple. With the Episcopal lectionary cycle being three years (Years A, B, and C), there are fourteen sermons from Year A, thirteen from Year B and eleven from Year C, which was the reality of scheduling in the 2013-14, 2014-15, and 2015-16 calendar years.

The disclaimer that must be understood is this: None of the words presented here (or any of those still there on WordPress) have ever been spoken out loud before an audience

Advent to after Epiphany Sermons: From the Untrained Mind

of any kind. In that sense, they are imaginary orations.

My imagination stems from the movie *Forest Gump* and the scenes where Forest would be seen at a bus stop telling his life story to strangers. I imagine doing the same, only differently. I see my captive audience as one that is not forced to sit and wait for a bus to come take them some place they desire to be. Instead, they are seeking the goal of heaven, or at least some insight into Christian lessons. Christianity can be seen like a transit system that parallels public transportation.

Those who read my words will then be much like the ones Forest talked with: patiently bored; interested while waiting, but getting to one's destination on a planned schedule being more important; embarrassed by the thought that an imbecile has anything worthwhile to offer; outright rejection with ridicule; or willing recipients of an engaging story. Over the past five years many people have visited at my bus stop. Several have actually liked what they read and a few have felt something I wrote demanded that they make a comment.

Like what Forest shared at his bus stop, everything I offer is designed as a friendly exchange with strangers. It is my story, not the story of anyone else. The commonality of the lectionary readings and how they make me remember my life story makes me share what I saw, what I felt, and what I think needs to happen for me to get on that bus to heaven. After all, everyone going to a bus stop is there for the same purpose, even if the ends of their rides differ. As I am waiting like everyone else, I remember my life with words, based on images passing before my mind's eye. The reality of my memories being expressed can seem like I am looking at someone sitting right next to me on the bus stop bench, talking to him or her. My memories of my life can become so vivid that it seems like I am telling others what to do, when that is not the case at all. I have become God, through the Mind of Christ, telling myself what God wants me to do. It is like preaching to the choir, when preacher and choir are all the same person – a one man band form of church.

The history that had me write imaginary sermons is based on my relationship with my wife. My wife would become an Episcopal priest, but before she made that transformation she was a church-lady Episcopalian. She was raised in that religious denomination as a girl and had a renewed commitment, as to the depth of her involvement with that branch of Christianity, before we met. Thus, I found myself becoming acquainted with that form of religious worship.

I had been unchurched for roughly forty years, prior to being introduced to Episcopalianism. In that time I had not been heathen, in regards to belief in God and Jesus Christ. I had become disenchanted with organized religion at the age of sixteen and repulsed completely by my mid-twenties, due to the televangelism that so blatantly besmirched Christianity as a form of entertainment, with actors crying crocodile tears while they begged for money, promising ministries that offered Jesus theme parks to their paying fans. My first wife was raised a Methodist, and I set aside my dislike for churches on Christmas and Easter and whenever the nearby church offered reasonably priced softball leagues.

For as little as my church involvement had been, I never

stopped feeling that I could talk with God at any time. My childhood religious upbringing had instilled a sense of closeness to God that made prayer be informal and constant. For as wayward as my life would roam, I always felt that God was with me, watching out for me. I never attempted to shame anyone for their religious beliefs or commitments to organized religion; but I rarely felt a need to go to a church, even though I often begged God for His forgiveness after feeling the guilt of sin.

My life changed completely in 2001. I began wandering down the path God had always planned for me to walk, knowing that I would wander the path I had taken to get to that point. Everything in my life began to be seen clearly as purposeful and necessary, grooming me for the road ahead. I suddenly was given an ability to understand the writings of Nostradamus, even though what I was shown was just the grand scope of view. It would take me another seven years to reach the microscope level of detailed awareness.

It was during that time of my life that I began writing books that attempted to explain Nostradamus to the world. It was during that time of my life that I met the woman who would become my second wife. It was during that time of my life that I began regular attendance in Episcopalian churches.

God brought my wife and I together, for the purpose of walking our chosen paths that led to God. My wife had ideas of serving the Episcopalian Church as a priest. I had ideas about telling the world about Nostradamus being an Apostle of Jesus Christ. Once God joined our paths together, my wife had a plan to serve God as an ordained priest

(Episcopalian schooled and metaphysically educated) and I had a plan to serve God as an unordained priest (metaphysically schooled and divinely educated). My wife and I, together, became like two sides of the same coin, as two souls with the same purpose, from different perspectives.

Sunday after Sunday my wife and I sat in a pew and listened to one lame sermon after another. As I read the handout bulletin that had the Scriptural readings printed on them, I was reading them with an ability to understand, based on the similarity of writing style I found in Scripture and that by Nostradamus. By being able to make sense of Nostradamus, the meanings of the Scripture readings became obvious to me. However, as obvious as it was to me, that clarity was not being expressed in pulpit oratory.

Each Sunday my wife and I would discuss this absence of explanation in church. My wife agreed with me. She confessed that she had never known so much was contained in the verses read aloud, as she had never placed great interest in reading the Holy Bible. The more we discussed these matters, the deeper our faith in God became. My wife wanted to fulfill an absence in the Episcopal Church with divine insight and holy knowledge. I wanted to tell the world that every book of the Holy Bible had been written by servants of God, just as Nostradamus had written a most holy book that was unrecognized as such.

My wife and I began a ministry of learning, where we attended bible study classes, lectionary classes, and began visiting a variety of Episcopal churches to listen to a variety of priests giving sermons. We found that the education of Episcopal priests did not allow them to see or promote the meaning that was found hidden in the Holy Scriptures, lingering at the origin language level, while demanding divine assistance in discerning the truth. Instead of the accepting my offerings (while my wife patiently observed and listened), my observations were often rejected outright, questioned as to where I had read such things, and tossed out like dirty bath water when I admitted I had to pedigree, such as a degree from a divinity school.

This was the same rejection I faced when telling others that Nostradamus was misunderstood, due to a mistaken desire to read divine syntax are paraphrased English. My wife, always the smarter of the two of us, saw that being able to attend seminary was dependent on not rocking the boat (or nave). She realized it would be impossible for her to serve God as an Episcopal priest, if the Episcopal Church banned her from seminary school. So, she was discerned, approved, and selected for official education (she already possessed a PhD. From academia), my wife was further down the path from church-lady to ordained priest. Meanwhile, I continued to focus on writing books about Nostradamus, leaving my religious interpretations for another time. Then, it was off to seminary together, my wife the student and me the spouse.

While in seminary, my wife and I lived in an enchanted land that was reminiscent of Disney World. Everywhere we turned there was someone in costume, with the whole campus like a movie set. Visiting for a week allows one to be mesmerized by the pretense, but living there and working there bring about an ugly sense of reality. The seminarians are more often than not college drinking buddies and frat house pranksters. There were few who wanted to talk about their core faith after classes were over.

Robert Tippett

As a way to make three years pass by without screaming, "No! This can't be!" I wrote and self-published four books that explained Nostradamus and his prophecies. My busy work allowed my wife the luxury of not being distracted by my negativity.

In May 2013, my wife graduated from seminary and was soon after ordained as a deacon for the Episcopal Church, Diocese of Mississippi. She interviewed and was offered a medium-sized town parish, which she gladly accepted. In the month before her official start, I began to write sermons that were based on the Episcopal Lectionary, from which my wife's sermons would be based. I determined that I would maintain this program for an entire three-year cycle. I not only had written a sermon for the first Sunday that my wife would officially begin ministering to her new flock, but had several sermons written for the following several Sundays.

I wrote those sermons for myself, but also as discussion material between my wife and me. My wife read every one of my sermons over that three-year cycle (completed in about 32 months). She occasionally used a snippet or a paraphrase from something I had written, never referencing me directly (per my request). Because my sermons were written about my life, which is highly unique (as everyone's life is), they can only be presented by me. Still, my words had an influence on my wife, just as her words influenced me.

I originally posted my sermons on a GoDaddy website, but the expense to maintain it did not match the results. When I ended the idea of having a website for both Nostradamus and Christian writings (separately groups), I created

Advent to after Epiphany Sermons: From the Untrained Mind

free WordPress blogs and reposted them there. When the idea of a blog named "Bus Stop Sermons" came to be, I subtitled that name with "From the Untrained Mind." That subtitle is also placed on this book, with the reasoning being that I have no diploma that gives me an official pulpit, no official approval to lead a flock of followers, and no vast educational history of study that proves me intellectually adept at sermon writing. But, then, I don't believe Jesus, nor the first many waves of true Christian Apostles and Saints had sheepskins from the University of the Holy Spirit.

The subtitle should be obvious, because everything on my "Bus Stop Sermons" blog and everything from there republished here comes from one who has no training in preaching sermons. My wife, and all officially ordained priests, are "trained" to preach and also "trained" to follow ritual and protocol. That education, more than giving theology students the secrets to obtaining the hidden meaning that Holy Scripture contains, "trains" them to do a sermon that is close to being only twelve minutes in length.

As I was rereading the sermons that I presented for Lent, it seems I also tried to keep away from any depth of explanation. By staying on a path that was based on my life and how the readings played out in my life's likes and experiences, I doubt anyone would walk out on me, if I were ordained and had a congregation to which I would preach my messages.

I once had a fellow parishioner confide to me that he became an Episcopalian simply because of the short sermons. He had been of a more 'southern' denomination, which had a preacher present two hour sermons, with everyone expected to stay after church and eat and get to know one another more. My wife also had to conform to those constraints; but like me, she had to prepare her sermons and print them out so she would not go off track and take too long. If I were to ad lib one of my sermons, I imagine I could wander for a couple of hours easy.

When I say "mind," I do that to differentiate the source of my knowledge. It is not from a brain that has studies the Holy Bible for decades. Like my wife had spent little time in her early history reading Scripture, I too was very Biblical illiterate. I knew the basic Bible Stories, but there was so much that the lectionary exposed me to that I barely recognized. When I took a course designed to educate laypersons for ministry, I was in a class of Episcopalians who knew just as little. However, I was better prepared from having studied before going to classes, and often from having written about what the course focused on each week.

The point of an "untrained mind" is not to be a statement about how full of wisdom I am or how deeply I have read books about the meaning of Scripture, without ever getting a diploma (or even a gold star on a report), because there are not many people (if any) that see Scripture like I see it. Just as when I was learning to read the divine language that is ever-present in the writings of Nostradamus, there was no human being who was teaching a course in how to do that. The "untrained mind" is then metaphor for an openness to receive the Spirit of knowledge and speak the truth. While the brain functions in this process, it is not the organ originating higher thoughts. It simply receives them and then I have to figure the meaning by following impulses of insight.

Advent to after Epiphany Sermons: From the Untrained Mind

As a twist of irony, I was raised in an Assembly of God church. That church is known for being in the "Pentecostal" branch of Christian denominations. The name "Pentecostal" is based on the Day of Pentecost, when disciples suddenly began "speaking in tongues." Many times I witnessed people (one woman more than others) stand up in church and begin making sudden, loud, unintelligible repetitive noises, with hands raised high. For some reason, Pentecostals believe making such noises constitutes being filled with the Holy Spirit. As I was sixteen when I voluntarily left that denomination, and had received some "training" in how to become tongue-tied and appear to be "speaking in tongues," I never believed making throat noises served any purpose; but then I was too young and ignorant to really know what was going on in church at that age.

Many years later, while in a church Bible study class, a young man said the unintelligible noises have to then be interpreted by someone who is fluent in "speaking in tongues." Supposedly, after a public display of noise making, someone then stands up and explains, "She said (this or that)." In all my youthful years of attending an Assembly of God church, where regularly the same woman would put on her display, I never heard anyone stand up and explain what she had said. All I heard were whispered "Praise the Lords" and then the pastor would continue where he left off. As such, I can assure everyone that "speaking in tongues" has absolutely nothing to do with making unintelligible noises.

What I do is the reality of "speaking in tongues," where the Greek word "*glōssais*" is translated as "tongues," but also can say "languages." Acts 2 sets up how pilgrims (Jews and Israelites) from many different places marveled at how the Apostles suddenly began "speaking in other languages" (from the Greek "*lalein heterais glōssais*"), due to the Holy Spirit making them speak in the tongues of others. Understanding Nostradamus meant the Holy Spirit made me see the text of Nostradamus (the literal Old French, not the English paraphrases) and be led to see how vast the meaning was. Learning how to read in that divine "tongue" (via the Holy Spirit, as it must be with me to see the truth) means I interpret that which was spoken in tongues. Like the young man said, I prove that to be true. People read Holy Scripture and sit silently, not knowing what has been said (although some whisper "Praise the Lord"). I stand up to interpret what was stated.

I share this history not to make myself seem special. Anyone who devotes him or herself to God and sincerely prays for His guidance, can likewise do what I do. Just remember what I said about seeing only the grand scope when I first started understanding Nostradamus. It took years of dedication and devotion to follow the whispers of insight and see the depth of truth that would be revealed through divine texts.

It then becomes a test at the bus stop. Like the one woman that told Forest, after he said, "Isn't that your bus?" She just waved her hand and said, "There will be another one." She wanted to hear more about what he had to say. That is what a good sermon does. It lights a fire of interest. It burns within one's heart so they cannot ignore the call to "Look deeper" anymore. I pray these sermons will ignite others to be filled with the Holy Spirit and preach their own bus stop sermons.

Advent to after Epiphany Sermons: From the Untrained Mind

Seasons Named Advent, Christmas and Epiphany

The liturgical seasons are not haphazard. They are by design. This is the final book in this series that represents sermons written over a three-year cycle of the Episcopal Lectionary. I began that journey on the sixth Sunday after Pentecost, in Year C. I ended it after the fifth Sunday after Pentecost, in Year C, three years later. I began where I began, so my ending point led to the point of starting. The liturgical calendar has to be seen as flexible like that too.

The liturgical year is a three-year cycle with a beginning point and an ending point. The ending point is Christ the King Sunday, which ends the Ordinary season after Pentecost. The beginning point is Advent. Advent begins a new Church Year.

The point of Advent is to lead one to Christmas, a day that normally does not fall on a Sunday. Christmas Day then leads to the after Christmas period, which is twelve days long. That leads ends with the Epiphany, which also is usually in the middle of a week and not on a Sunday. The Epiphany begins a 'minor' Ordinary season, which leads one to the season of Lent. Thus, there are roughly three

Advent to after Epiphany Sermons: Seasons Named

months of time between the end of the Ordinary after Pentecost part of the calendar, until Lent. Those three seasons are the focus of this book.

What is missed in this yearly view is the whole view of a three-year cycle. Advent marks the beginning of each liturgical calendar year and the Ordinary after Pentecost season marks the ending of each year; but the three liturgical calendar years are not the same. This means one complete cycle has three points of beginning and three point of ending.

Christians should recognize the value of the number three as being more than coincidental. Three is the number of the Trinity, which is Father, Son, and Holy Spirit. Each are viewed as separate, while the mystique of this comes when three combine as one. This should be seen as why the catholic [universal] churches have three years designated to represent the wholeness of a three-year cycle as presented scripturally.

The liturgical calendar that is basically followed by those churches most closely descended from the Church of Rome, which follows an established whole-view of the Holy Bible over a three-year period of time, struggles to explain the symbolism of that division by seasons. The splinter churches that developed after the Reformation maintain the markers of Christmas and Easter, but are free to roam the Holy Bible on their own courses, independently. Thus, the wide gamut of Christians are either raised to follow a church-led pattern of worship or raised to follow a pastor-led one.

This inconsistency in teaching the whole view's logic and

Robert Tippett

reasoning, as metaphor to guide Christians to service to God, means many Christians make the mistake of thinking a church year begins with the birth of Jesus (Christmas) and ends with his death (Easter). That lack of education means more Christians attend church services on those two occasions, while seeing the rest of the year as optional in attendance. That is the mistake of not knowing why churches are a necessity, as deemed by God.

When I was a child, my mother took me to an Assembly of God church four times a week: Tuesday night, Friday night, and Sunday services in the morning and the night. On the drive from our house to the church, we passed by a Methodist church. As Christmas neared each year, that church would set up a large outdoor wreath with four large light-bulb-lit candles. Each week there would be a candle lit, until all four were lit right before Christmas. I asked my mother why the church did that (as ours did not) and she explained the candles marked the four weeks before Christmas.

That was all I understood about the season called Advent. I do not know that my mother told me that Methodist church called their lighting of electric outdoor candles "Advent." All I knew was when I saw that wreath set up, it was counting down the days until Christmas. However, that meant little to my young brain, as I already knew when Christmas was coming. I knew that when the Sears 'Wish Book' arrived in the mail and Norelco began repeating their commercials on television, with Santa riding a cordless shaver in the snow.

Every year since I was a child, the signs of Christmas coming have become more and more commercialized,

Advent to after Epiphany Sermons: Seasons Named

beginning earlier and earlier. Traditionally, the Christmas season was set off by the Macy's Thanksgiving Day parade. A shopping frenzy would begin the following day, which would come to be known as "Black Friday." However, with the advent of the Internet age and the demise of brick and mortar retail stores (such as Macy's), the competition to offer the first sales for Christmas has no firm boundary.

Thanksgiving evening is now open game for shopping in stores. Still, online stores offer big sales for Christmas items, beginning after Halloween. The inflation rate has caused the 'price of Christmas' to go so high, more time is needed to make all the purchases and then begin making the revolving payments to credit cards.

During my working career at United Parcel Service, I developed a deep-seated restriction on the happiness and joy that the Christmas season (Advent) should bring. Thanksgiving marked the great onslaught of 'peak season,' when Christmas packages multiplied like rabbits. The 'free hire' period began in late September, when temporary workers would be seasonal hires and not guaranteed a Teamster-sponsored job after a normal training period (full-time or part-time). New hires meant rookies thrown to the package wolves, with me in management and the one who was chewed out by bosses if anything wrong ever happened - at a time when everything wrong was set up to happen. All year long I dreaded hearing the words "It's Christmas time!"

The reason for the season (actually two seasons rolled into one) is the birth of Jesus. To Christians, especially those in the West, in particular those in the United States of America, birthdays are times when parties are thrown, guests are invited, and presents are given. That idea of gift giving is rooted in the Magi giving Jesus (and Joseph and Mary) the gifts of gold, frankincense and myrrh. However, since Jesus, Joseph and Mary are long gone, Christians now think it is still required that Jesus be given gifts, which in turn are given to all the family members that identify as being believer in Jesus as the Christ child born.

That attitude transforms the meaning of Advent into the mad dash to spend currency (charged on credit cards) on gifts, which are then wrapped and hidden away until the time accepted as when the first gifts were given to baby Jesus. Some seem to believe the Magi came at night, so one present is allowed to be opened on Christmas Eve. Still, the majority wait until the first child jumps on a parent's chest at 5:45 AM, screaming, "Wake up! It's Christmas!"

For as much as Advent has degenerated into the time for gathering possessions and making things neatly presentable, the season after Christmas is when there is a mess of new toys and gadgets all around, none having found a place (or a time) to be stored away. All the wrapping paper becomes large plastic bags of trash set by the curb. Few realize the Twelve Days of Christmas come after Christmas, not before. Fewer think the Magi came by the manger on January 6, nearly two weeks after Jesus was born on December 25. Fewer still have any idea of what an Epiphany means.

The problem with this mindset is all the focus is placed on Jesus. Yes. Jesus was born, he lived and died. His life is important for all Christians to know. However, to limit God to only one Son becomes the sin of playing a god on earth.

Advent to after Epiphany Sermons: Seasons Named

That dawning of awareness says, "You must become the resurrection of Jesus." When that becomes your understanding, then the elders who were divinely inspired to create a three-year lectionary cycle [i.e.: Apostles; Saints] did so with everything set up to become your celebration of the birth of Christ within your body of flesh. It becomes a reflection of your personal Epiphany, realizing God's Holy Spirit is holding you up and projecting your actions forward.

That divine presence is due to your death of self-ego and your resurrection as the Son of God. With that marriage of your soul to God, you then leave the warmth of a personalized church pew and you go out into the world preaching the Gospel. In your Year A, you come to know the Father. In your Year B, you come to know the Son. In your Year C, you come to know the Holy Spirit. After a complete cycle of God within you, then you are a full-fledged Saint walking the face of the earth.

By understanding that, it becomes clear that the Holy Bible is a reflection of three things: the Prophecy of the <u>Coming of Christ</u>; the Coming of Christ; and the Continued Coming of Christ. That is the framework for the Trinity in writing. Everything begins with Prophecy and that is the true meaning of Advent.

A Season Named Advent

The word "advent" is defined as such: "The coming or arrival of something or someone that is important or worthy of note." (The Free Dictionary by Farlex, utilizing American Heritage Dictionary) The etymology is from the

Latin "*adventus*," from the Old French "*advenir*," meaning "arrival to come." The usage implies an anticipation or expectation that lies in the future.

When one realizes that the Advent of Jesus was long before his coming, based on the Prophets of the Old Testament, with even the angel that foretold Joseph and Mary of a coming miracle birth, that was longer than four Sundays. Mary's pregnancy would have been nine months. This means the period of time that is roughly one month needs to be analyzed symbolically.

For weeks equates to one-thirteenth of a year. If one were to take the average lifespan of a normal American (76), then the period of Advent equates to 9.88 years or roughly a decade. This means the symbolism of the Advent is as a period of necessary preparation prior to an expected arrival.

In the case that one wants to be 'pregnant' with God's child, the expectation of Christmas might not bring that gift under the tree. Many married couple try to get pregnant and fail, which a repeated theme in the Holy Bible. This means ten years of trying might be one's expectation, where not getting your wish the first time failure arises is no reason to quit trying.

A biblical example is that of Jacob working for Laban for seven years, expecting Rachel, only to be rewarded with Leah. Because his expectations had not been met, Jacob then worked for Laban seven more years to finally get the woman of his dreams. With Jacob living to be 147 years of age, fourteen years equates to roughly one-tenth of his life. That means Jacob's 'Advent' was fourteen years long. However, he had no clue what that period of waiting meant at that stage of his life.

The season reflected by Advent occurs before Christmas, meaning rebirth follows a period of birth into a flawed human body. A flawed human body is not born from its mother's womb, as it is a product of the world over a number of years. A baby is born without the maturity of human sexuality, such that a child reaches maturity at puberty. Thus, children are designated as neuter gender until that time "arrives" in their lives.

The "advent" of puberty is a known event in everyone's life. It is when the age of innocence is lost. In that way, the Israelites were known as the "children of God" when Moses led them out of the womb of Egypt and to the verge of their "promised" land. That "promise" was the "Advent" of adulthood. The same loss of innocence that the maturity of land ownership gave them made them responsible for what they did to maintain their gift of land.

This makes Advent be synonymous with the same responsibility for one's own soul, after one has entered the world as self-sufficient. The promise of maturity in body, however, does not equate to the prophecy of the coming of Jesus Christ. This is where one's upbringing plays a role as to when a mature child is heading to that Advent.

Christian parents will raise their children with a sense of right and wrong, which is a basic teaching of the religious practices performed by Christian denominations. In this process, a child will be baptized by water, either the Christening of an infant or the dunking of a youth in a baptismal pool. That ritual act symbolically announces to the child that its soul is promised to God. Still, that is not a prophecy of one's Advent, as not every child will mature to a coming of Christ.

The act of baptism by water can be seen as the parable told by Jesus about the ten virgins. All were deemed bridesmaids, as they had been promised in marriage to God, the bridegroom. Of those ten, half would be deemed foolish, because they did not do the necessary work to prepare for their true Advent.

This becomes the meaning of Paul's encouragement to "mature in Christ." The acts required to reach a personal Advent are the acts that demand one keep a vessel of oil for one's lamp. The lamp is symbolic of one's baptism by water, such that someone else gave a child (or virgin) the expectation of salvation (the light that avoids the outer darkness). The oil is the works of faith, which stem from having been taught the morals of religion. Thus, it is up to the mature person (again a virgin, as that denotes puberty having been reached) to maintain a commitment to God, which is the price paid for vigilance, to stay awake.

In the parable told by Jesus about the Prodigal Son, we see a child reaching puberty in the younger son demanding his share of inheritance. The son then left home and went out on his own into the world. There, the son found the world preys on innocent lambs, stripping them bare of morals and religious values, as those are only the outer clothing worn by human adults. That makes the memories of the son, recalling how even the slaves were treated well by his father, was an inner value instilled before he matured and left home on his own. His longing to return home was his inner teaching reminding him he had lost the way, which called to him through his conscience to mature in Christ.

When the prodigal son left the world of sin and walked the road back home to his father's house, he began his Advent. As such, many children who are raised by parents that do nothing to give their children even empty lamps, where they are left to their own wiles to figure out how to put oil in them so light shines, they are not left out of this opportunity. This is where one who has indeed matured in Christ, who experienced Christ coming AND continues that promise as Jesus Christ reborn, the children that grow into lost and forsaken adults (Gentiles) are given lamps, filled with oil, by the servants of God (His wives).

Once an adult has been given this hope for the future, they become like the prodigal son and go out on their own, leaving the Saint he or she encountered behind. It was to such adults given the lamps of salvation by Apostles that the epistles of the Saints were written. The letters of Peter, Paul, James and John were the gifts of oil to keep the light burning in those lamps. Still, the engagement promise of a virgin or bridesmaid leads one to the world of sin - the marketplace where the wise virgins told the foolish virgins to go, as if salvation can be bought.

To fully commit to God as His wife means entering a personal Advent, which comes from knowing the darkness of the world. Without knowing the value of the oil in the lamp, without fighting swine for slop during a famine, one will foolishly think salvation is given at birth, because someone told him or her that salvation was assured by water sprinkles. Thus, the true meaning of Advent is when one does like the prodigal son and surrenders one's right to selfishness and walks the road back home to the father's house alone, reduced in ego to the level of complete servitude.

It is at that time in one's life when one happily lights the candles of true promise, which are symbolized in the Advent wreath. The four Sundays might turn into ten years of patience and waiting on the Father. The four Sundays might be like Jacob finding out he needs to bargain for another seven years of labors before his true love is his. The four Sundays might just be four minutes of sacrifice during wartime, which seems like an eternity. The length of time is the last thing one dwells upon, when one has entered a personal Advent, because it is the promise within one's heart that makes all the work be worth the wait.

A Season Named Christmas

The etymology of the word "Christmas," according to Webster's Dictionary is "Middle English *Christemasse*, from Old English *Cristes mæsse*, literally, Christ's mass." While that history leads one to intuit the word "mass" as (capitalized) meaning a Eucharistic rite, where wafers and wine are served - thus a Mass in honor of Christ - that becomes a flawed circular argument that denies the word "mass" (non-capitalized) existed before Christians began honoring Christ in Eucharistic ritual and the question was raised, "What do we call this ritual?" One must realize the truth of a Christ Mass.

Again referring to Webster's for information about the history of the word "mass," their website explains a secondary noun etymology as such: "Middle English *masse*, from Anglo-French, from Latin *massa*, from Greek *maza*; akin to Greek *massein* to knead — more at MINGLE." In that sense, the word "mass" becomes synonymous with "accumulate, build-up, concentrate, and gather," as "amass." (Webster's) Still, that understanding needs to be grasped as how Roman Catholics began to apply "mass" to Christ.

In an article posted online by the website *Aleteia*, entitled "Why do Catholics call their main church services "Mass"?", the author[1] explained: "The English word "Mass" comes from the Latin word *missa*, which means to be "sent." He then added, "The word is used during the conclusion of the celebration, when the priest or deacon says in Latin, *Ite, missa est.* The literal translation of that phrase is, "Go, it has been sent.""

In that article, Thomas Aquinas was quoted as explaining the usage of "*Ite, missa est*" as the dismissal in a church service. Thomas stated in his work *Suma Theologiae*, "the victim [Jesus] has been sent to God through the angel, so that it may be accepted by God." As a "dismissal" at a standard "Mass," is a priest's announcement that God has received His Son and knows the followers of the Son are continuing the Spirit. From that awareness, the author summarized the use of "Mass" means, "a starting-point for a lifelong journey of Christian witness" and so Christians "may be beacons of light, set on a hill for all to see."[2]

That fits the scenario I presented about the Advent being when one has been given a lamp as a bridesmaid of God, by which the light of Christ can shine. Because the body of Jesus has been received by the Father, the beacon of light that Jesus of Nazareth was then continues to shine through the bodies of flesh, whose souls have been engaged to God. Upon the completion of that engagement (the Advent),

---

[1] Philip Kosloski, published on 8/24/2017.
[2] Ibid

then the coming of Christ (Christmas) is the rebirth of the Son into new mature flesh (regardless on the human gender one's flesh beholds).

This means "Christmas" is a perfectly chosen name for a recognition and celebration of the coming of Christ. It is not personal because God sent His Son into the world as one baby, named Jesus. If that were to be the case, then everyone would recognize December 25 each year as "Jesusmas." The "Christ" ("*Christos* "), while it is the Greek replacement word for "Messiah" ("*mashiach* "), is still a title that means "the Anointed one."

Certainly, Jesus was "Anointed" by God at birth, but the purpose of the true Apostles who were divinely inspired to create a lectionary cycle that fit each true Christian (also an Apostle-Saint) was **not** to remember when baby Jesus was brought into the world. It was to designate one day each year for each true **Christ**ian to commemorate the day he or she was reborn as Jesus Christ. While Jesus was the prototype of the Christ, he was not "Christian," as he was a Jew. Therefore, Christmas must be seen as a time for Christians to be recognized, as those who have individually become reborn as Jesus Christ.

As for that day, historians and scholars (usually those not divinely inspired) will argue and propose theories as to why December 25 is recognized as the birthday of Jesus. Some will conject that the date was chosen by Roman Church leaders, as a way to take advantage of the pagan recognition of the Winter festival. Some will offer that there is evidence Jesus actually could have been born on that day. Since there is no way to prove their conjecture and theories, the people calling themselves Christians do not worry

Advent to after Epiphany Sermons: Seasons Named

themselves with such facts; they just enjoy the celebration of giving gifts to one another.

When one realizes the season of Christmas (twelve days long, so either one or two Sundays[3]) is to recognize one's own personal birth of Jesus Christ within, then one realizes December 25 is not a date that accurately states when one began to speak in foreign tongues, like the first Apostles did on Pentecost Sunday. Understanding that makes one able to see the logic used by the first organizing Saints of Christianity, who determined a symbolic date for this personal recognition.

I have just recently published a book that has its roots in a dawning (a divine inspiration) that made me realize the Son of God would not be born by chance, or haphazardly. God's Son would be born in the daytime, not at night. God's Son would be born when the days were long, not short. Finally, God's Son would be born on a Sabbath, not any other day deemed less holy. That dawning came to me as Christmas was nearing, which makes more sense as to why the recognition of the birth of the Christ-child comes in winter.

The Winter Solstice occurs each year in December, either on the 21st or 22nd. When that event occurs, the Northern Hemisphere experiences the longest night. According to what I have heard stated about the pagan worship of Sol (the Roman god representative of the sun), for three days the sun is seen as dead, because it appears to be motionless in the sky. After three days of death, it beings to rise and

---

[3] When Christmas falls on a Sunday, it is called Christmas Day. The following Sunday is then always January 1 or New Year's Day. Instead of calling this "the First Sunday after Christmas," it is called "The Holy Name Sunday." This occurs in a cycle of 6-5-6-11 years, due to Leap Years.

the days become longer. This becomes a time to celebrate that return promise of life returning to the land. Of this ancient belief, the Wikipedia article entitled "Winter solstice" says, "direct observation of the solstice by amateurs is impossible because the sun moves too slowly or appears to stand still (the meaning of "solstice")."

The symbolism of three days dead can certainly be applied to the time Jesus was hanging dead on the cross, taken down and prepared for burial, and his body being placed in the tomb of Joseph of Arimathea. That Easter event of death can then be attributed to a timing that is parallel to the relationship the sun [light] has to the earth [humanity], when the sun is at its nadir that reflects when the light of life has left the world. That symbolism must then be made personal, as reflecting the darkest depths of one's life reaching the point of despair makes giving up on the world, as offering any redeeming values, (death) become the only option.

Because Christmas is not recognized on the Winter Solstice, but three days later (Christmas Eve - Christmas Day), the originating Saints that determined that date did so as a way of symbolically stating the resurrection of Easter Sunday. That then means that baby Jesus is not born each year; he is risen each year. The personalization for each true Christian is then the date that he or she was reborn in his name.

Perhaps, to better grasp this symbolism, so the focus is not on the actual Jesus but the individual who has allowed God to place His Son within his or her flesh, one needs to take one's eyes off Jesus and place them on Lazarus, the brother of Mary and Martha. The news of his illness was sent to

Jesus, prior to his death. That becomes symbolic of seeing the light of the sun going lower and lower in the sky. For Jesus to say, "Lazarus is only sleeping," that is symbolic of the sun reaching its nadir and Lazarus had indeed died. Then, after Lazarus died on the day the news was delivered to him, Jesus returned to Bethany three days later. When sorrow ruled that day, Jesus spoke, "Lazarus! Come out!" and Lazarus was alive again. The sun was again rising in the sky, which becomes symbolic of that event.

On a personal level **You** become synonymous with Lazarus. The weight of the world is the disease you have come down with. Your personal nadir or Winter Solstice is when you finally die of self-ego, realizing there is nothing of value you can offer the world and the world offers you no hope. At that depth of despair, you send out a call to Jesus to come save you; but Jesus will not come before your ego has completely died. The symbolism of December 25th is then when Jesus returns to where your **self** has been lain. When Jesus cries out to you, "Come out!" then that becomes your rebirth, your Christmas.

What needs to be grasped is the same death and resurrection would happen to Jesus. Jesus was alive in a body of flesh but alive in the flesh means death, unless one has married one's soul to God. When Jesus calls out, "Come out!" he is there for the one who has truly given up his or her self-ego and died a figurative death. The resurrection is not caused by Jesus, but by God. Just as God raised Jesus, so too did God raise Lazarus. Only God can resurrect a dead mortal in the flesh to everlasting life. Jesus came to become Lazarus, even though Jesus remained in his body as Jesus. Lazarus became Jesus reborn in new flesh, just as Jesus becomes reborn in the flesh of **all** true Christians.

When one is able to see the meaning behind Christmas as being when God sent His Son into each true Christian, with the rebirth being the equivalent of Easter Sunday, then one needs to look at the symbolism of the Twelve Days of Christmas, as that is the season that follows that rebirth. To see that truth, one needs to then look at the forty days the risen Jesus remained with his disciples.

According to John, "Jesus did many other things as well [during his time risen]. If every one of them were written down, I suppose that even the whole world would not have room for the books that would be written." To sum that up as the follow-up to having been reborn as Jesus Christ, the time between Christmas and the Epiphany is one of learning.

In a couple of sermons within this book is an explanation of the symbolism that is the Twelve Days of Christmas. I will not go over that here, but know each of the twelve days symbolizes, in number, the whole scope of learning that is the foundation of Christianity. The Holy Bible becomes the cornerstone that is Jesus Christ, built into every true Christian.

If one were to use the percentage of a normal lifespan, such that the four weeks of Advent equates to thirteen percent of one's life (9.88 years), the twelve days is relative to about two and a half years. That figure can be rounded up into Year A, plus Year B, plus the half of a year that is Advent to Pentecost; or, a cycle of the Father, the Son, and the Holy Spirit. Therefore, the season after Christmas becomes a **real** thirst for knowledge that comes through the lectionary schedule; and, this is personally motivated, when one is no longer content with listening and doing nothing.

The twelve days also must be seen as a number chosen by the original Saints that established the lectionary cycle. In my research for the book *The Star of Bethlehem: The Timing of the Life of Jesus* I determined the dates of Jesus' birth and the Magi's arrival in Bethlehem. There was not a twelve-day time lapse between those two events. Before I can to that divine enlightenment, no one had any proof that there was twelve days between the two. It is, therefore, a manufactured number of days, just as December 25 is a symbolic date on the calendar. Thus, twelve becomes a number that can reflect a cycle of the sun through the zodiac, or a year's time, while also being a repeated theme in the Holy Bible, when the number twelve appears.

I see the symbolism of the twelve days after Christmas as a time of completion. That was the age of Jesus when he was left behind in the Temple. With the symbolism of Christmas being the event in one's life, when God has sent His Son into a new body of flesh, the twelve days symbolizes a maturity of that presence, which causes one so filled with the Holy Spirit to continuously acts in ways that please God. The length of time it takes for one to reach the Epiphany is dependent on the individual's rate of learning and God's judgment as to when the individual is prepared to take on more responsibility.

A Season Named Epiphany

The word "epiphany" [not capitalized] is defined as: "a sudden, intuitive perception of or insight into the reality or essential meaning of something, usually initiated by some simple, homely, or commonplace occurrence or experience." (Dictionary.com) The same source defines the capitalized word as: "a Christian festival, observed on January 6, commemorating the manifestation of Christ to the gentiles in the persons of the Magi; Twelfth-day." These two definitions do not seem to mesh smoothly, which is why most Christians do not realize the symbolism of this name.

Part of the confusion, I believe, is the improper placing of this name on the life of Jesus. It should be placed on each individual true Christian. The arrival of the Magi must not be misconstrued as "Gentiles" coming before Jesus, because the Magi were most-holy priests that had been led by God to anoint a newborn king. One should presume they were of Judaic descent, who remained in Babylon, under Persian control. In that sense, the magi should be seen like Daniel and Ruth, not as Gentiles.

This makes baby Jesus, Mary and Joseph in no way be the recipients of sudden insight from an experience that would have to be deemed far from commonplace. The holy parents had both been told by the angel Gabriel that a most-holy child was coming; so, to have priests from the east showing up with symbolic gifts of coronation would have seemed like **more** of the works of God. Jesus did not experience awe by the experience; so, that leaves that definition to be applied to the individual Christian, who after being born as the resurrection of Jesus Christ is then anointed with the gifts of the Holy Spirit.

Imagine you spending two and a half to three years delving deeply into the lectionary readings, Sunday by Sunday. See yourself as becoming involved with Bible Studies classes and filled with a desire to discuss the readings with other Christians. If you spent that much time in your adult life searching, throughout the weeks and not just on Sunday, the Lord sees that desire coming from your heart. Your brain takes time to soften the barriers it has previously placed around your heart. After your commitment to marriage is shown through the symbolic time called "after Christmas" (the Twelve Days), God sends His 'wise men' to anoint you with the gifts of His Holy Spirit. The Christ King has then arrived in you.

A personal day of Epiphany comes when you hear an inner voice leading you to go beyond all the opinions written in books and published on blogs. Your Epiphany is when you clearly see what others take for granted as some misconstruction of the truth. Your Epiphany comes when you suddenly have intuitive perception about the meaning of Scripture.

That is the Epiphany of realizing Scripture is written in a foreign tongue [Greek or Hebrew], which you have never learned; but you suddenly start looking up the original languages, because you are led by the Holy Spirit to speak in tongues you were never taught to know. Your Epiphany is to suddenly intuit you are doing religious things in ways you had never done before.

Certainly, one can see how an Epiphany becomes relative to the transformation of the disciples into Apostles or Saints. They had spent three years of their lives in complete attendance to the needs and teachings of Jesus, their Master and Rabbi. They had spent their "lectionary cycle" proving their love and devotion to God, as their Christmas season of learning. Then, as Jesus died and was buried, they too went 'underground,' hiding themselves in shame - their nadir. However, when Jesus was risen and stood where they hid, then they were given the gift of the presence of Jesus Christ among them.

That day when Jesus suddenly appeared inside the locked door of an upstairs room, the disciples had the Epiphany of the resurrection. That was not and ending but a beginning, a new direction begun in their lives. That event ended their time as disciples by their receipt of the Holy Spirit - marriage of their souls to God - leading them to a time of intense training. That Easter Sunday evening event meant a season began that could only come after that Epiphany.

While it is easy to see the transformation of the disciples fitting the event of an Epiphany, it is not as clear how their season after the Epiphany evolved. This is where Christians today are less like the disciples who knew Jesus in the flesh and more like Paul. Paul's Epiphany occurred after he encountered Jesus Christ, who appeared suddenly as a light from heaven, asking Paul, "Saul, Saul, why do you persecute me?" It was then that Paul (then known as Saul) went blind for three days - his Easter death of self - his pre-Christmas nadir.

That transformation, where Saul would be renamed as Paul, is parallel to the Epiphany Jacob had, when he wrestled with an unnamed figure all night long. The one Jacob wrestled with was himself. He fought for control of his own ego and self-will. When morning came, Jacob's hip became lame, a source of eternal pain, which became a permanent reminder to Jacob of the limitations one's ego places on one's soul. Jacob was then told his name would be changed to Israel, "because you have struggled with God and with humans and have overcome." (Genesis 32:28)

Advent to after Epiphany Sermons: Seasons Named

In both the cases of Israel and Paul, their Epiphanies became events that marked them as priests of God. While not clearly stated, Israel would become the one who would become Moses-like to his children and their children's children. The foundations of the religion that would become more clearly developed through Moses was instilled within the Israelite people, making them observe different rituals and teachings than the other people of the world [Egypt]. Thus, the transformation of the Epiphany is from follower to leader, from disciple to rabbi, from unsaved soul to a soul married to God, reborn as His Son (regardless of one's human gender).

This leads to the meaning of the after the Epiphany season. It becomes synonymous with the ministry of Apostles, with the caveat being it is not the full-fledged ministry that comes after the Pentecost. This needs explaining.

Each year in the Church calendar there ate two Ordinary seasons. One is the Ordinary after Pentecost season (the half-year period of ministry) and the other is the Ordinary after the Epiphany season (the five to eight weeks of ministry). The use of the capitalized word "Ordinary" means "to be Ordained," even though the weeks of each season is listed as numbered Sundays after an event. The Episcopal Church has someone in each diocese who goes by the title "Canon of the Ordinary," which means he is the guide for all who have been Ordained into ministry by the Episcopal Church diocese.

According to the Church, the Ordinary after the Epiphany season is not truly considered "Ordinary," simply because a priest can only be Ordained one time (like only one baptism). This rejection of the after Epiphany season as not being truly Ordinary says the after the Epiphany season is like a trial run. In seminary terms, it is called a seminarian's Curricular Practical Training (CPT). In the disciples of Jesus terms, it was when his disciples were sent out with talents of the Holy Spirit, on a temporary basis.

This means the event of the Epiphany - a personal experience of becoming God's bride - is followed by the wonders of learning the talents given by the Holy Spirit (the symbolism of the Magi bearing the gifts of anointment), although learning how to use those talents is not a full-fledged ministry assignment. It is when one must take the birth of Jesus Christ within one's soul and use that presence to come to know God as His Son reborn.

To be able to see one's personal experience of the gifts of God's Holy Spirit, of which Paul listed, is to practice those gifts as often as possible. Just like a child receives his or her new gifts at Christmas, the excitement is followed by the delight of actually putting those new gifts to work. No one in his or her right mind would receive a desired gift and simply say, "That's nice. I'll just wrap it back up and keep it as a memory." Gifts received are meant to be put to use.

This concept is then the explanation of the after the Epiphany season, which ends on *Mardi Gras*, or Fat Tuesday. This fattening is intended to be in preparation for the testing that comes during the season (forty days) of Lent. Thus, the purpose of the period of time after the Epiphany is to hone the skills of the Holy Spirit's gifts, so one can pass the test of fasting.

The final two weeks of the season after the Epiphany is referred to (by some) as Carnival. This is when King Cakes are popular. The etymology of the word "carnival" is from the Late Lain "*carne levare*," which means "remove meat." According to the Wikipedia article on "Carnival," it states: "The word *carne* may also be translated as flesh, producing "a farewell to the flesh " A farewell to the flesh means the enhancement of a soul, so it is ready to do battle with Satan, over control of one's flesh. Fat Tuesday, or Shrove Tuesday, is on the eve of Ash Wednesday, when one's body of flesh has been reduced to ash, a figurative death of the flesh's control over the soul.

This means the true testing of one's rebirth as Jesus Christ is when one has come to the point of complete sacrifice of self-ego and self-will, as an obedient wife of the Father, who then fully gives birth to His Son. All of the temptations of the world - Satan's domain - can then easily be combated by Scripture (the gifts of prophecy and understanding prophecy). A successful testing in this wilderness of the soul is the ability to command Satan to "Get behind me," which is not the individual speaking but the Lord.

It should be understood that Satan enters this period of learning, when new Christians practice using the gifts of the Holy Spirit. As such, pagan souls hear the word "Carnival" and interpret it as meaning "a phrase embraced by certain carnival celebrants to embolden the festival's carefree spirit." (Wikipedia article on "Carnival") A carefree spirit is that of a lost soul and lost souls will try to persuade those newly resurrected as Jesus Christ to just pretend to be Jesus, just as they do. That is the symbolism of wearing masks that hide the true self underneath, during *Mardi Gras*.

The parallel to be seen here comes on the eve of Sainthood,

when All Hallows Eve become the pagan worship of the dead, when the masks of Halloween confuse the sanctity of the symbolism. *Mardi Gras*, as a concluding event in Carnival, is likewise a distraction from the true purpose of fattening. Instead of fattening on the Word of God and His talents given, it becomes a time to lust in debauchery, so one's flesh will be satiated with sin until a return to wickedness afterwards. A momentary sacrifice of one thing (during Lent) then will symbolize a false commitment to God as one's husband.

Conclusion

The sermons contained in this collection come from the Advent seasons of 2013 to 2015. The after Christmas sermons were those that bridged 2013 and 2014, 2014 and 2015, and 2015 and 2016. The sermons from the Sundays after the Epiphany were written in the years 2014 to 2016. Those actual dates can be felt in the words, where I speak of the current events of those times. That is not why I publish this book of sermons; nor is it why I published any of the books in this series, which all stem from those calendar years.

The subtitle of this series is "From the Untrained Mind." I am that untrained minister, fictitiously preaching at a bus stop, because I have no degree from a seminary or theological school, which goes along with a paid job at some church that is owned and operated by a religious organization. That is the fundamental meaning of this trilogy of seasons that spread over (on average) twelve weeks each year, or almost a quarter of a year's time.

In all of my pretense of speaking to a congregation, which was modeled in my mind's eye as that where my wife was a parish priest, I was acting like a child who woke up on Christmas morning and unwrapped a gift from God Almighty that held in it the *Book of Heaven: How to be a Holy Minister*. For three year's time, through the Years A. B, and C of the Episcopal Lectionary, I preached. Like a child pretending to be a grown-up, my wife read every one of my sermons, like a good mother encouraging her child. Because I publicly published them on my WordPress blog, others read them too; and, over time I amassed some followers - my congregation - my riders waiting at my bus stop.

I attended seminary with my wife, as a spouse, not a student. After she graduated and was Ordained, I felt the need to write sermons, just as my wife would be needing to do. I had been called to serve God in a different way than my wife, a calling that I had responded favorably to a dozen years prior. Most of that time I wrote about the meaning of Nostradamus, who I was led to see as an Apostle in the name of Jesus Christ. While my wife was in seminary, I began to spend more and more time writing about the meaning of Scripture; but, I had basically left the preaching and teaching on that topic to the professionals.

When I wrote my first sermon in my private, personal commitment to God, it was about the meaning of the reading selections for the Sixth Sunday after Pentecost, in Year C. By the time Advent came around that same calendar year, it initiated a cycle change, to Year A. However, **MY** Advent began during the Pentecost season.

This is how the cycle of named seasons in the Churches that are Catholic-based (Universal) are symbolic for personal growth and development in service to the Lord God.

Everyone who personally experiences the childbirth of Mary, when a most holy child came into the world, is truly a Christian. The reason for the seasons is **not** to remember that Jesus was born into the world, lived in the world, died in the world, resurrected into the world, and ascended from the world to sit by the Father's right hand. The reason is to become Jesus Christ returned into the world.

Charles Schultz, the *Peanuts* cartoonist who was known to draw Christian-themed characters, much like C. S. Lewis used words to make similar symbolic statements, drew a four-frame cartoon that sums up what is learned by the repetition of the three liturgical years. Linus told Charlie Brown he had read a book, which was about a man, who lived and died. The end. Charlie Brown, chin in hands as he leaned on the stone wall, said, "Gee. It makes it feel like you knew the man."

The point of the lectionary cycle is to **deeply feel** you know Jesus, because you have become him reborn. You must desire to read his book because you love God with all your heart. Your love of God has become a marriage that blends your soul with the Holy Spirit, so all your soul then belongs to God. Your love of God has evolved your human brain into the Mind of Christ, so you love God with all your mind. That is the deep insight that must come from a four-frame *Peanuts* cartoon.

Your Advent comes whenever you marry God. Your Christmas comes whenever God elevates your soul to that of His Son. Your Epiphany is when the Jesus within has been crowned and your body, it then anointed as the Christ reborn. Your getting fat off the talents that God feeds your season after the Epiphany.

In my sermons, you will read the me of five to seven years ago writing. You will notice that each of my sermons is personal to me, pulling from my life experiences, my likes and my memories. I do not think I am unique, so my life can somehow reflect upon your life; but all God's children are different. The point of anyone who preaches from the truth of Christ within is not to tell anyone, "Be like me." Every time someone hears a priest, minister, pastor, or rabbi give the impression, "Be like Jesus," the reality is that is an impossibility. Self-will cannot make one Jesus Christ resurrected. Without first marrying God and becoming completely subservient to His Will, one will only experience failure trying to be like Jesus. That is the meaning of **all** one's heart, mind and soul being the prerequisite.

I have written sermons for a complete three-year lectionary cycle. I have posted interpretations of Scripture on the Internet for many years. I have self-published over ten books that have Christian themes. However, the way God uses me is not the model that anyone else needs to follow.

The model is found in the Gospels and Epistles, in the Old Testament Psalms and Prophets. It is to fully submit to God and stop trying to remain you. You have to become Jesus resurrected and for that to ever happen, you must marry God.

A personal Advent does not come if the invitation sent by the King to attend His Son's wedding is tossed away and his servants persecuted to death. It does not happen if you just show up dressed as you (not Jesus Christ) at the wedding banquet of Heaven. When Jesus said, "Many are called, few are chosen," the truth of that statement says,

"You have been called," if you call yourself a Christian. However, if you are not now, presently, serving God as a minister to those who seek God in their lives, then **You** have not chosen that service to the Father.

The whole three-year lectionary cycle becomes like a by-stander watching a merry-go-round. In order to grab the brass ring, you have to get on the ride. Once you get on, you never want to get off. Advent is then purchasing a ticket and getting in line, filled with the anticipation of a child knowing Christmas is coming. Christmas is then selecting the horse or carriage that you will sit upon, which will reflect how God will use you. Epiphany is taking the brass ring as you cycle by and the time after the Epiphany is the joy of knowing you have to tell others how wonderful this merry-go-round is.

It is my hope, through making these sermons available for public consumption, that you will read the full list of Scriptural readings, from which each sermon comes. The readings are the sources that influences my words; but the length of a sermon can only be a nibble that is intended to be served as an invitation to marry God. That engagement comes from learning what a potential husband offers a bride-to-be. In that sense, each sermon offered is like a wafer passed out by a priest at an Episcopal church altar rail. The sip of wine that fills one's being with desire can only come from your personal contact with God and the communion that comes from drinking from His holy chalice.

I hope this explanation of the name meanings found in the first quarter of the Episcopal lectionary seasons helps you make the decision to serve God as His wife (regardless of human gender). God wants your soul. Jesus Christ wants your body to be his. God and Christ want your mind to be led by the Holy Spirit.

Advent, Christmas and Epiphany Sermons

YEAR A

Advent

YEAR A

First Sunday of Advent

YEAR A

December 1, 2013

Relevant readings:
Isaiah 2:1-5
Psalm 122
Romans 13:11-14
Matthew 24:36-44

Advent and Being there

Happy New Year!

We begin a new year in the church's cycle of the lessons we teach of God and Christ. May Christ be born anew in you, through the presence of God's Holy Spirit. We are upon the

Advent Sermons: First Sunday of Advent, Year A

Advent of Year A.

Today we begin reading from the Book of Matthew, saying goodbye, for the time being, to Luke.

In the themes presented in the readings today, you might have noticed the repeating of the word "house," along with instructions to be "awake."

We heard of the house of God and Jacob, the house of the LORD, and the house of David. Jesus told of an owner's house being broken into.

Paul told us to wake from sleep. Jesus told us how staying awake prevents break-ins.

When I began to ponder these reading and think about the way "house" has become a word of a physical building, in our modern vernacular, I flashed back to a scene from one of my favorite movies, *Being There*.

In that scene, the character Chance, who is a gardener, is mistakenly received as Chauncey Gardiner, by the higher-class people he has encountered ... by chance.

While recuperating from an injury at the mansion of those people, who accidentally hit Chance with their luxury car, the following conversation ensues:

EVE (the wife of a rich old husband)
Won't your injury prevent you from attending to business, Mr. Gardiner?

CHANCE

No. It won't do that.

EVE
... Would you like us to notify anyone for you?

CHANCE
No. The Old Man died and Louise left.

(There is a moment of silence.)

EVE
Oh. I'm very sorry. Well, if you have any need for any of our facilities, please do not hesitate to ask.

RAND (the rich old husband)
Do you need a secretary?

CHANCE
No, thank you. My house has been closed.

RAND
Oh. When you say 'Your house has been closed', you mean to say that your business was shut down?

CHANCE
Yes. Shut down and locked by the attorneys.

RAND
What'd I tell you? Kid-lawyers! The S.E.C.! Damn them!

This movie makes a statement about misunderstandings leading to false relationships, when there is nothing more at play than hearing what one wants to hear, or hearing what one is capable of hearing.

Advent Sermons: First Sunday of Advent, Year A

Chance is a simpleton. He hears the word "house" and can only think in terms of a physical building, the place where he had lived his entire life, tending its garden.

Eve and Rand are wise and worldly. They live in a "mansion," the French word meaning "house," but they think of "houses" as companies and corporations, places of business and financial securities.

The movie was based on the book by a Polish author, Jerzy Kosinski. There have been reports that he plagiarized the plot from the book *Nicodemus Dyzma*. Kosinski said, in an interview about his novella, his working title was the code word "Blank Page," or sometimes the German word "*Dasein*," which means, "Being there" or "There being." He considered "*Dasein*" as the name of the book, but chose the English equivalent, which we know it as today.

Kosinski delighted in the interest in his book, something stolen from the house of another author. *Being There* was identified as a work, by philosophically minded critics, in the vein of Heidegger, a German existential philosopher. The book filled Peter Sellers with a strong emotional sense of being, as he identified with the character Chance. Peter Sellers, who starred in many successful movies, most notably the Pink Panther series, felt like he was Chance the gardener.

That emotion was so strong in Sellers that he tried for ten years to have *Being There* made into a movie, even considering financing it himself, because he felt the story must be told AND he must star as the character that represented the true Peter Sellers.

The last scene in the movie shows Chance the gardener walking on top of the water of a lake, going out about ten feet, then stopping. He then bent over and slowly plunged his umbrella all the way down into the water and then brought it back out. He then continued walking on the water as the movie ended. Peter Sellers added that scene, as there is nothing in the book that tells of that ending. Peter Sellers wanted everyone to know that Chance the gardener represented purity.

Take away all the things of this world that we wrap around our bodies – things which weigh us down and keep us from having true faith, blind faith in God – and we sink in that water after taking the first step.

In a way, Jesus is telling us, through Matthew's words, "You need an Ark to reach heaven in, or you need to be pure enough to walk on water when the flood of your end comes." When that flood comes and it is your end, it is too late to start building an Ark. The flood will come at an unexpected hour, so be alert at all times.

Paul says being alert comes by putting on the "armor of light," meaning as long as the light shines upon us, we stay awake and we are prepared to act honorably. That armor is the Holy Spirit within, so that we project Jesus outwardly. The light is the day being near.

Isaiah said, "Come, let us go up to the mountain of the LORD, to the house of the God of Jacob, that he may teach us his ways." That "mountain," which is the "highest," which "shall be raised above the hills," is Christ. That "house of the God of Jacob" is the "business" of Jesus.

Advent Sermons: First Sunday of Advent, Year A

That "house" is the family of Christ, the continuing of the new bloodline, as God's chosen priests. In that "house" is the teaching of the LORD's ways, which comes from the Holy Spirit enlightening us from within our heart-center. We each must be a "house" of the LORD.

When God told Isaiah to write, "Learn, so we may walk in his paths," God is saying walk on water. Be pure of heart. Unwrap yourself from the cloaks of darkness that weigh you down and cover that light. Stop thinking with a brain that is so easily distracted by the material realm – the science of observation, where seeing is believing. Let go of the worldly trappings. Take a leap of faith. Let your heart elevate you.

David wrote in his psalm, "Peace be within your walls and quietness within your towers." He was referring to Jerusalem, the capital of Israel.

The place that became known as Jerusalem was in existence prior to the children of Israel arriving. It was called "Salem," which is synonymous with the Hebrew word "*Shalom*," meaning "Peace." The Hebrew word that is most closely related to "*Jeru*" means "Rain." A "Rain of Peace" leads to a flood of emotion.

Jerusalem is also seen as meaning, "Foundation of Peace, Teacher of Peace," and "Possession of Peace."

Psalm 122 can then be seen as asking God to make the "house of David" be the "Place of peace." We should see ourselves as the New Jerusalem, with Jesus coming from the "house of David" into us to reside.

We must become the house of the LORD and let His light shine through us as innocence, simplicity, honor and purity.

Once we find ourselves "Being There," we will be ready for the coming of the Son of Man

… whenever that may be.

May the peace of the LORD be always with you.

Amen

Second Sunday of Advent

YEAR A

December 8, 2013

Relevant readings:
Isaiah 11:1-10
Psalm 72:1-7, 18-19
Romans 15:4-13
Matthew 3:1-12

What would you like for Christmas?

We are now just seventeen days from Christmas, the symbolic birthday of Jesus. Today is the second Sunday of the Advent liturgical season. Last Sunday we saw a duality presented. Two would be on earth, but only one would go to Heaven. The other one would be left behind.

Advent Sermons: Second Sunday of Advent, Year A

That represented a choice that was up to the individuals: wake up and save your soul, or dream your time away and let your ticket to Heaven be stolen.

Today we have more duality presented, on many levels. We read of the righteous and the wicked, the wolf and the lamb, the leopard and the kid, the calf and the lion, the cow and the bear, the lion and the ox, the child and the snake, the poor and the oppressor, the sun and the moon, the Gentiles and the Jews, the wilderness and Jerusalem, the Temple servants and the wild priest, the baptism with water and the baptism with the Holy Spirit, and the wheat and the chaff.

Each is representative of a choice that we all have to make. We choose to be one or the other … in a symbolic way.

The last Sunday in November, during the evening, my wife went to a local church here. She went to attend a special blessing service. My wife, being an Episcopal priest, then attended a church that is not of the Episcopalian denomination.

Lord knows, most Episcopalians have better things to do on Sunday evenings than go to a church.

When my wife got home, she said she saw some of the members of her church there. She saw members who had attended the morning service she celebrated.

My wife said those members apologized to her when they met in that other church, for being there, for listening to another preacher's sermon.

My wife told them not to worry, because she found it refreshing to be at a Christian service that was not Episcopalian, simply because it had been a long time since she had last attended one. There was a difference that she witnessed, from a new perspective.

I imagine, if the minister who preached that night had known my wife was a priest for the competition, he might have pointed at her and cried out, like John the Baptist, "You viper!"

Fortunately, I advised my wife not to wear her collar, so she was only identified by those she knew.

There is nothing wrong with what my wife did. And there is nothing wrong with what the members of her church did, by going to other churches and listening to other sermons. It is good to hear people preach about the meaning of the Scriptures.

In the Gospel reading today, we see something similar took place at the Jordan River. The people who regularly attended their synagogues, and those who would listen to sermons at the Temple, where their rabbis were most probably Pharisees or Sadducees, those people also went to be baptized by John.

Of course, as Matthew told, some Pharisees and Sadducees showed up at the Jordan for John to baptize them too.

Do you think everyone going to see John the Baptist was playing it safe … just in case? What could it hurt to have your sins washed clean?

Advent Sermons: Second Sunday of Advent, Year A

After all, Naaman washed off his leprosy ... a symbolic sin ... by bathing seven times in the same river. The water of the Jordan River had to be seen as having some healing properties.

But, then, if the Pharisees and Sadducees saw John the Baptist as a threat, like they would see Jesus, maybe they went to get baptized just so they could get some kind of evidence that John was breaking a law? Maybe they were trying to get the goods on him.

John certainly wasn't too happy to see the Pharisees and Sadducees show up at his place of symbolic cleansing. "What are you doing here, you deadly snakes?" he asked.

Remember ... the snake is a symbol of slick tricks. It uses wily intellect to destroy souls. So, John was calling them out as being tricky.

Still, John said he would symbolically wash them clean .... He would wash them because those priests were not the pure lambs they made the people think they were. Sure, they knew the Law and they condemned those whom they deemed to be sinners, but they knew they were sinners too. By going to John, they could be exposed as being just like the common folk ... full of sins. In that way, they were no closer to Heaven than the next guy.

This is another duality ... the shepherd and the sheep.

Imagine last week's lesson on duality, where the shepherd and the sheep were in the field together, and the shepherd (the awake and alert one) gets called away, leaving the sheep alone. What happens to the sheep then?

This is where the duality lesson comes into play. The shepherd prepares one of the sheep to become a shepherd of the flock ... at least a leader of sheep ... one who will stand up as a ram and defend the flock.

Without the shepherd, a decision must be made. Sink or swim? Eat or be eaten? We have to make the choice between death or salvation, being a sinner or a saint.

You can only be one at a time.

Most likely, people are sinners in need of a good scrubbing. Still, people wish we could be saints.

Therein lies another problem. We wish. We hope. That is good, but it does not remove the sin and make us saints.

For people with serious problems, like alcoholism or drug addiction, they find themselves deep in a trap they cannot easily get out of. They get so far in that they cannot even tell what is reality and what is illusion. The first step of recovery from those problems is admission that a problem exists. They cannot kick the habit without facing up to their addiction and admitting they do have a serious problem that must stop.

Imagine how going to the river to be dunked by John was an admission of a problem with sin, which the Jews felt they had. Simply by going to the synagogue wasn't enough to make them stop. They felt dirty and sought out John.

They must have thought, "I just can't stop sinning."

Advent Sermons: Second Sunday of Advent, Year A

For Christians, we amend that confession to say, "I just can't make the full commitment to being a saint."

Going to listen to more than one person preach, or going to be baptized by water after going to a temple and listening to someone tell you what sinners do, is then a confession of sins, an admission that a problem exists … but that is just the first step.

Imagine an alcoholic coming out of an AA meeting, having just stood up in front of the group, admitting a problem with drinking. Then, imagine after the meeting is over the same person going across town to a bar, getting drunk once again.

What was it Flip Wilson used to say? "The devil made me do it?"

That is the same thing as going to a church, getting on your knees and confessing you are a sinner; and then going out after church and committing sins all over again.

That is what we all do … to some degree. Because we come to church regularly, we probably sin much less than other heathens, those who never go to church and those who commit heinous crimes. Still, our sins keep us coming back.

We come back because we all seem to seek out leaders … shepherds … sponsors … someone other than ourselves … to help save us from sinning again. In that projecting kind of way, we like to listen to sermons.

Sometimes we feel like it helps to get a second opinion.

In the Isaiah reading today, we hear the prophecy of a coming Messiah, one who would have the spirit of the LORD rest on him. From that spirit would come Heaven, where none of the earthly duality exists.

In Heaven, there is no reason to fear lions, and tigers, and bears. Isaiah prophesied that this one to come would bring that peaceful coexistence to the earth.

In Paul's letter to the Romans, we read him referring to that reading in Isaiah. He said Jesus was the one prophesied. Paul also said, "May the God of hope fill you with all joy and peace in believing, so that you may abound in hope by the power of the Holy Spirit."

The duality of Matthew's verses comes down to hearing John tell the people around him that he was not the one. There would come one much greater, one who would baptize with the Holy Spirit and fire. John is prophesying the Advent of Jesus, who would be the Christ.

The Advent of Jesus Christ must be internal to us, at which point it will project externally.

You have to choose between being baptized with water (a physical element) or spirit (of God). Being cleansed of your sins symbolically … up to that point in time of being cleaned, but not the times still to come … is temporary, like a bath or shower. Being cleansed of your sins by God is permanent. Sins are then completely gone: past, present, and future.

Advent Sermons: Second Sunday of Advent, Year A

To admit a problem means you must maintain a commitment to put that problem behind you. To do that, you have to choose to be baptized with the Holy Spirit and fire, which accepts the power of hope that keeps one from ever sinning again.

Sinner ... or Saint?

There was a Belgian surrealist artist name René Magritte. Perhaps you have seen some of his paintings. He painted one that is named *Son of Man*, which depicts a man wearing a top coat and bowler hat, with his face blocked from view by a green apple. Magritte painted several pictures where human faces were missing.

He enjoyed the surrealism of transparency and illusion. This can be summed up as the way René Magritte saw the reality of an earthly existence.

When we choose to be filled with the Holy Spirit and fire, we become like a René Magritte painting. The surreal becomes real. The spiritual overcomes the physical.

We are no longer the most important person in our lives. The ego has stepped aside. God tells us what to do, and we gladly accept that suggestion. We live to make God happy.

As we go through December and anticipate, with joy, a remembrance of Jesus being born again, remember that Jesus wants us to be baptized with the Holy Spirit. God baptizes His faithful as the first step to be reborn as His Son.

According to AA and their twelve-step program, baptism

by the Holy Spirit and fire is the equivalent to their twelfth step. It is the goal an addict must seek.

First, we have to admit we have a problem and need that baptism. Then, by receiving the spirit of dedication and with the help of others who share our goal, we can commit to taking all the steps necessary to eliminate the problem of uncontrollable sin.

After we have voluntarily chosen to be filled with the Holy Spirit, letting Christ lead our actions, we can then sponsor others to be likewise filled. We can give to others, as has been given to us.

The spirit of giving is what this season is about. Advent is when the spirit of giving abounds, as we anticipate the coming of Jesus. It is the spirit of Christ giving us hope.

The question now is, "What do **you** want for Christmas?"

Amen

Advent Sermons: Second Sunday of Advent, Year A

Third Sunday of Advent

YEAR A

December 15, 2013

Relevant readings:
Isaiah 35:1-10
Psalm 146:4-9
 or Canticle 15
  [or Canticle 3]
James 5:7-10
Matthew 11:2-11

Pay attention. God is talking to you.

Reading this Gospel this week made me think of the movie, *Taxi Driver*, where a young Robert DeNiro was looking

Advent Sermons: Third Sunday of Advent, Year A

into his mirror, practicing making his new attachment to his arm work, saying, "You talking to me?" He said it over and over.

"You talking to me?" "You talking to me?" "Who do you think you're talking to?" "I'm the only one here ... you talking to me?"

DeNiro's character, Travis, was upset about the way the world of New York City had become, so he was planning on being a tough guy by cleaning up some of the filth.

Jerusalem under Roman domination was similar to some degree. John the Baptist was similar to Travis, in that regard. He wanted to fight the criminals who were against God.

He must have thought Jesus would fight likewise.

Therefore, it seems that Jesus was somewhat miffed by the disciples of John the Baptist, when they came to tell Jesus their leader was in prison AND he had sent a message to inquire, "Are you the one, or should we wait some more?"

"You talking to me?"

Jesus said, "Tell John what you have witnessed and what has been spread around town by word of mouth. Jesus heals the sick, raises the dead, cures the lame, deaf, and dumb, all while bringing good news to the poor."

"You talking to me?"

Jesus told the disciples of John, "Go back and tell John

that anyone who takes no offense at me will be blessed by God."

One of the translations of that statement has Jesus saying, "Whosoever shall find no occasion of stumbling in me." Another, "Who has no doubts about me." Still another, "He that shall not be scandalized by me," as well as, "To whom I shall not be the cause of falling into sin." Two more say, "Who does not stumble and fall because of my claims," and "He that may not be stumbled in me."

Thus, Jesus was saying to the disciples of John, "Go tell him he is not in prison because of my actions. So, as long as he is not blaming me for his troubles, then he is blessed by God."

When the two followers of John left, Jesus begins asking, "What did you go into the wilderness to see?"

He quizzed, "Were you looking to find just one reed shaking in the wind?"

A reed shaken by the wind means one that bends to whichever direction the wind is blowing. So, were the people going into the wilderness to see someone who would believe Jesus was the Messiah one day, when that person was free to stand in the baptismal pool of the Jordan River, but then doubt that belief when that person finds himself in jail, with no one pulling the walls down to free him?

Were you looking to find someone symbolically announcing he was a king by dressing in fine linen and fancy, soft robes (most likely purple)?

Advent Sermons: Third Sunday of Advent, Year A

Such a king would be someone from the house of David, returning with the Torah in one hand and a sling in the other. That king would boldly ask, "Where is the giant called the Roman Empire?"

Would they really go out into the wilderness to find a wild man wearing such Temple garments?

Were they going to see a prophet?

Sure, they thought that, but their minds were filled with images of a returned Elijah, riding a chariot of fire, with the glow of God upon his face. The prophets had already spoken, so another prophet was not what they were looking for.

Besides, the people who wandered out from Jerusalem were known more for killing prophets, more than anointing them with oil and pronouncing them kings. If they were to see a prophet, they wanted to see it be the Messiah King, with a band of angels carrying the Ark of the Covenant alongside.

Jesus asked those questions rhetorically. He knew why the people went to see John the Baptist. It was because they were full of sin and wanted someone to make them clean. Someone who could wash away the dirt of sinful living would be nice to see.

Now, they saw a man who was in prison and crying about whether or not Jesus was the one. Had not John said there would be one who would come after him, one so great that John would be unworthy to stoop and untie the straps of his sandals?

Was John questioning Jesus a symbolic act of stooping so

low as to try that?

Was Jesus rebuffing John's question not proof that John was unworthy of doing that, thus proof that Jesus was the one to come after him?

Jesus was the one with a message sent by God, so he was the one to see. Jesus would prepare the people for the path to heaven, by telling them what they needed to change first.

Washing with water was not enough. They had to wash their minds clean, so their bodies would sin no more.

As holy as the people thought John the Baptist was, he admitted he was unworthy, when compared to the one he knew would come later. But the people thought he was the one.

God speaks through Jesus:

"You thought he was me?"

"Open your eyes and see the truth!"

"Open your ears and hear the truth!"

"Get up off your beggar's blanket and walk the path of righteousness!"

"Open that mouth that has been quiet about what is wrong with the world and praise God that the world may be saved through Jesus Christ!"

"Here is your God! Be strong and do not fear!"

Advent Sermons: Third Sunday of Advent, Year A

> "I am sending YOU my Son in whom I am well pleased. Listen to him!"

Is God talking through Jesus to me?

Yes. He most certainly is.

We are now ten days from Christmas and our recognition of the birthday of Jesus the Christ.

Last Sunday we saw John the Baptist call out the leaders of the Temple and the keepers of the Law. He called them "vipers."

We saw how the coming of heaven on earth would bring eternity to the faithful, such that the ox and the bear would eat straw and the leopard would lie down with the kid.

The symbolism was how heaven is not a place where food is necessary. Animals lie down just to be friendly and take in the scenery. Chewing straw is just a laid-back thing to do, when one has an eternity on one's hands ... or hooves ... or paws.

Today, in the Isaiah reading, we have a picture painted for us about the coming of Christ. It begins by stating why Christ will need to come. It then goes into what he will do when here. It then moves on to tell what those who meet Christ will have to do.

Yes. We have responsibilities too.

John the Baptist rebuked the Pharisees and Sadducees

because he saw them as failing to holding up their end of the Covenant. They were taking advantage of God. They believed they were doing all they needed to do to get to heaven. They were, instead, like deadly snakes, killing the innocent children of God who stuck their hands into their holes in the ground.

The symbolism of Isaiah's reading today is another one of those duality things. Today, we see the wilderness and the dry land, versus the waters breaking in the wilderness, the streams in the desert, pools covering the burning sand, and spring water coming like a drinking fountain from the ground.

In Ezekiel 37, we heard God ask if dry bones could live again. In Isaiah, we see how flesh is to dry bones as water is to dry land.

The symbolism of water is emotions. The land needs water, just as bones need flesh. We must do more than go through the motions of faith. We must have a deep-rooted emotional attachment.

Just as we cannot live more than a few days without water, we cannot get to heaven without a strong emotional desire to get there.

Israel was dried out after centuries of mismanaging their agreement with God. It was the same ole same ole, looking for a little excitement to spice things up … maybe a little idol worship here and a little sexual liberation there. Who's gonna notice?

Jesus coming into our lives is all we need. The spring of

Advent Sermons: Third Sunday of Advent, Year A

God flows through us in the form of the Holy Spirit.

Jesus is born as a baby in a manger once a year, to spice up our lives with gifts and bows and pagan lights on trees; but what is most important is Jesus Christ being the model for each of us to live up to.

We cannot do that by self-will or good intentions. Those always end up going awry.

It is not easy living like Jesus, but it is not impossible.

Jesus came to show us it is possible, with God's help. With God's help we will all support each other in that quest.

God wants us to be happy and to rejoice and sing … not just in this building, but everywhere we go, for the rest of eternity.

Amen

Fourth Sunday of Advent

YEAR A

December 22, 2013

Relevant readings:
Isaiah 7:10-16
Psalm 80:1-7, 16-18
Romans 1:1-7
Matthew 1:18-25

You're all invited to Jesus' birthday party!

Here we are on the Sunday before Christmas. We will celebrate the birth of our Savior on Wednesday.

Today we prepare for that event by remembering the virginal birth, the miracle of Jesus; and, we remember that it was prophesied by Isaiah.

December 25th is marked as the birthday of Jesus, and we see the baby Jesus in the manger where Mary gave birth, with him as "baby Jesus," all wrapped up in swaddling blankets.

Compare that to your birthday.

We all have a birthday each year. So, does everyone come to see you then?

Does everyone throw you a party and pass around pictures of you "in the buff," when you were just a baby on a rug or all sudsy taking a bath?

Probably not.

We recognize our birthdays as celebrations of a new year completed, with all of the accomplishments up to that point recognized, and all of the promise of a new year to come praised.

Make a wish and blow out the candles!

The same counting of past accomplishments and promises to come should be something to look forward to this coming Wednesday.

Christ is two thousand thirteen years old (there about) … and still going strong!

We wish him another two thousand plus years to come.

That is where we play a role … in **that** celebration of the promise ahead.

As remarkable as it is that an angel would announce the birth to shepherds, and wise men from the east would find their way to a little place in Bethlehem … guided by a shining light … it is us, and all those before us, who take from that birth the promise of the past, and keep Christ alive now, and in the future.

In the reading from Isaiah, we heard the LORD speaking to Ahaz. God said, "Ask a sign of the LORD your God; let it be deep as Hell or high as Heaven."

God was telling Ahaz to ask for proof that He was real and Ahaz wasn't just pretending to believe in the One God.

To ask for a sign was to put God to the test. It meant to say, "Prove yourself! Make yourself known so I will know to serve only you and tell everyone I meet to face you as well, or suffer the consequences!"

Maybe he could have asked God to heal someone?

Maybe he could have asked God to make him rich beyond his wildest dreams?

Maybe he could have asked to be the smartest man on the planet?

Maybe he could have asked for all women to fall madly in love with him, just from a glance?

Advent Sermons: Fourth Sunday of Advent, Year A

Maybe he could have asked for all of the above?

God was saying, "Make a wish, Ahaz."

Ahaz would not test the LORD.

It is good to know just who this Ahaz guy was, if you don't know. He has some history of interest.

Ahaz was the son and successor of King Jotham of Judah. He wrecked Judah by worshiping every god other than the LORD. According to one website, Ahaz "looted the temple and gave the consecrated utensils, and even the bronze bulls that carry Solomon's seal, to the king of Assyria." He sought military assistance from the Assyrians in his war against King Pekah of Israel. Ahaz even burned his own sons as sacrifices to idols.

To sum it up, Ahaz wasn't very faithful to the Lord his God, so he did not need any proof that he was going the wrong way.

Isaiah wrote that the LORD would give a sign without Ahaz asking for one. The sign would be named Immanuel. In Hebrew, the name Immanuel means, "God is with us." Thus, when Jesus was born, God was physically with the world.

In Matthew, we read that the angel told Joseph to name his son Jesus. In Hebrew that is Yehsua (a.k.a. Joshua), which means, "YHWH is salvation." Thus, God not only was with us, but God was with us for the purpose of saving us.

Ahaz was not trying to save anyone. He was trying to lead

everyone to a place opposite of Heaven. That is why we need to be saved … so we don't go to Hell.

Going to Hell is a lot easier than going to Heaven. It doesn't require proof from the Lord.

The world is a place of pretty wrapped presents that are just waiting for us to gleefully unwrap and become lost in. They say the best things in life are free … but try telling that to the Apple Corporation, AT&T, the I.R.S., and everything else that has us shackled as slaves to our lust, to our thinking we NEED so much … too much.

We get caught up in the incense, frankincense and myrrh that were given to the baby Jesus.

We get caught up in replacing a real Saint Nickolas, a man who was known for his secret gift-giving (putting a coin in people's shoes that were left outside the front door), with a Santa Claus that can be photographed at the mall.

Enter the money-changers, who could barely wait for the Thanksgiving turkey thermometer to pop out, before opening the doors to their shops of business.

Christmas is about giving.

It is about God giving the world His Son, our Savior. It is not about selling us Jesus.

Jesus was born, according to our calculations and calendar configurations, two thousand thirteen years ago. The number 2013 is the Year of Our Lord (*Annus Deus*), what A.D. stands for.

Advent Sermons: Fourth Sunday of Advent, Year A

In Jesus' three years of ministry in Judea he gave miracles to the people. He did that by healing the sick, making the lame walk, the blind see, the deaf to hear, and the downtrodden to be able to be uplifted.

He gave his disciples his words of wisdom; and, after his death, resurrection, and ascension, he gave them the Holy Spirit. So, the gift of Jesus Christ could become the gift that keeps on giving.

Paul was given the Holy Spirit without having known Jesus the man. We are like Paul in that sense, as have been all other Christians past and those with us now, as those who awoke one morning to find the gift of God in one's heart. We represent the present of two thousand years of Christianity.

Wednesday, December 25, 2013, we celebrate this gift as a call to serve and be set apart, as Paul wrote to the Romans. We can be apostles ... if we test the LORD.

We can set apart the gospel of God ... if we ask for proof.

We can be given grace and apostleship to bring about the obedience of faith, for the sake of Jesus Christ.

We can answer the call to belong to Jesus Christ.

All of those gifts can be ours, but we cannot buy them in stores.

We cannot get them by acting like Ahaz ... as if we know who Santa Claus is and we have resentment that no one other than us will be paying Walmart for what makes people happy.

I imagine it is the Ahaz type people of the world who love those commercials about diamond rings and fancy jewelry being a sign of God's love surrounding them.

I've seen one commercial where Santa Claus goes into his "stable" of fancy cars and the Mercedes or the BMW twinkles like Rudolph, saying, "Let me be your sleigh tonight."

Isaiah said to Ahaz, "Is it too little for you to weary mortals, that you weary my God also?"

We weary mortals when we make it seem that God rewards human flesh with fancy things, all while there are so many of human flesh who can barely stay alive, much less buy a BMW or hear bystanders whisper about someone, "He went to Jared."

Please, don't get me wrong. Giving is good. Making people happy is good.

That is not the reason an angel came to Joseph and told him that Mary would bear a son conceived by the Holy Spirit.

Christmas is about receiving a gift from God, which means we have to believe in God to believe in Jesus as Christ.

We have to test the LORD to prove he is real in spiritual ways.

We have to test the LORD by letting baby Jesus become a miracle birth within us.

We must rejoice, "Immanuel!" "God is with me!"

We must praise "Jeshua!" "God is salvation" through Jesus in me!

These are the gifts of the season …

And on Jesus' birthday, if we make that our wish, it can come true.

Amen

Christmas

YEAR A

First Sunday after Christmas

YEAR A

December 29, 2013

Relevant readings:
Isaiah 61:10-62:3
Psalm 147 or 147:13-21
Galatians 3:23-25; 4:4-7
John 1:1-18

In the beginning was, is, and will be Logos

Zion (or Sion) means "highest point." This word is often seen as a reference to the city named Jerusalem. Yet, the political movement called Zionism supports a State of Zion, where the reference is to what was once the land given by God to His people, the children of Israel. As such, the body surrounding the center has reached its highest point.

Some say Jerusalem is a combined form of "*Yara-shalem*," which means "completeness, soundness, or wholeness [from *shalem*] is cast [from *yara*]." Still, others believe Jerusalem means "Rain of Peace" or "Foundation of Peace." When it is seen as "*yahu-shalem*" it means, "the wholeness of God."

It is important to understand name meanings.

Otherwise, we read "Zion" and "Jerusalem" and we think of a place on the map. We think of a physical representation of symbolic energy.

In David's psalm, he sings, "Worship the LORD, O Jerusalem; praise your God, O Zion." Worship the LORD from center to edge, from body and soul.

In Isaiah's song we hear him sing, "For Zion's sake I will not keep silent, and for Jerusalem's sake I will not rest." Again, the two are interconnected, for one to thrive, the other must also.

The tendency is to think those two historic men of God were advising Israelites, from a place on earth, a land known as Israel, to praise God. We can lose sight of the duality of city and state; but in one way they were speaking as one whole. However, in essence they were saying, "To reach the highest point O people, do not keep silent. Praise your God to the highest. Worship the LORD for a wholeness with God, so that a foundation of peace will not rest."

This past Wednesday we celebrated the symbolic birth of Jesus.

Today we read from Isaiah and see the garments of salvation being draped around us with that birth. We now have available to us a robe of righteousness.

It is now us who must become married to the spirit of Christ, as welcoming God's gift to us from His presence … as us being His gift to the world ... in the name of His Son, Jesus.

David told us what we become once Jesus is within us … as God sends forth his word and melts the coldness that had kept us the slaves of the Law.

Paul said the Law only kept us in a pen, because without that rule over us, we would become lost, scatter without a shepherd.

Being lost means we lose faith. The Law of Moses trains us to wait patiently in that pen until Jesus comes so we might be justified by faith. Once justified, we rule ourselves ... when Jesus is within our hearts, we no longer need a disciplinarian to oversee us. We no longer notice the pen that keeps us.

John said Jesus brings light to the darkness. The darkness is what keeps us separate from God. Jesus shines the way to God.

John said, "And the Word became flesh and lived among us," so we see Jesus as the Word.

John also wrote, "In the beginning was the Word, and the Word was with God, and the Word was God."

To understand how Jesus is the Word becoming flesh, we need to understand the word "Word."

The Greek word written by John the Beloved was "*Logos.*" That Greek word means, "word," but it also means, "Reason or discourse," rooted from *legein*, meaning "to speak."

Strong's Concordance lists "*logos*" as meaning, "from *legw - lego* 3004; something said (including the thought); by implication, a topic (subject of discourse), also reasoning (the mental faculty) or motive; by extension, a computation; specially, (with the article in John) the Divine Expression (i.e. Christ):--account, cause, communication, X concerning, doctrine, fame, X have to do, intent, matter, mouth, preaching, question, reason, + reckon, remove, say(-ing), shew, X speaker, speech, talk, thing, + none of these things move me, tidings, treatise, utterance, word, work."

Strong's aligns "*logos*" with meaning that is synonymous with "cause, motivation, and intent."

Thus, the "Word" is from the **Mind** of God, as God's **Plan** for the world. This means John wrote, "In the beginning was the **Plan** [for Jesus], and the **Intent** [of Jesus] was with God, and the **Motivation** [of Jesus] was God."

When Jesus was born, "the **Reasoning** [of Jesus] became flesh and lived among us."

To understand this Idea, look at how John the Beloved

wrote about the beginning, when Jesus was with God. John wrote, "All things came into being through him," where "him" is God.

That is the beginning of Creation … well before John the Beloved came into the picture. Therefore, John is speaking from the position of wisdom, brought upon him through the Holy Spirit.

Perhaps it is confusing when we read John write, "There was a man sent from God, whose name was John." Later, shown in parentheses, we read, "John testified to him and cried out, "This was he whom I said, 'He who comes after me ranks ahead of me because he was before me."

Who the heck was John?

Was John the author of the Gospel of John? No. Was John a reference to the Baptist? No, because that really makes no sense, because Jesus was not "before" John the Baptist, if he was "after" him AND "before" is not the same as "ahead of."

The naming of John is like the mention of Zion and Jerusalem, by Isaiah and David. It is a name so familiar; we assume it referred ONLY to a person of Biblical past, just as we knew Zion and Jerusalem are ONLY historical places. But, when we read in a way that limits and restricts like that, we then miss so much information. We miss a wealth of insight.

John is the English version of the Greek name *Ioannes*, and that was derived from the Hebrew name *Johanan* (properly *Yochanan*). The Hebrew meaning of that name is "Yahweh is gracious."

The name Jesus (or *Iesous* [Greek], a form of the Aramaic name *Yeshu'a*) is a contracted form of Joshua, which means, "Yahweh is salvation." Thus, the flesh of God was Jesus, and Jesus is God's graciousness to the world, so Jesus is john, in the lower case, becoming a descriptive term of him.

However, look at the Greek capitalization of John and someone who speaks about Jesus as, "He who comes after me ranks ahead of me because he was before me." Then think about the Son of God, who was the Plan, Motivation, Idea and Intent of Jesus, and one finds Adam.

The name Adam is the Hebrew word for "man." As the first "Man" who was the Son of God, Adam was a John … a statement of God's graciousness to the world.

Rather than be the first "man," Adam was the first "Son of God," the first "Son as Man," who was part of God's master plan to bring light to a world that only knew darkness. Only Adam was not that light.

Adam was created by God to testify to the light. Adam was placed on earth "to express or declare a strong belief, especially to make a declaration of faith; to support, bear witness, to serve as evidence" [definitions of "testify"] to the light. That means Adam was the originator of **the** lineage that would produce Jesus.

Thus, when one reads verse 15 - the parenthesized statement on your handout - it means, "Adam, God's first example of graciousness on the earthly plane, the first Son of Man, was a declaration of faith for a lineage to follow, leading to Jesus, as God's salvation to a world of darkness.

Adam, as John, then cried out, "Jesus is he of whom I said, "Jesus comes after me by thousands of years, yet he ranks ahead of me as the Intent, the Motivation, the Idea, and the Cause that brought about my presence, because Jesus was before me in the Wisdom of God's Mind, who Planned a light for a darkened world surrounding mankind."

From God's fullness, as a child born in the flesh named Jesus, we have all received grace upon grace. We had a line of priests establish the grace of worship to the One God, through Adam and all the Patriarchs, all the faithful who remained true to the Word, the Plan, the Intent, and the Purpose of Christ.

The Law indeed was given through Moses, another in the lineage of Adam, as a disciplinarian that demands devotion, and who tests the will of the people. From that state of will, Jesus was sent to bring grace and truth.

Paul was repeating this in his letter to the Galatians, when he said, "We are no longer slaves to a disciplinarian, once we receive the gift of God, God's Salvation to the world, the Purpose of Jesus Christ."

Through the law we can be redeemed and be adopted as the children of God. This happens when we allow God to send the Spirit of his Son into our hearts, so we cry out, "Father!"

Last Wednesday was the beginning of a new year for God's gift of Salvation to the world. Let it reignite or let it begin a new spirit within you.

Amen

Second Sunday after Christmas

YEAR A

January 5, 2014

Relevant readings:
Jeremiah 31:7-14
Psalm 84 or 84:1-8
Ephesians 1:3-6,15-19a
Matthew 2:13-15,19-23
  or Luke 2:41-52
  or Matthew 2:1-12

Jesus the boy preacher

In the reading options for today, there are three readings that focus in on the life of Jesus after his birth, beyond the

Christmas Sermons: Second Sunday after Christmas, Year A

nativity, with one reaching as far as when he was twelve. Two are from Matthew, with one of the stories being of the wise men stopping to inform King Herod why they are in Judea – to see the newborn King of the Jews. The other tells of Joseph having a dream where he was told to take baby Jesus and Mary to Egypt, because Herod was planning to kill the newborn.

Today it is the choice from the Book of Luke that I want to talk deeply about. That selection is when Jesus was twelve years old and when he was mistakenly left behind in Jerusalem, after Passover.

In that story, Jesus is found in the Temple, surrounded by elder rabbis. The rabbis are amazed at the level of knowledge such a young boy has. Jesus listens, he answers questions accurately, and he asks the right questions as well.

When Joseph and Mary find Jesus, he has a somewhat immature response, by saying, "Where else should I be but in my Father's house?"

Now, in the book *The Infancy Gospel of Thomas* (not a canonical book) there are several stories about Jesus as a growing child. Some tell how this immaturity glimpse given in Luke's Gospel is supported.

Think about this concept for a moment.

Jesus was born as the image of God in the flesh. We most regularly see him as an adult having amazing abilities. Those were abilities that were available to him from the beginning, but his body had to grow and develop, including his brain, so he could learn to master those special talents.

As the Son of Man, Jesus possessed the same free will we all are given by God; but free will AND amazing powers at his disposal … that took some harnessing.

We truly begin to see the adult Jesus developing in this account in Luke. We have moved beyond his birth as a baby, and see him as a preteen, when he was accidentally left behind. In a way, it is at his "coming out party," when we first encounter the focus and purpose Jesus had, through the Holy Spirit.

Prior to beginning his full-time ministry, Jesus was an attendee at a wedding banquet. The host ran out of wine. Jesus did not volunteer to turn water into wine. He was content just sitting back, enjoying the event, and taking everything in as it came. Instead, Mary, his mother, tells Jesus, "Fix the wine shortage problem, son."

Again, we see a wee bit of that edge, the hint of an attitude. "Woman, mind your own business," he says, or something of that nature. It was the same type of response as we read today in Matthew, "Where else should I be other than in my Father's house?"

Still, after turning water into wine, Jesus did not begin his ministry right away. He spent forty days in the wilderness first, preparing himself for what he knew lay ahead of him.

In other words, Jesus had the power when he was a toddler, something akin to Superboy, before Superboy grew into Superman. Scholars who have looked deeply into *The Infancy Gospel of Thomas* say that Jesus acts much like a mythological hero – a half-human / half-god entity – who knew he had powers unlike the other boys in the neighborhood.

Christmas Sermons: Second Sunday after Christmas, Year A

He was, at times, impish and insolent.

That is where good parenting comes into play.

In the Gospel reading today, and for the one back on Christmas Eve, we twice feel how Mary took delight in Jesus. When the shepherds came and told Joseph and Mary how an angel had told them that a Messiah had been born, Luke wrote, "But Mary treasured all these words and pondered them in her heart." Again, in today's reading, after Jesus leaves Jerusalem with his parents and goes back to Nazareth. Luke wrote, "His mother treasured all these things in her heart."

Jesus was tempered by his mother's love. His Father, God, would have disciplined Jesus if he ventured too far and abused his special talent – like Icarus flying too close to the Sun, he would have learned lessons of failure – life lessons. But by having loving parents, Jesus was shaped into a fine, young thirty-something-year old, who was then ready to begin a world-altering ministry.

I think back to when I was in my youth, going to a Pentecostal church.

Occasionally, we would have traveling evangelists come visit. They would stay for some length of time, usually a week, preaching multiple times while there. For instance, they probably drove in on Monday, because the church offered services on Tuesday and Friday evenings. Then, they would stay for the two services offered on Sunday, in the morning and the evening.

One traveling evangelist I remember was a boy my age,

who came with his family, all of who sang and preached. He was a red-headed ten-year old, bible-thumping, fire and brimstone preacher. He wore a powder blue suit, with a tie that he would loosen mid-way through the sermon. He would pace the altar, yell and point at the audience, all of which got the congregation moved. The boy was quite animated.

Not too long ago, I watched a boy that was four years old doing, basically, the same thing; although, I will give that ten-year-old boy credit for preaching a better sermon. The four-year-old that I saw on TV did not yet have an advanced vocabulary, which that traveling ten year old had.

Not to burst any bubbles, but I believe those child ministers are fakes. As sad as that is to say, there are no four-ten-year-old preacher boys who are going to guide you to salvation.

After one of the services that the ten-year-old preacher boy preached in our church, he invited some of us kids to the mobile home the family traveled in. It was parked in the church parking lot. All we local boys were in awe of him, so we gathered around, like he was a celebrity of merit.

This boy lit up a cigarette. He told us it was all fake. His dad (himself a preacher) taught him to act that way.

<ppphhhhhhhpppppphhhhhhppppphhhhhhhh>

All the air went out of that balloon then. That bubble was forever burst. I wanted to believe, because my mother wanted me to grow up and be a preacher ... and I wanted to please my mother.

Now, that boy and I were the same age. Hopefully, he grew up into a true preacher, actually believing what he said, rather than putting on an act - putting on a show that the people want to see. I can't say what happened in his case.

The point is this: A ministry of truth takes time to develop. Jesus took thirty-something years to learn his religion, to find self-control, to test God's power, and to pray to his Father, before he ever began to take his "act" on the road.

Take, for example, the disciples of Jesus. They all spent three years following Jesus around, seeing to his every need. They were given a temporary commission, and some came back amazed at how the power they were given made others kneel before them. That power left them, after their commission; and, up to the Last Supper, they were what I call "dumb as stumps," spiritually speaking.

"Where did you say your father lived again?" Philip asked, while getting drunk after the Seder meal.

It was not until after they had their own forty days in the wilderness, with a resurrected Jesus before his Ascension - boot camp with the Messiah - that their training fully hit them; and then, like a rush of wind, they were filled with the Holy Spirit.

In comparison, you do not apply for a CEO position for some Forbes 500 company, simply because you think that would be a good job to have, when you have yet to even work in a mail room. Experience matters.

Jeremiah sang about what it takes to reach Heaven. You

have to be a remnant of Israel. That means you have to know what having lost everything means, before you can know the motivation of gaining something.

You have to wail from sorrow, before you can get the most from laughter and dance. You have to be alone and cold, before you can appreciate the warmth of a shepherd taking you into his arms.

Paul put it beautifully in his letter to the Ephesians. He wrote, "I have heard of your faith, and your love toward all the Apostles who have died for Christ, as saints."

Paul then prayed for those Apostles-in-training, saying, "I pray that the God of our Lord Jesus Christ may give you a spirit of wisdom and revelation."

He went on to say more as he prayed, "so that, with the eyes of your heart enlightened, you may know what is the hope to which he has called you."

You do not fake that.

You do not flip a switch and begin acting like an Apostle.

You know that is true as soon as you see the first hungry lion rushing towards you in an arena filled with non-believing Romans. That's when you start yelling, "I was only kidding! I'm not really a Christian!"

Paul had maturity. Paul had experience. Paul saw the spirit of Jesus and he was possessed with the Holy Spirit.

Paul was beaten for his newfound beliefs. Paul was stoned

Christmas Sermons: Second Sunday after Christmas, Year A

and left for dead because of his newfound faith. Paul was imprisoned multiple times because he believed in Jesus Christ, because the Holy Spirit was with Paul.

Paul had the Holy Spirit for the purpose of leading many others to the same eternal source of power. All who were so filled, through Paul, found the life of an Apostle required total commitment.

From that experience, Paul wrote to his fellows in Ephesus, saying "[there] is immeasurable greatness [from] his power, for us who believe."

Jesus had to learn how to let that power shine, without misuse. Paul had to learn the same thing.

As a twelve-year-old boy, Jesus knew things. He knew power. Still, he had to learn love is the greatest power of all.

When you have the ability to heal the sick, raise the dead, disappear in the middle of a mob, and even walk on water, it takes maturity to let someone kill you.

Because Jesus experienced love, from Joseph and Mary, who protected him and provided for him, and disciplined him, Jesus was prepared to let his powers be set aside, so that his love could be released to fill so many others.

Patience. Prayer. Practice.

Then ... receive the spirit.

Deep breath.

Hold it in.

Amen

Epiphany

YEAR A

First Sunday after the Epiphany

YEAR A

January 12, 2014

Relevant readings:
Isaiah 42:1-9
Psalm 29
Acts 10:34-43
Matthew 3:13-17

The epiphany of understanding King Cakes

Last Monday was Epiphany. This is the first Sunday after. Who brought the king cake?

Epiphany Sermons: First Sunday after the Epiphany, Year A

The season of Mardi Gras is upon us. It is Carnival time. It is time to celebrate the new king's crowning, before we head into Lent. God's promised king is here! Long live the king!

For myself, having not grown up Catholic or Episcopal, and having not grown up along the gulf coast of Florida, Alabama, Mississippi or anywhere in Louisiana, I never knew Mardi Gras. I certainly knew nothing about king cakes, until a neighbor of mine introduced me to them by bringing one to our family, as a gift.

They were true Cajuns and told me the cakes were a tradition. They said there was a small plastic baby baked into the cake and there was some meaning to being the one who got the piece with the baby in it.

The cake was sweet. There was a plastic baby in it. And, I had no idea why it was called a "king cake." I might have thought … if I thought anything about it … that it was named after Martin Luther King.

It was relatively recent that I learned Mardi Gras was related to a holy season. Prior to that, I had only associated Mardi Gras with New Orleans, and (to be honest) I saw all the revelry, costumes, and beads as a sign of decadence, not something divinely manifested.

I misunderstood the meaning behind the celebration and I did not understand the season of Epiphany.

Maybe, if some of you have religious backgrounds similar as mine, you have struggled with understanding the Mardi Gras season too.

For those that know this already, please bear with me.

The words "*Mardi Gras*" are French, meaning "Fat Tuesday." That is the day before "Ash Wednesday." So, we have entered into in the fattening season, before we go through forty days of sacrifice, during Lent.

As for the meaning of king cakes, I looked that up. There are two schools of thought on them. One is based on the cake coming with a crown around it. The crown is removed and the cake is divided and passed out. The one who finds the bean or baby gets to wear the crown. The "winner" becomes king for the day.

The other idea says this: If you get the piece of cake with the bean or baby in it, then you bring the king cake tomorrow (or the next time) … up until Fat Tuesday.

Either way, there is a "tag, you're it" concept behind the consumption of a fattening food.

This is then complimentary to the meaning of "Epiphany," which is seen as a "divine manifestation." The baby (or bean) represents Jesus, who has been born of divine origin.

The season of Epiphany is marked as beginning when Jesus is baptized by John the Baptist, in the Jordan River. At that time, the skies opened and the voice of God said, "This is my Son, the Beloved, with whom I am well pleased."

That was an epiphany for Jesus.

That reading from Matthew, however, cannot be the only

focus for today. What Matthew wrote needs to be incorporated with the other readings that accompany it.

Clearly, in Isaiah, we see how Jesus was to be the "servant upheld by God, in whom God's soul delights." In other words, God was "well pleased."

In David's psalm (Psalm 29), we see how "the LORD shall give his people the blessing of peace." That peace and goodwill towards men is what Jesus was to the world.

In the Book of Acts, Peter proclaimed, "You know the message he sent to the people of Israel, preaching peace by Jesus Christ – he is Lord of all." Christ is the king. All praise the Lord, Christ the King!

Still, the message of Epiphany, as symbolized by the baby in the king cake, has to be seen as God sending the light of Jesus to the world, through a divine manifestation. That light was sent to give "light to all nations, to open the eyes that are blind, to bring out the prisoners from the dungeon, from the prison those who sit in darkness."

Jesus is that light, and Jesus would come to find "a dimly burning wick [that] he (would) not quench." Instead, Jesus would fan the flames to that dimly burning wick, so the light rose and still shines brightly. Still, to maintain that brightness, Jesus needs lots of new wicks … constantly.

In that way, Christians are the keeper of the flame, the bearer of the light of Jesus, reborn as the Christ.

As Peter said, "[Christ] commanded us to preach to the people and to testify that (Jesus) is the one ordained by

God." Peter, a disciple elevated to the level of Apostle, was ordered, as in ordained, to preach as a witness to Jesus Christ. Thus, all of the Apostles were ordained as well, as the keepers of the flame, to bring continuous light to a darkened world.

Christianity is the light of Christ spread by Apostles. Apostles are ordained by Jesus Christ. Apostles speak as Jesus, the Beloved, with whom God was, is, and always be well pleased. Apostles speak as Jesus Christ, through the Holy Spirit.

The one who gets the piece of the king cake with the bean or the baby in it is then symbolizing the one who has been blessed by God and filled with His Holy Spirit. That is the Apostle who gets to wear the crown of Christ, as the new flame that lights the way for others to follow.

As a cake can be seen as bread, made from flour, milk, and eggs, it represents the body of Jesus that must first be consumed and digested, in order to receive the spirit. As the one receiving the bean or baby, one is then also obligated … ordered and commanded … to try and let others to get the piece of king cake with the bean or baby inside.

The "tag, you're it" concept is what we should be celebrating each Epiphany season. We should be getting fat on the knowledge that "all the prophets testify about Jesus as Christ."

The Holy Spirit tells us what the Prophets meant. The Apostles, being filled with the Holy Spirit, teach the lessons of that meaning.

Epiphany Sermons: First Sunday after the Epiphany, Year A

We should be storing up enough faith and light so "that everyone who believes in him receives forgiveness of sins through his name." For that forgiveness, we need to understand what that means.

Peter said, "I truly understand that God shows no partiality, but in every nation anyone who fears him and does what is right is acceptable to him." That is a statement that being a chosen one of God is not enough to go to Heaven. Just because you get a piece of king cake, you are not forgiven of all sins because you believe somewhere in the cake is a bean or plastic baby.

You have to strive for that prize, keep trying, keep getting fat on the bread until you ignite with the spirit. You have to keep trying in order to get lasting forgiveness of sins.

When Peter said God showed no partiality, he meant the Jews were not saved and forgiven of sins because they professed faith in God. Both Israel and Judah professed that faith as they were being overrun and enslaved by conquering forces. If only they acted from a fear of God, doing rightful things, then the outcome might have been different. If only their ACTS had been like those of Apostles, they would they be saved.

When you get the slice of cake with the bean or baby in it, the symbolism is you have received the Holy Spirit. You have been reborn as Jesus, still at the infant stage. You then do rightful things because you know the power of the LORD within you. When you know the peace of the LORD as a state of pure enlightenment, then you never want to leave state, much less forfeit it.

By being filled with the Holy Spirit, your acts will forever more be acceptable to God. Your acts will be to get others to realize the same ecstatic state if bliss you have been gifted. You want to teach them what you see in the words of prophecy.

As an Apostle, you want to open eyes so they too can see. You want to open ears so they can hear the voice of God speaking to them. You want to send to them, by their faith in Jesus Christ, what you have. With the mind of Christ in you, then you become the Advocate others need to find. You meet other Christians, true seekers of truth, and tell them to open their hearts and receive the Holy Spirit.

You want to say, "Tag. Now you have it."

So, if you have a slice of king cake this season, but yours does not have the bean inside, no baby Jesus, then cheer up. There's still time! Keep trying! Don't give up.

This season is all about getting fat with that knowledge and faith. When Lent comes, we fast and trust that our acts will be sustained through a God-given power and inner peace. If we survive the forty-day training camp, with Jesus Christ as our Drill Instructor, then we can begin our ministry as a servant of the LORD. That ministry lasts for the remainder of a lifetime.

On that day, when you "get the bean" that you feel deep within you, the heavens will open to us individually. Each of us so fortunate will be able to see the Spirit of God descending like a dove and alighting on us, as Apostles of Christ. Our inner ears will be capable of hearing the voice of God say, "This Spirit within you, guiding you, is my

Son's Spirit, the Beloved, with whom I am well pleased."

Walk in love, as Christ loved us and gave himself up for us, a fragrant offering and sacrifice to God.

Amen

Second Sunday after the Epiphany

YEAR A

January 19, 2014

Relevant readings:
Isaiah 49:1-7
Psalm 40:1-12
1 Corinthians 1:1-9
John 1:29-42

Will Jesus be staying at your place?

In this season of Epiphany, we now see Jesus as the anointed one, the Messiah, with the dove of heaven upon him. Two disciples of John the Baptist have heard that Jesus is the Lamb of God.

Epiphany Sermons: Second Sunday after the Epiphany, Year A

Those two ask Jesus, "Where are you staying?"

It can be assumed, from the Wilderness perspective, in which John the Baptist stayed and spent his time, when not dunking Jews in the waters of the Jordan River near Jericho, they knew Jesus was going home after his baptism. The two disciples wanted to know where Jesus was headed.

They asked "Where do you live, brother Jesus?"

The Greek word written is "*meno*." That word translates to mean, "To remain, abide," as reference to a place; but the same word also can state, "to sojourn," in reference to a destination.

Still, in a in context to time, the question posed can be understood as asking, "Jesus, will you last?"

In reference to a state or condition, it posed the question, "Are you the awaited one? Can we trust there will not be another like you?" After all, the ones asking were followers of John the baptizer.

Jesus answered that question by saying, "*erchomai* **kai** *horao*," which translates as, "you should come **and** you should see." Still, as a more profound statement, where the "and" connects two responses, Jesus says to them:

"You should find the answer to your question …

AND …

you should experience that answer."

Such a response cannot be read as flippant, or the disciples would have never followed Jesus. The world "should" is stating the condition of obligation and duty, as a condition of expectation. After all, they were disciples of John the Baptist, and discipleship comes with responsibilities, as "learners" and "students."

We are not told how long the group walked after that conversation, or to where they might have stopped before going to Galilee; but they followed Jesus and were amazed enough to have Andrew get up and go to get his brother, Peter (Simon Peter). From that, we can assume that Jesus was not mute during that time spent traveling. He must have spoken to his new followers, so the disciples' eyes were opened and their ears could hear things never heard before, coming from John.

They found the answer to their question through an emotional connection to Jesus. Their hearts were opened and they were experiencing the one prophesied to come. They could feel that as truth, even though their brains still did not know anything for certain.

This was unlike their experience with John the Baptist, who they knew and had followed until finding Jesus. Crowds came to have their sins washed away, but I can imagine there was a temporary feeling surrounding that activity ... especially when the same people would return to be cleaned over and over again.

I imagine, for Andrew and the unnamed disciple, and for the third convert – Cephas, Pierre, Stony, or "the Rock" – or the one commonly called Peter, what they found and what they experienced was their Epiphany. They felt how

Epiphany Sermons: Second Sunday after the Epiphany, Year A

special Jesus was.

They would aid Jesus' ministry, like interns. Jesus needed an entourage, those who would tour with him as gofers, set-up men, or roadies.

Thus, the disciples of Jesus were called by God before their births too. While in their mother's wombs they also were named as servants of the LORD.

Because they followed Jesus, they were planned to serve the Lord through Christ. As Apostles, the disciples would no longer serve the needs of a man named Jesus; but they would serve God as extended bodies that would become duplicate hearts and minds, as was Jesus.

The song of Isaiah that was read today is a deep vision, where Isaiah is channeling a spiritual conversation between the man Jacob and the LORD.

Near the end we read of "The Redeemer of Israel and his Holy One." That would be Jesus. This parallels the recount of John the Beloved, where John the Baptist calls Jesus "the Son of God."

If one follows the conversation in Isaiah carefully, one sees Jesus was to be the Redeemer of the failure brought about by Jacob's descendants, the Israelites. It was a failure to maintain their commitment that promised, "my God has become my strength."

That was the **intent**, such that the children of Israel represented the Word in the beginning, before a people would be born, named while in the mother's womb. The land named

Israel became their womb of development.

But Jacob failed God. His strength was not the One God, Jehovah (Yahweh), but more than one god, *elohim* – saying, "my **gods** have become my strength." That strength would fail Israel and those descendants would become scattered, requiring restoration to the survivors.

In Hebrew, the word for Redeemer is "*qu'al*." Its use is relative to a kinsman, in particular one marrying a widow who is without a male heir. A Redeemer, a "*qu'al*," is one who is genetically linked to the widow, in a family relationship, a relative. By marrying a woman solely to produce a male heir, that widow can then lay claim on the property of her deceased husband. That is because the inheritance would be claimed by the widow's new son.

What was lost is then returned.

This means that Israel had failed to produce a rightful heir to the heavenly kingdom. Instead, it had turned away from God, worshiping idols, so that both Israel and Judah became "deeply despised" and "abhorred by the Gentile nations." Those enemies rose up and defeated Israel before it could produce a righteous heir. The Israelites ... the Jews ... would become the slaves of rulers not of their own bloodline. Like widows without heirs, they had no right to claim what had been lost through death.

In that way, Jesus would Redeem God's Plan for Israel, the *logos* of His servant, as the one produced that would return God's Intent to a priestly people.

Redemption would not be the land - that known as Judea or

Epiphany Sermons: Second Sunday after the Epiphany, Year A

Palestine. The Romans would keep that. Later, the Turks would lay claim.

Instead, Redemption would be through the installation of priests serving the One God, through the Redeemer Jesus Christ. The baby in the womb is born. There is a male heir to serve the LORD.

Isaiah even wrote who would be found propagating those "of man" (the meaning of the name Andrew) with "a Church" (the symbolism of "the Rock" of Saint Peter), demonstrating how "God is gracious through Apostles," with the "salvation of God" coming through Jesus Christ.

Isaiah wrote, "Kings shall see and stand up, princes, and they shall prostrate themselves."

Those are the Kings of Europe. They would become the princes of Christ, whereas the Jews would never prostrate themselves before Jesus. The Jews would forever long for a return to the lost land, to a lost prominence as God's chosen people, while missing the **purpose** for which they were chosen.

Thus, the Redemption of the intent of Israel, which manifest through the Word made flesh, is through the princes of Christianity. They became the male heirs to the throne.

That is where we all come in ... because we are Christians.

Still, it is easier to say, "I am a Christian," than it is to act Christian, without any statements being made.

We are as Paul wrote to the Ephesians: "I am called to be

an apostle of Christ Jesus by the will of God."

The will of God is different than the will of Paul. It is different than the will of Robert. It is different than the will of any one human being.

The will of God is found by "those who are sanctified in Christ Jesus, called to be saints, together with all those who in every place call on the name of our Lord Jesus Christ, both their Lord and ours."

That is a true Christian; and, it is to those who find "Grace to you and peace from God our Father and the Lord Jesus Christ."

Think about it …

Israel was a nation of people who thought all they had to do was go around telling Gentiles, "We are chosen by God. We are special. All we have to do is be a descendant of one of the Tribes of Israel. All we have to do is say we believe in God."

When they failed ... from acting like whatever they did was through the grace of God ... they found out the hard way that they were wrong. However, the first Christians were Jews who believed, like those two disciples of John the Baptist, who followed Jesus to find why they were chosen, and to experience first-hand how to serve God.

That is why we recognize Epiphany each year.

Just as the dove of heaven lit on Jesus and stayed there, it would also lite on the Apostles. Through the past two thou-

Epiphany Sermons: Second Sunday after the Epiphany, Year A

sand years, it has stayed on all the Saints. Likewise, we too must have to have our own Epiphany and recognize Jesus is on a sojourn in us, individually - mind, body, and soul.

We have to call out to Jesus, "Hey! What can we do to have you abide in us?"

Jesus will say, "Seek me and you will find me.

"And"

"Follow my lead and experience what it means to be an Apostle … learn from the rabbi how to be a saint."

Then, as David sang, "Wait patiently for the LORD to put a new song in your mouth."

Find happiness through trust in the LORD.

Experience how "In the roll of the book it is written, 'I love to do your will,' because "Your righteousness is not hidden in my heart."

Let the dove of heaven shine light on you and remain there.

Amen

Third Sunday after the Epiphany

YEAR A

January 26, 2014

Relevant readings:
Isaiah 9:1-4
Psalm 27:1, 5-13
1 Corinthians 1:10-18
Matthew 4:12-23

Understanding the day of Midian

In chapter three of Matthew, we read of John the Baptist baptizing Jesus. The heavens opened, a dove lit on Jesus, and the voice of God was heard. That was in the Jordan River, which created the border between the Roman territories of Judea and Perea.

Epiphany Sermons: Third Sunday after the Epiphany, Year A

In chapter four of Matthew we read of Jesus spending forty days in the wilderness. During that time he was tested by the devil and attended by angels. After those forty days, Matthew immediately tells of Jesus hearing the news of John the Baptist being arrested.

John the Baptist lived in the Judaean Wilderness and that wilderness extended (and still does) from eastern Jerusalem to Jericho, which is by the Jordan River. So, after being baptized Jesus was already on the eastern edge of that wilderness.

So, making sure we are following the logistics properly, Jesus began his Lenten period as part of his return from his baptism experience. Jesus then heard the news of John's arrest, at which time Matthew said Jesus "withdrew to Galilee." The question is, "Withdrew from where?"

After we read John's account of Jesus' baptism, he then wrote of Jesus' first encounter with Peter and Andrew. They are identified as disciples of John the Baptist. On the next day after his baptism, Jesus was seen leaving the Jordan River area by those two disciples. One of the two called to Jesus, saying, "Look, the Lamb of God!"

John goes on to tell how the two disciples asked Jesus, "Where do you stay?" Jesus replied, "Come and see."

Jesus went to Galilee the next day, possibly after staying with friends near Jerusalem that night. Galilee was the territory governed by Herod Antipas. It was Antipas who arrested John the Baptist, with that arrest taking place two days after Jesus' baptism. So, one can assume Peter and

Andrew went with Jesus to Galilee; and, it was in a Galilean wilderness that Jesus was tested by Satan.

It can be assumed that Peter and Andrew, and James and John, sons of Zebedee, were also Galileans, who accompanied Jesus there as a statement of faith; but also as it was not out of the way for them. We don't read of them spending forty days with Jesus in the wilderness, watching him fast, pray, reflect, and tell the devil to get out of his way. That would require the dedication of disciples; but they were not quite there yet.

Thus, when Matthew wrote of John the Baptist's arrest, he wrote, "Jesus withdrew to Galilee." That was most probably the where his forty-days of sacrifice had taken place.

That news caused Jesus to seek his homeland as a place of solitude before beginning his ministry full bore. He had to be tested first.

Nazareth is in the region known as Galilee, to the west of the Sea of Galilee. The land surrounding Nazareth is that which was first given to the tribes of Jacob's sons, Zebulun and Naphtali. That was where Isaiah prophesied the light for those who walked in darkness would come, as a glorious and joyful light shining.

Now, because John wrote in his gospel how Jesus told two disciples of John the Baptist to come and see where he stayed, before beginning his Lenten period, we know they had already met when he saw them fishing on the Sea of Galilee. A relationship had begun, and the two who would become Jesus' first disciples still did not know that would be their call. They came to Galilee with Jesus, they saw he stayed in Nazareth, then when they - as disciples of John the Baptist - went to their own homes in that territory. When they also heard of their leader's imprisonment, they left Jesus alone, so they could regroup also.

Matthew says Simon-Peter and Andrew were fishers. That is a statement of their "day jobs," when not being called by John, with instructions to help him do some more baptisms next month. The Sea of Galilee would attract people whose profession was fishing. That is the biggest place nearby, so with no John to follow, and with Jesus on a camping trip, they went back to work.

When Matthew wrote that Jesus saw Peter and Andrew (two brothers) casting nets as fishers, Jesus was back from his forty days in the wilderness. He had moved from Nazareth to Capernaum, on the northern shore of the sea. While walking about, Jesus saw two men he recognized.

He knew they were disciples of John the Baptist. He knew John the Baptist was in prison, so they were back to their old job. That means when Jesus called to them this time, saying, "Follow me and I will make you fishers of men," he said that to people who knew him … in some way. Jesus was saying, "Hey, you disciples of John, I will make you disciples of God."

That explains why they "immediately left their nets and followed him." Still, when Jesus came upon James and John, with their father Zebedee, they too immediately left their father and followed Jesus. I imagine the fishers got together after a day on the water and told tales to get to know one another. Peter and Andrew might have told stories of this guy Jesus, the Lamb of God.

From then, Jesus began working miracles and his disciples came and saw it all. As they say, "The rest is history."

I believe during this Epiphany season, it is important to find new ways to see aspects of old lessons that take us that extra inch forward, towards a level of unconditional faith, with understanding being a solid foundation for that faith to be built upon. We come to hear a sermon and we see something we questioned before in a new light of understanding. Each time we read the same verses we need to see them in a way that we had not seen prior.

Sometimes we read things and get confused. We mean to look something up or ask someone what they think; but sometimes we think not knowing is a sign of a lack of faith. Often, we forget to find the answers that clear things up. We don't ask question from embarrassment. However, we need to have a firm grasp on those answers.

We must ask the questions, no matter how dumb they may seem. Even if it is like asking Jesus, "Your father's house? Did you ever tell us where that was? Is it in Nazareth?"

One tiny part of today's reading from Isaiah can be one of those confusing bits. We hear it; but because we are not Jewish and do not spend Sabbaths deeply going over the written word, we are not "versed" in all the meanings of names and the history of places. The Jews of Isaiah's Judah would have, but we are much farther removed, so we miss small things.

I am referring to where Isaiah told how the coming light would remove the yoke of burden from across their shoulders of those in darkness. It would be broken as "on the day of Midian."

Raise your hand if you understand "on the day of Midian."

<look for raised hands>

Okay, for those of you who are not recalling what "on the day of Midian" means, let me tell that story. It comes from chapter seven (mostly), in the Book of Judges.

It begins with the man named Jerubbaal, which means, "Let Baal contend against him." We know Jerubbaal better as Gideon; and, Gideon was God's help sent to His struggling people, who were under the thumb of the Midianites.

The Midianites had built shrines to Baal and Asherah (the wife of Baal) in the Promised Land, which Gideon tore down. He contended with Baal, which caused the Midianites to come after Gideon and those who he led.

Gideon asked God to help, and God said, "You have too many soldiers. Tell those who want to go home to go home." Gideon did and his troops dropped from 32,000 to 10,000.

God said, "That is still too many. Send the troops still left under your command to the river and see how many lap the water like dogs or bow down to drink from the river."

A well-trained soldier knows to always be on guard for attack. One is not on guard when one becomes more concerned with drinking water than guarding one's safety. A good warrior looks around, while placing his hand in the water and bringing a sip to his tongue. A fool gets down like a dog to drink.

Gideon counted three hundred men who did not know basic military safety procedures, like how to drink water from a stream.

God said, "With three hundred men I will save you." God would save them because Gideon had only three hundred fools to face a mighty foe with. Any victory could only be attributed to the power of God, which would be pitted against the power of Baal.

The Midianites were camped, with the "Amalekites and all the children of the east," in the valley below Gideon's troops. Their numbers were so great it was "like grasshoppers for multitude; and their camels were without number, as the sand by the sea side for multitude."

So, the odds were three hundred fools to many thousands in the Midianite army.

The three hundred were divided by Gideon into companies of one hundred each. Each man was given a lamp to place inside a jar; and, each man was given a trumpet. Then they "contended against" the army of Midian at night.

The spread out and moved into positions just outside the three watch posts for the Midian camp. Then the three hundred each broke the jars and held high the lamps. With their lights now visible in the darkness, each man then blew his trumpet. It appeared a superior force was making a surprise attack.

Epiphany Sermons: Third Sunday after the Epiphany, Year A

The result was fear striking the Midianites, so that they ran, leaving everything behind. Gideon then called for the other armies of Israel to give chase, and all the Midianites were overrun and their leaders killed. So, "on the day of Midian" means when a great victory was brought about by God.

Knowing that, we see Isaiah's prophecy of the coming of Jesus, as the light for those who walked in darkness. Jesus would break the jar hiding the light, which was the control the Temple had over the people. God exposed the fears of those who keep that imbalance in place, through the light of Jesus. Jesus would begin to trumpet, "Repent, for the kingdom of heaven has come near."

The yoke of oppression would be broken, just "as on the day of Midian," through the advent of Christianity. Only twelve disciples, and their families, would bring fright to the Roman Empire, winning the hearts of a greater world. From the beginning of just a few, thousands would then respond to the call to drive the darkness away.

Just like the victory over the Midianites, the victory of Christ is due to God. Jesus is like Gideon, a.k.a. Jerubbaal, as another one who contended against Baal.

The disciples were the fools, the soldiers who lapped water like dogs. Throughout the Gospels we read how the Resurrected Jesus had whipped his ragtag army of fools into shape, during his ministry, but more so before his Ascension. Those who had been unskilled priests for God were immediately elevated into miracle workers on the Day of Pentecost. They had been volunteers for the cause, as followers and attendants to the needs of Jesus, but they never dreamed they would do anything more than watch Jesus go against evil.

Other than their temporary powers when the Commission of Twelve was sent, followed by that of seventy, the disciples lapped water like dogs, bowing down to drink-in all that Jesus said. It seemed to just go in one ear and out the other.

Are we no different today?

We follow. We do what we are told. We watch Jesus sacrifice for us. We watch Jesus perform miracles. We have difficulty remembering all the details we hear. We think we have no special talents to contend against the Baal's of sin, disease, or death.

But we are taking the first steps. We are following as fishers of souls. We are asked to accept the invitation and let God be our eyes, so we can perceive in new ways.

In time, our day will come. Be patient, our jar will be broken and the light will shine through us. Expect a miracle and it will happen, through faith.

Amen

Epiphany Sermons: Third Sunday after the Epiphany, Year A

Fourth Sunday after the Epiphany

The Presentation of Jesus in the Temple

YEAR A

February 2, 2014

Relevant readings:
Malachi 3:1-4
Psalm 84
 or Psalm 24:7-10
Hebrews 2:14-18
Luke 2:22-40

Epiphany Sermons: Fourth Sunday after the Epiphany, Year A

A purification of flesh and blood

In the reading from the letter to the Hebrews, we are told, "Since God's children share flesh and blood, Jesus himself likewise shared the same things." I think that is a statement that needs some deeper reflection.

If one goes and types in "flesh and blood" into a search engine, one can find that "flesh and blood" is an idiom. Literally, those three words together mean, "A living human body, especially with reference to its natural limitations; a human being." Figuratively, the saying means, "the quality of being alive."

One source says it bears the meaning, "if you say that someone is flesh and blood, you mean that they have feelings or faults that are natural because they are human."

We read what Paul wrote and seeing his words causes our conditioned minds to think in terms of an idiom. Then, when we read and hear, "Jesus himself likewise shared the same things," we think Jesus had flaws and faults because he was human, just like us.

Then, when we read and hear of baby Jesus being taken to the temple for purification, we tend to jump to a conclusion that Jesus was impure and needed to be cleansed.

To a small degree all of that is true; but there is a deeper meaning that can easily be missed.

The word "flesh" alone bears the meaning of flawed, of

being human, of being alive. The word "blood" is where we overlook the obvious.

Think about the times when you use the words "flesh and blood." You talk to your children using those words. Your parents use those words to you. It means more then, as the statement, "You are my human being," because it is a statement of relationship. To say, "You are of my own flesh and blood," you are referring to an offspring, someone who sprang from your loins, sharing flesh that looks like you, sharing blood that came from you.

The word "blood" bears a definition that means, "Descent from a common ancestor; parental lineage. Family relationship; kinship." We need to see that in the readings today.

Paul wrote, "Since God's children share flesh and blood." Therefore, he was not talking generally, but instead making reference to a link through family relationship, a parental lineage, as children descended from God.

This is then not a statement about the whole of the human race. It is referring to a select subset of humanity. Thus, this statement is put into a letter addressed to "Hebrews." That was a distinction that separated a part from the whole classified as "human," being those human beings who routinely communicated with the language of Hebrew. Today, those people are generally called Jews. Jews, while sharing a common religion, are a race of people too. The Hebrew people are related to one another, through flesh and through DNA ... blood.

Jesus, being a descendant of the house of David, as a Jew, shared the same things as other Jews. He shared a heritage, tradition, and culture with the Hebrew speaking people. "Therefore he had to become like his brothers and sisters in every respect, so that he might be a merciful and faithful high priest in the service of God."

That statement says that Jesus was destined to lead the Jews, where the Temple priests had failed to lead. Thus, as Paul wrote, God had to send his Son as a Jewish human being, "to make a sacrifice of atonement for the sins of the people."

The Day of Atonement is a Jewish holy day, called *Yom* (Day) *Kippur* (Atonement). One of the ceremonies that takes place on *Yom Kippur* is the release of the scapegoat. A goat ceremoniously takes on the burden of the sins of the people, and it is then outcast into the desert. In a way, Jesus was also outcast by the Jewish people. However, it is more the other way around, where Jesus has outcast the Jews, although he still took their sins upon himself.

The sins of the Jewish people were their failure to be dedicated priests for God. Since the beginning, when they were given the land promised them, they wanted a king – so they could be like other people. A king would allow only one to be responsible to God as a priest, so all the rest could go and play like special children. They too were chosen to be priests, but they wanted all the benefits of being a priest, with none of the testing.

Paul wrote, "Because (Jesus) himself was tested by what he suffered, he was able to help those who are being tested." Those who "are being tested" (in the present tense of Paul's time), were those who were the first Christians. Those consisted of Jews and Gentiles; but in the letter to the Hebrews,

Paul was talking directly to the Jews of Christianity.

In today's time, Paul's words still apply. Those who "are being tested" now are us, and all Christians. Today, only a small portion of Christians are Jewish, maintaining their laws in addition to the amendments of the New Covenant. That means Gentiles are now to be tested, with testing meaning suffering, as Paul wrote.

The prophet Malachi wrote of testing that comes from God's messenger. We read that from the Old Testament today, because we believe Jesus was that messenger.

Malachi asked, "Who can endure the day of his coming, and who can stand when he appears?"

Jesus came around 4 BC,[1] and then he left around 29-30 AD (give or take). However, Jesus said he would return, so Malachi's questions still apply.

Who can endure the day of his return? Who would still be there in two thousand years?

Who can stand when he reappears? Who will rise when Jesus returns?

Malachi said, "He is like a refiner's fire and like fuller's soap." He said, "He will purify the descendants of Levi and refine them like gold and silver, until they present offerings to the LORD in righteousness."

This is metaphor for Jesus returning value to God's priests.

---

[1] In 2014, I made an assumption that was common. By late 2016 I had determined Jesus was born in 9 BCE (-008 Julian Date). I have since written about this in the book The Star of Bethlehem: The Timing of the Life of Jesus.

Epiphany Sermons: Fourth Sunday after the Epiphany, Year A

They will be tested by fire, so their precious metals separate from the dirt, rock, and other metals of lesser value, which lesser priests will have allowed to be attached to them. They will be washed in lye soap, beaten on rocks, and made soft and full as fine linen robes should be.

Jesus will make worthy priests, ones that "will be pleasing to the LORD."

Thus, we need to ask ourselves: Are we tested? Are we worthy?

In Luke, we read of Jesus being presented in the Temple, as required by the law in Leviticus. The "purification process" is for Mary and her first born son, due to the discharge of blood during Jesus' birth. Both are deemed sinners, where the sins of the child are due to it having the blood of his mother inside it. That is a statement of mitochondrial DNA association, where lineage is traceable through blood and tissue … flesh and blood.

Simeon, whose name means "He who hears," came into the temple to serve in the purification process. Mary, according to the Law, could not touch any holy thing or go into any sanctuary, until forty days had passed after childbirth. Jesus would have been circumcised on day 8 (according to Law), and Simeon would then make inspections and ask pertinent questions, with everything being part of a ritual ceremony of cleansing - making the rough wool full and soft. However, when Simeon took Jesus in his arms, he immediately knew Jesus was special for the world.

Simeon said to a baby only forty-one days old, whom he had never laid eyes or hands on before, here is "a light for revelation to the Gentiles and for glory to your people Israel." If the name holds true, then Simeon spoke the words he heard, as a priest for the One God. The voice of flesh and blood, sourced in the divine mind.

Then, there was a widow who had lived in the temple for many years, continuously worshiping, fasting, and praying, who overheard Simeon and his conversation with the amazed parents, Joseph and Mary. Her name was Anna, a name that means "compassion." She began praising God, and telling others about having the Messiah now among them. She told this "to all who were looking for redemption of Jerusalem."

Mary was supposed to bring a lamb for sacrifice, but we read two turtle doves were sacrificed instead. The Law stated that if one cannot afford a lamb, then turtle doves (or pigeons) could be substituted. They would have been purchased from the vendors on the steps outside the Temple. That was what was sacrificed as part of the purification process for Mary and Jesus.

The reason Mary did not bring a lamb is the family had traveled "up to Jerusalem" from Egypt, where then had fled to avoid the death decree ordered by Herod I, or Herod the Great. Herod had died, thus making their return safe. The exclamations made by Anna, to all who came into the temple compound, would not endanger the family. Thus, when the required purification process was finished, "they returned to Galilee, to their own town of Nazareth."

In this season of epiphany, we are not called to remember that Jesus was a Jew and lived by the Law of Moses. We are not related to Jesus by physical blood. We would not know Jesus from Adam, if it had not been for acts of Jews who were first filled with the Holy Spirit, who were led to become true priests for God, causing them to reach out to us Gentiles, allowing our ancestors to receive the Holy Spirit, becoming Christians too.

That is the significance we recognize with our Communion, our Eucharist. As human beings we share the flesh of Jesus, the body of Christianity, through a physical wafer. Beyond that physical relationship, we spiritually share the blood of Jesus, through the spirited wine that enters our bloodstream, making us symbolically related to Jesus in essence. We become of the lineage of priests that the children of God were created to be. We become linked to Jesus through the Holy Spirit.

Jesus was sent to redeem the children of God who failed to live up to the standards God set. They were only the flesh, and while they had the genetics of Adam in their blood, they were not willing to receive the spirit of purpose, of intent to lead the world as God planned.

The saying goes, "What goes around comes around." We are the latest version of the children of God. Therefore, the warnings of the prophets apply to us, the same as they applied to them.

Are we failing to serve God as He intended, as priests, who not only use words to spread the news of Jesus Christ, but also live in the spirit of Christ?

Are we leading by example?

Or, are we a reflection of those needing redemption?

May Christ give us all strength to accept the testing of suffering, so that we may live in the glory of God's people.

Amen

Fifth Sunday after the Epiphany

YEAR A

February 9, 2014

> **Relevant readings:**
> Isaiah 58:1-12
> Psalm 112:1-10
> 1 Corinthians 2:1-16
> Matthew 5:13-20

How to fast and atone for lost New Year's resolutions

According to the Jewish Encyclopedia, under "Fasting and Fast Days," it is said, "The Rabbis compared fasting to sacrifice, and considered the affliction of one's body as the offering up of one's blood and fat upon the altar."

That source goes on to state, "Of regular fixed fast-days the Jewish calendar has comparatively few. Besides the Day of Atonement, which is the only fast-day prescribed by the Mosaic law, there were established after the Captivity four regular fast-days in commemoration of the various sad events that had befallen the nation during that period."

According to the website Hebrew for Christians, two other days of fast were recognized from rabbinical literature, bringing the total of official fast days to seven.

Perhaps it is mere coincidence, or perhaps it is through the all-knowing mind of God, but in the Isaiah reading today there are seven times the words "fast" or "fasting" appear.

1. God spoke through Isaiah, saying, "Why do we (the Jews) **fast**, but you (God) do not see?"

2. "Look, you (the people) serve your own interest on your **fast** day,"

3. "Look, you (the people) **fast** only to quarrel and to fight"

4. "Such **fasting** as you (the people) do today will not make your voice heard on high."

5. "Is such the **fast** that I (the LORD) choose [supposed to be] a day to humble oneself?"

6. "Will you (the people) call this a **fast** [to bow down like a bulrush and to lie in sackcloth and ashes]?

7. "Is not this the **fast** that I choose: to loose the bonds of injustice, to undo the thongs of the yoke, to let the oppressed go free?"

Seven times said, with each use indicating the people had changed the Law, to suit their own needs, as if ceremonial fasting was a quick-fix and the fast-track to heaven.

God said the fast He chose was to share your bread with the hungry; to bring the homeless into your house; to cover the naked; to not hide from your own kin.

God then said through Isaiah, **IF** you are doing those things, **THEN** "your light shall break forth like the dawn."

He said, **THEN** "your healing shall spring up quickly; your vindicator shall go before you, (and) the glory of the LORD shall be your rear guard."

How many times did Jesus fast, according to what we know in the Gospels?

The answer is once, just as the Lord commanded, by Law. In Matthew, chapter four, verse two, we read, "And after (Jesus) had fasted for forty days and forty nights, then he became hungry."

A day of "fasting" is usually seen as "abstaining from food and drink," where "drink" means beverages other than water. The intent of "food" can mean abstinence from meat, with a forty day fast implying a minimum of eating unleavened bread, which would have less chance of molding.

Epiphany Sermons: Fifth Sunday after the Epiphany, Year A

The Jewish Day of Atonement (*Yom Kippur*) is the one day each year that the Law demands a child of Israel fast. The Day of Atonement is the holiest day of the Jewish calendar, and it represents the day that Moses returned from the mount with the tablets inscribed by God.

That day occurred forty days after Moses ascended Mount Sinai; so, the fast of Jesus (what we call Lent) reflects a "Season of *Teshuvah*," or the "Period of Repentance," the same as Moses experienced. It is a time of purification, and as such the children of Israel were purified through the Law sent by Moses.

And the Jews, those who would welcome Jesus as the Messiah, would become purified through the new covenant sent by Jesus.

In the Gospel reading from Matthew, we hear Jesus asking the crowds of Jews who came to be near him, "If salt has lost its taste, how can its saltiness be restored?"

The answer is a re-purification. Each year, God commanded a day of atonement be recognized. Each year, the ten days before that day of repentance are recognized as the Days of Awe. That period commences with *Rosh Hosana*, the New Year, or the "Head of the Year."

The days of awe are for prayer and meditation, where all wrongs one has done against others must be repented and forgiveness sought. The Day of Atonement is when one's wrongs against God can be forgiven. The Ten Days are therefore an opportunity to mend one's ways in order to alter the judgment of God in one's favor – Do unto others as you would have God do unto you.

Atonement and purification are like taking an unlit stick and turning it into a torch, or striking a match to candlewicks upon a lampstand. Salt that has lost its saltiness can have its saltiness restored in the same way, by becoming a "light of the world."

Fasting, as a ritual for anything other than repentance, so one can become restored to service for God, will do nothing towards getting one to heaven.

The season of Lent (which is the Season of *Teshuvah*) has been altered to be a period of ceremonial sacrifice, where some vice is set aside for forty days. It has become like a New Year's resolution; but instead of our Lenten commitments being for a whole year, they are just for forty days.

Who thinks giving up chocolate for forty days will get you to heaven?

Who thinks forty days of playing only nine holes of golf, instead of eighteen each week, is a great sacrifice of purification and repentance?

Jesus said, according to Matthew, "I have not come to abolish the law or the prophets, but to fulfill."

Jesus said, "Until heaven and earth pass away, not one letter, not one stroke of a letter, will pass from the law until all is accomplished."

In this period of Epiphany, are we preparing to have ourselves to be lit anew as servants to God's commandments, to be priests who will free the oppressed and break every yoke? Are we prepared to become lights for the world?

Are we readying ourselves to shine before others, so they may see our good works?

Or, will we find ourselves "no longer good for anything," worthy of only being "thrown out" and walked on, like dirt, like the dust of the material plane we come from?

Paul wrote to Apostles in Corinth, explaining to them, "Remember we are special. We have been enabled to speak God's wisdom, which is secret and hidden from normal people."

Paul rekindled the Corinthians by saying, "We have seen what no eye has seen, nor ear heard." He said it was written that no "human heart conceived what God has prepared for those who love him."

If you only follow God's commandments to Moses, you can never achieve the Holy Spirit and God's wisdom. If you do not know God's commandments, how can you ever conceive what the Holy Spirit is?

Of those who do not follow the Law, Paul wrote, "Those who are unspiritual do not receive the gifts of God's spirit, for they are foolishness to [those gifts]. They are unable to understand [the gifts of the Holy Spirit] because they are spiritually discerned."

"They are spiritually discerned" means they must be properly investigated, fully questioned, completely examined. Anything less than "proper, fully, and complete" discernment means an inability to understand the Holy Spirit, the gift of God.

Because there are those who do not have a full year to dedicate to God, because there are crowds of followers who only want healing, but are unwilling to teach others how to heal, the light of Christianity's promise goes unrewarded. Still, it beacons to those in darkness.

Whoever breaks one of the least of God's commandments, and teaches others to do the same, will be called least in the kingdom of heaven. You are salt without taste, earthbound.

But whoever abides by all the commandments and teaches them will be called great in the kingdom of heaven.

Teaching in a school requires a degree from a university. Teaching the covenants of God and Christ goes beyond what any colleges or universities know to teach. One needs a degree from God, which shows you have completed all the requirements of gaining wisdom AND you stand prepared to pass that wisdom on.

We have entered a new year, already nine days into February.

How are those New Year's resolutions working for you?

It is hard to make things happen alone; but with God's gift, with God as your rear guard, you can work miracles.

Can you hear the call?

Amen

Epiphany Sermons: Fifth Sunday after the Epiphany, Year A

Sixth Sunday after the Epiphany

YEAR A

February 16, 2014

Relevant readings:
Deuteronomy 30:15-20
 or Sirach 15:15-20
Psalm 119:1-8
1 Corinthians 3:1-9
Matthew 5:21-37

Making the grades for graduation day

Here we are on the sixth Sunday after the Epiphany. There are three weeks before the first Sunday of Lent. So, we are still getting fat, in preparation for the yearly period of sacrifice. Mardi Gras (meaning Fat Tuesday) will be on March 4th, sixteen days from today.

We should be getting fat on the Holy Spirit. That means not fat on sin, to the point we must wear masks and costumes so we can parade one's sinful self in public.

Instead, we should be having our own Epiphany, our own sudden manifestation of the meaning of the Holy Spirit. Our own comprehension of reality should dawn on us as a sudden intuitive realization. Through individual epiphanies, we must confess our sins sincerely, and then spend Lent in repentance.

Without that epiphany to thrive on, our time of sacrifice will fail.

Failure is common. Anyone who fails to make the necessary sacrifices will not be alone. As the sayings go, "Misery loves company" and "There is safety in numbers."

In the parable of the wedding banquet, a metaphor of one's entrance into the heavenly kingdom, Jesus concluded, "Many are invited but few are chosen."

Today's readings focus on the choice we must make during the season after the Epiphany.

Do we sacrifice? Or, do we stay with the status quo – the way things are now and have been?

Today we read from Ecclesiasticus. That is the Roman Church's name for the book containing the All-Virtuous Wisdom of Sirach. The name of that book was changed to

Ecclesiasticus because the wisdom of Sirach states what the Church stands for. The Latin word "*ecclesia*" (from the Greek "*ekklesia*") means "an assembly of the people," from which we translate "church."

Today's selected reading focuses on how Sirach said, "Before each person are life and death, whichever one chooses will be given."

That wisdom then ends by saying, "[God] has not given anyone permission to sin."

In other words, individually we can make the right choice or we can make the wrong choice. Through free will the choice is each of ours to make.

The alternate Old Testament reading for today is from Deuteronomy, where Moses talked about not choosing to obey the commandments of the LORD. He too said it is between choosing life and death, to which he added, either blessings or curses are received in return. The choice, again, is each of ours to make.

David sang a song of praise, where he promised that obeying the commandments of the LORD brought happiness. He pointed out there is an "all or nothing" clause, when he sang to God, "You laid down your commandments, that we should fully keep them."

In our educational process, both public and private, we get accustomed to 65-70% being a score constituting a minimally passing grade – a "D." A few "D"s are allowed in a educational program of study, but for the most part a "C" (between 71-80%) is the regular minimum expectation for passing.

In a school life that never seems to end, a lot of times we get by without being fully committed to a subject. How often have people winged it? How often have we flashed a smile and hoped to catch a break? How many times have we made some correct guesses on multiple choice tests and got by?

After all, if we are rewarded with certificates, diplomas, and degrees, for having completed an important task, while having given little more than minimal effort, was it worth it?

In my case, in hindsight, from the 20-20 clarity of mature vision, I must have graduated from high school simply because they felt the seat that I was taking up could be better served by giving it to a student who might actually care about learning. I have few memories of applying myself to study and homework. I have more memories of the cold feeling of knowing I was about to fail another test ... miserably.

Regardless of one's success in the systems of public education, in the school of spiritual life, where our religious dedication and observance to God is graded, there is only one test, and only one passing score. Nothing short of perfection will allow for graduation. Each one of us must be 100% right, when the day of that big test comes.

Jesus stressed that in the Gospel reading from Matthew today. He reminded those around him of the laws against murder, of bearing false witness against a neighbor, those forbidding adultery and those against coveting a neighbor's wife. There was no "gray area" to consider. There was no minimum amount of wrong answers allowed.

Jesus said it would be better to cut off a body part, whichever one led to a sin, in order to make that 100% grade, than it would be to come in under perfection and go to hell.

All .... Or nothing.

100 .... Or zero.

The choice is ours to make, but the wisdom of Sirach, as well as Jesus, says, "God has not given anyone permission to sin."

Paul wrote to the Corinthians and referred to them as his "brothers and sisters." He addressed them as being like babies, not capable of digesting solid food. They were just kindergartners, still being nursed along; nowhere close to being tested on their compliance to the Law, and much less the new covenant of Christ.

As babies, they were "still of the flesh." Instead of minds led by the Holy Spirit, they were still amazed by their physical attributes, just like how babies contemplate their feet, taste their toes and hands, love physical touches, delight in melodic songs, and enjoy the colorful mobiles we hang over their cribs for them to gaze at.

Babies "behave according to human inclinations." When they physically grow up, into mature bodies, they still behave according to human inclinations. So, grown bodies are still babes spiritually. We become jealous of others who say they know the Holy Spirit. We argue and quarrel over

Epiphany Sermons: Sixth Sunday after the Epiphany, Year A

whose version of the Holy Spirit is better.

That is a sub-100% way to be.

The "flesh" needs the Law, or it will wander aimlessly, forever mistaking sensual delights as spiritual surrogates. As such, the Law becomes a prison for everyone. The Law is a wall of safety that has been built around us, designed to keep us within those safe limits.

The Pharisees were like the sentries who walked along the walls, looking down on the people from the parameters of that wall of Law. They could see who stayed within those limits; but more importantly (to them), they could see who was sneaking outside the Law. They could tell who was sinning here and there, and then sneaking back into the prison that the Law created.

Paul told us, as we read a few weeks back, that Jesus came to free us from the prison that the Law represented. However, that freedom was not from Jesus abolishing the Law. He came to fulfill it. Therefore, there is no escaping the physical boundaries the Law is designed to establish.

Jesus frees us from the Law by telling us to stop trying to make the Law our standard of measure. The Law represents a 70% score. That is because the Law has holes in it, like gates, which allow easy access to sin. We pile laws upon laws to cover those walkways into the gray areas, to justify wrong answers; but those paths are still outside the Law, thus sin.

Jesus is telling us to go inside ourselves, to our hearts. Open them and ask the Holy Spirit to come reside in us. If we let the Holy Spirit run our lives, we never go beyond the Law, because we never need to worry about what limits we can go to, before having to turn back.

We move beyond the "flesh" state and enter the "spirit" state.

Earlier this month, Jay Leno retired from *The Tonight Show*. His final week he had on his favorite guests. One was a native of the South (Texas), Matthew McConaughey. Matthew McConaughey remembered his first time on *The Tonight Show* and how nervous he was. He said Jay came back to the Green Room and offered him a tip, one that he used to get through his nervous first appearance on TV, and a tip he said he has used ever since.

He said, "Jay told me to just want to be here."

That is good advice. If you ever try to go somewhere you really don't want to go, you will fail miserably. I did not want to go to high school. I passed simply because no one cared. I wanted to go back to college and complete my degree. I graduated with honors, because I cared. I wanted to be there.

The same works in the school of spiritual life. You just have to want to offer true repentance to the Lord. You just have to care.

You just have to want to be filled with the Holy Spirit.

You just have to want to be led by the mind of Christ.

You just have to want God to live in your heart.

Epiphany Sermons: Sixth Sunday after the Epiphany, Year A

You just have to want to be free from figuring out if the Law lets you do this, but not that.

You just have to want to be happy by not bringing shame upon yourself.

You just have to want to please God and not anyone else.

You just have to want to choose life over death.

(pause)

Certainly, that is easier said than done.

(pause)

We all want to graduate with honors, to be assured our souls will reach Heaven ... but it is so hard; and, it requires so much sacrifice.

We look around and see so many other people who are not sacrificing. People tell us to stop spoiling their party, to get with it and have fun.

"*Carp Diem*, Seize the day!" they say. That becomes the kind of fun that you always regret afterwards, when the hangover comes.

Happiness is more than a cheap thrill. Happiness is more than a delight of the flesh. Happiness is more than what pleases our five physical senses.

Happiness is the satisfaction of knowing you are on the

right track. Happiness is a slap on the back, a hug, and a hand reaching out to help you get back up and continue on your way.

Paul wrote to the Corinthians, telling them Christians all have a purpose. It does not matter if one Christian's purpose is different than another Christian's. Some plant and some water, but all serve their purpose together. It is not up to us to choose what role we play for God.

Being Christian means we each serve God, so God chooses how He will use us ... after we choose to serve only Him.

We must know that we are not the only ones making that choice. We serve alongside others who also serve God, but in ways that compliment what we each do in that service.

This is the concept of "Love your neighbor as yourself." You love those who are also serving God, by being together, by working together, and by living our lives in dedication to God together.

As Christians, we are neighbors. We are led to support one another, just like Paul supported the Corinthians, through deeds and words of support.

We, as Christians, are God's field, God's building. We represent the body of Christ, so we may be filled with the Spirit of Christ. We are the Church that serves God, through Christ.

In this season of the Epiphany, where we celebrate the Christ child being born of the flesh, we must challenge ourselves to experience our own realization as Christians in the flesh ... as babies readying for solid food. We should ask ourselves, individually, "Am I happy with my service to God?"

Are we preparing for the sacrifices that are required for our ultimate graduation?

Are we supporting others in their plans to sacrifice, and are we being supported likewise?

Are we amid neighbors, in a position to succeed?

The choice is each of ours to make. Whichever we choose, life or death, that will be given to us.

Amen

Seventh Sunday after the Epiphany

YEAR A

February 23, 2014

Relevant readings:
Leviticus 19:1-2,9-18
Psalm 119:33-40
1 Corinthians 3:10-11, 16-23
Matthew 5:38-48

All along the watchtowers the faithful keep their view

Moses obeyed God when he told the "congregation of the people of Israel ... You shall be holy, for I the LORD your

Epiphany Sermons: Seventh Sunday after the Epiphany, Year A

God am holy."

Paul told the Corinthians ... a church of early Christians ... "You are God's temple" and "God's temple is holy."

Jesus told those Jews who followed him to the mount to hear him preach, "Be perfect, therefore, as your heavenly Father is perfect."

David wrote the lyrics, "Turn my eyes from watching what is worthless," and "Fulfill your promise to your servant."

Paul warned, "Let no one boast about human leaders. For all things are yours – all things belong to you, and you belong to Christ, and Christ belongs to God."

Now this seems to be fairly clear directives to follow. A Christian is no different than a child of Israel, with each being a member of the "congregation of people" who believe in God.

God set laws for his people to follow, which sets the parameters from which holiness can be identified.

"See that boundary? Do **NOT** go beyond that boundary!" sayeth the Law.

It is an all or nothing line in the sand. You are either holy or unholy, based on how well you respect the laws.

Now, Paul said, "You are God's temple." Let's examine that concept for a moment, incorporating the law with that.

The laws represent the walls of the temple. The Ten Commandments represent the "watch towers" along the wall, positioned at strategic points, so a view of that which is both beyond and within the walls can be seen.

That makes the temple appear like a fortress, a defensive structure that has to be guarded. We have to know what the laws are and we have to have imaginary sentries in our heads to warn us. Our inner voice is trained to shout out, "Stop! You are not allowed beyond this point!"

The reason we have to have sentries is we like to hang out along the wall and imagine what it is like "on the other side."

When it has been said, "The grass is always greener on the other side," that is the way an unholy act can seem to someone who hangs out along the wall of holiness.

You see others beyond the law doing everything you are **not** allowed, by law, to do. You do not do certain things simply because God told Moses those laws.

Still, you rarely see any sinners being struck by God's lightning.

People murder and go free or don't get caught.

People steal the life savings of others and get light sentences or government bailouts.

Divorce is commonplace. Marriage is confused. Sexual sterility has become the trend.

It has become fashionable to covet the unwanted children

of other nations, both as adoptions and marriages.

The world goes 24/7 and as it does the Sabbath gets lost in the hustle-bustle.

A nation that once was one hundred percent God-fearing now argues over whose sect is better, with more and more Americans not believing in God at all.

When we stand on the ramparts of the temple and look out and see someone we know - a loved one - beyond the boundaries of the wall of law, we become lost.

We don't know what to do.

If we preach to those who we deem sinners, we get laughed at. We put our tails between our legs when someone asks us questions about the law, which we do not know the answers to. We struggle with judging the sins of others because we know what guilt feels like. We want absolution for our own sins.

It is so easy to say, "It is beyond my control."

It is so easy to say, "My church is what I count on. I give money and time to my church so it can fight for good over evil for me. I pray for my church to call upon God to right this nation, to heal this world."

We think, "The Church is big enough to fight evil and those who are beyond its walls of defense," but there are those who are trying to scale its walls and bash its gates in with battering rams.

Meanwhile, we leave these walls every Sunday and often go outside the boundaries of the laws – by driving long distances and going shopping on Sunday afternoon (the Christian version of the Sabbath).

We are living among those attacking the Church; doing many of the things they are doing, trying to maintain low profiles.

Moses said, "If you are to be one of the congregation of God, then you must be holy."

Paul said, "You are the temple of God, so you must be holy."

Jesus said, "You must be perfect because God is perfect."

None of that is a commandment to the whole world. It only applies to those who will be priests for the One God. You are not told, "You must be a holy priest." You have a choice.

But the choice is either all or nothing ... holy or unholy ... servant of God or servant of self.

Many are invited, but few are chosen. That means most are offered God's hand in marriage, but very few take Him up on that proposal.

Jesus actually tells us what to do if we are to make the choice to serve God, to be holy, to be perfect.

He said we have to go beyond the walls of the laws.

Epiphany Sermons: Seventh Sunday after the Epiphany, Year A

We must go beyond the walls of the laws without breaking the laws.

When Paul said we have to be the temple of God, that means God is in our hearts, with Christ in our minds.

Paul said, "You belong to Christ, and Christ belongs to God." That means, "Christ is always in your thoughts, and Christ's thoughts are all coming from God."

You can only be holy ... you can only be perfect ... when you stop worrying about what you can and can't do and just stand aside and let Christ lead your bag of flesh and bones around.

Christ makes you perfect. Not the other way around. You will never be perfect as you alone.

The walls of the laws were where the Pharisees lived. They manned the towers and from that vantage point they could see where everyone went. They saw sinners as being the only ones who walked around outside the walls. They persecuted Jesus because they saw him there.

"Sinner!" they cried.

The Pharisees and their watchmen shouted warnings, which scared the congregation of people who were supposed to be holy ... who were supposed to be individual temples of God ... who were supposed to each be a priest for God.

They were scared because they felt guilt, without knowing how to make themselves stop sinning ... without knowing how to not get caught. To stop living as a sinner among sinners is such a large responsibility to carry upon one's shoulders ... so much stress to contend with ... such an uphill climb that wears one down.

The congregation of the people of Israel always backslid and fell away from God. Like in a trance, they would wake up finding themselves mired outside the walls of the law, wallowing in sin. From guilt they would pray for forgiveness.

God would send them a judge, which would snap them back to their senses. They would rejoice for a time, then begin to pace along the walls, inside the temple of laws. Forty years later, they would repeat the same cycle of fall and rise, sin and be cleansed.

Then, the people asked Samuel to tell God they wanted a king to bear all the responsibility. They peered out beyond the temple sanctuary and saw other nations had kings. They longed for what those sinners had. They wanted a head for the land to be the one to fight evil. They wanted him closely advised by the Temple. They wanted an institution of government, like those the unholy had, to rule over them. "Give us a human to be our shepherd of holiness," they demanded.

David was a shepherd, if you recall, before he was anointed by Samuel to be the king the people sought.

They were given that, but after three kings – Saul, David and Solomon ... that institution ... that Church ... split.

A house divided cannot stand ... so both halves fell.

Epiphany Sermons: Seventh Sunday after the Epiphany, Year A

The problem comes from wise men being allowed to run the show. Human shepherds so often become pied pipers, offering irresponsible promises that people of herd mentality blindly follow. Human leaders can only lead everyone to ruin.

Paul warned the Corinthians, "Do not deceive yourselves."

Do not put all your eggs in a basket that worships something less than God – like a leader, like a Church.

Paul wrote, "If you think that you are wise in this age, you should become fools so that you may become wise."

You have to fail and admit, "Oh what a fool am I," before you can see that nobody is going to lead you to heaven other than you.

You cannot lead yourself there without Christ in your mind and God in your heart.

You cannot get to heaven with sin between your toes and on the soles of your feet … even though you look pretty clean to the rest of you. God knows your heart. Christ knows your thoughts.

"Let no one boast about human leaders," Job wrote. "He catches the wise in their craftiness." "They are futile," said Isaiah. The serpent in Eden was the craftiest of the creatures, leading Adam and Eve to be influenced to act in evil ways.

You will not be holy simply by following behind someone you think is holy. You will not be a temple to God simply by going into a church. You will not be perfect in your actions simply by learning the laws.

Nothing has changed since Moses first told the congregation of the people of Israel, "You are to be holy because God is holy."

It has always been that … all or nothing.

It has been, ever since then, an exercise by the people to think of ways to change the "all or nothing" into a matter of degrees, through human cunning.

In this season of the Epiphany, with Lent rapidly approaching, it is time to have a "Come to Jesus meeting," in the real sense of those words.

You need to realize it is all or nothing, because only with Christ leading your thoughts and God leading your heart can you walk outside the walls of this church and still be within the laws.

May God be with you.

Amen

Last Sunday after the Epiphany

YEAR A

March 2, 2014

Relevant readings:
Exodus 24:12-18
Psalm 2
 or Psalm 99
2 Peter 1:16-21
Matthew 17:1-9

Get your climbing boots on and let's climb a high mountain to speak with God

This is the last Sunday of the season of Epiphany. This

Epiphany Sermons: Last Sunday after the Epiphany, Year A

coming Wednesday is Ash Wednesday, the first day of Lent.

Today's lessons focus on Moses and Jesus going up onto high mountains, each with assistants, where they both heard the voice of God.

Moses stayed forty days on Mt. Sinai, before he went down with the tablets. Jesus had already spent forty days in the wilderness, before beginning his ministry.

Both Moses and Jesus began their ascents after a six-day period. On the seventh day the glory of God shone forth.

Matthew begins his story by stating, "Six days after Peter acknowledged Jesus as the Christ." That marks a period of time that began at the end of chapter 16, when Matthew wrote how Peter acknowledged Jesus as the Messiah. That event took place in the district of Caesarea Philippi, where Jesus had led the disciples.

Caesarea Philippi was also a town, in the Roman province called Gaulanitis. Today, that region is known as the Golan Heights.

The Golan Heights had been part of Syria until the Six-Day War (1967), when the Israelis took control. They refused to relinquish control over a significant part of the Golan Heights afterwards, because of the strategic position of Mount Hermon.

Mount Hermon is only ten kilometers from the ancient town of Caesarea Philippi. There are actually three nearly equal peaks there, which rise to roughly 9,200 feet above sea level. Mount Hermon equates to a "high mountain," as

Peter called it.

The strategic advantage of that mountain range is it overlooks the Hawran Plateau and the city of Damascus. The highest peak of Mount Hermon is at an elevation that is 5,900 feet higher than the elevation of the plateau of Damascus.

Surrounding the Sea of Galilee are mountains, but they are only about 500 feet above the elevation of the surrounding terrain. The Sea of Galilee is actually around 700 feet below sea level, making the Jordan River Rift Valley seem more mountainous than it is.

Mount Tabor is one of the mountains in the area surrounding the Galilee region. On top of that mount is where a Christian church is dedicated to the transfiguration of Jesus. That is where many believe the transfiguration took place. However, Mt. Tabor is only 1,880 feet above sea level. That is not a "high mountain."

Mount Tabor is actually what is called a "monadnock," which is defined as, "a small mountain that rises abruptly from a gently sloping or virtually level surrounding plain." It is something like a place I was brought up near.

I was raised in the Atlanta, Georgia area and nearby was Stone Mountain. That is the world's largest exposed piece of granite, and it rises to an elevation of nearly 1,700 feet, with it being over 800 feet above the surrounding terrain. From the top of Stone Mountain, one has a panoramic view of Georgia, stretching for many miles. Stone Mountain is a tourist attraction because it is so accessible.

Epiphany Sermons: Last Sunday after the Epiphany, Year A

As a youth, I walked up Stone Mountain several times. There is a path along the gentle sloping side, with scenic spots along the way to stop and take a rest. As you near the top, the grade becomes steeper, so much that I would be on my hands and knees, grabbing hold of bumps in the rock surface, pulling with my hands and pushing with my feet, just to get up the last fifty yards. Once on top, there is a large, relatively flat area, with a building that has a gift shop and a bucket lift station. I climbed Stone Mountain by myself a few times.

In my early twenties, I climbed rock faces with friends, in and around Atlanta. Once, three of us climbed a rock wall at Tallulah Gorge, near where the Great Wallenda had set up towers for a tight rope performance years before. Only the towers still remained then.

We enjoyed rappelling down, just below where one tower stood, and then climbing up the shear wall there. We used only small cracks, nooks and crannies to place wedges (called "chocks") and to use for hand and foot holds. Of course, we were secured to a rope tied off to a tree at the top, which went through the hooks to the chocks and us. Three climbers in a row were secured by rope, hand and foot holds, and wedges in strong cracks in the rock. Smart climbers prepare, as the danger is from slipping and falling.

The rope would keep us from falling all the way down, even if you were the lowest climber. Still, a fall meant temporarily (at least) dangling upside down, hooked to the rope and the most secure chock holding, stopping the fall. There is always a danger if you hang upside down too long. A helmet helps you keep from being knocked unconscious; but when you climb as part of a team, someone will help you get upright.

The point of this lesson is it is too dangerous to climb "high mountains" alone.

High mountains, like Mount Hermon and Mount Sinai, are much taller than anything I ever attempted to climb. It makes sense to see how climbing such a mountain could require ropes and more than one climber, in order to safely reach the top.

We read elsewhere in the Gospels about Jesus going into the mountains near the Sea of Galilee to meditate and pray. He went alone at those times, leaving all the disciples behind to do other things. However, when Moses embarked to a high mountain, he took Joshua with him, leaving Aaron and Hur behind. Likewise, Jesus took three assistants, leaving the other nine disciples behind.

Mount Hermon is actually snow covered most of the year, and it is where the only ski resorts for Israel and Lebanon are located. Mount Sinai has an elevation of over 8,000 feet, and I watched a YouTube video the other day, showing Christian pilgrims making the ascent of that "high mountain." Those climbers were amazed that it was snowing; and they walked a path where snow was on the ground. The snow came from the clouds that were present; and one of the climbers remarked how it was so much like in Exodus, with the clouds surrounding the mountain.

It may very well be that Moses and Jesus took assistants to help in reaching the higher altitudes of those high mountains, because they knew they would encounter weather, either rain or snow. So, when we read, "Moses set out with his assistant Joshua," we can assume Joshua was going to assist with the climb, rather than assist Moses in his talk with God.

In Exodus we read how Moses went up "the cloud covered mountain," and "the cloud covered it for six days." We read in Matthew that "Six days after" … "Jesus took … and led them up a high mountain." It is said that "from the cloud a voice said, 'This is my Son, the Beloved.'" So, we know a cloud was nearby.

Whenever we see film of high mountains with clouds around them, we know there is weather there, with snow and winds making conditions hazardous. To think of clouds being around a high mountain for six days, imagine how much snow could be falling. High mountains are snowcapped because of clouds moving by, and clouds are water vapor mixing with the cold temperatures of high altitudes.

Think of the recent snow and ice we had, as little as that was. When the clouds were still overhead, the snow had a sleepy look to it. Then, after the clouds moved away and the sun came out … what happens to sun on white snow?

It can be blinding. Then think about Exodus where we read, "the glory of the LORD was like a devouring fire on top of the mountain in the sight of the people of Israel." The sun, that huge fireball in the sky, was reflecting brightly on a snow-covered Mount Sinai!

Now see how Matthew says, "[Jesus] was transfigured before them, and his face shone like the sun, and his clothes became dazzling white." Snow blindness is an eye problem that comes from "exposure to sunlight reflected from ice and snow, particularly at elevation." The technical name is photokeratitis, where the ultraviolet rays of the sun are not blocked from harming one's eyes.

Wikipedia reports, "Fresh snow reflects about 80% of the sun's UV radiation," and "this is especially a problem … at high altitudes, as with every thousand feet (approximately 305 meters) of elevation (above sea level), the intensity of UV rays increases by four percent."

So, let's imagine that Mount Hermon has had six days of snow, just as did Mount Sinai. The arid conditions of the area mean clouds bring snow to the high elevations, but nothing in the valley down below. Jesus knows God is coming to meet him, just as did Moses. Jesus takes three assistants and begins to hike up the mountain, into the snow, while the clouds are still there, making things white.

On the seventh day the Lord called out to Moses. On the seventh day God called out to the disciples. The seventh day is the Sabbath, the day of the Lord.

For us Christians, we call the Sabbath "Sun-day." The sun shone upon Moses and Joshua, just as the sun shone on Jesus, Peter, James, and John. The Sun came out from behind the cloud, into a blanket of pure white snow. That is symbolic of holiness.

What we get from today's Gospel reading is how, "[Jesus] was transfigured before them." Then we are told, "Suddenly there appeared to them Moses and Elijah, talking with [Jesus]." This is called the "Transfiguration."

Epiphany Sermons: Last Sunday after the Epiphany, Year A

The Greek word written is "*metemorphōthē*," which means, "he was transformed" or "he was transfigured." From "*meta*' – change – "*morph*" – form – we can see how Jesus changed form. It means the outward appearance of Jesus was altered.

His face "shone like the sun" and "his clothes became dazzling white." Jesus was exalted and glorified by the presence of the LORD, regardless of the presence of snow. However, the light on the snow could have altered the eyes of the disciples so they were allowed to see that transformation.

Peter wanted to build tabernacles, because God had instructed Moses to build one so the LORD could live among the people of Israel. If they knew they were going into snowy conditions, they would have brought tents and supplies, so Peter was simply asking if they should pitch tents for their guests.

God told him to be quiet and listen to Jesus, because things had transformed from the freedom from bondage in Egypt (Moses), to a nation split (Elijah), to an exiled people under Roman bondage (Jesus); but Jesus was going to transform the disciples; and, in return, they would transform many more of humanity.

Three disciples witnessed three forms of Christ. One who had died and was buried outside Israel, one who was born in Israel but left to ascend into heaven without dying, and one who would be born and die in Israel, but then resurrect and ascend. They saw a trinity in Jesus.

We read this today because we are about to spend forty

days on the mountain, so to speak, with the season of Lent coming. We need to have our own transformation.

Rather than spend forty days getting a Law to follow – to decide what little thing we can try to give up for less than a month and a half – we need to become like Jesus and change form. We need him to change from being something nebulous – like a cloud, as a super human – into someone who suddenly joins with us, talking to us from within.

Then we can hear the voice of Jesus as he tells us, "Get up and do not be afraid." We will go down the mountain together, knowing the security of our lifeline is tied to a power that will never fail. From there we can go well beyond forty days of sacrifice.

We need to understand why Peter wrote, "You will do well to be attentive to the prophetic message of Christ, as to a lamp shining in a dark place, until the day dawns and the morning star rises in your hearts."

May you be filled with the Holy Spirit so your faces shine like the sun.

Amen

Epiphany Sermons: Last Sunday after the Epiphany, Year A

Advent, Christmas and Epiphany Sermons

YEAR B

Advent

YEAR B

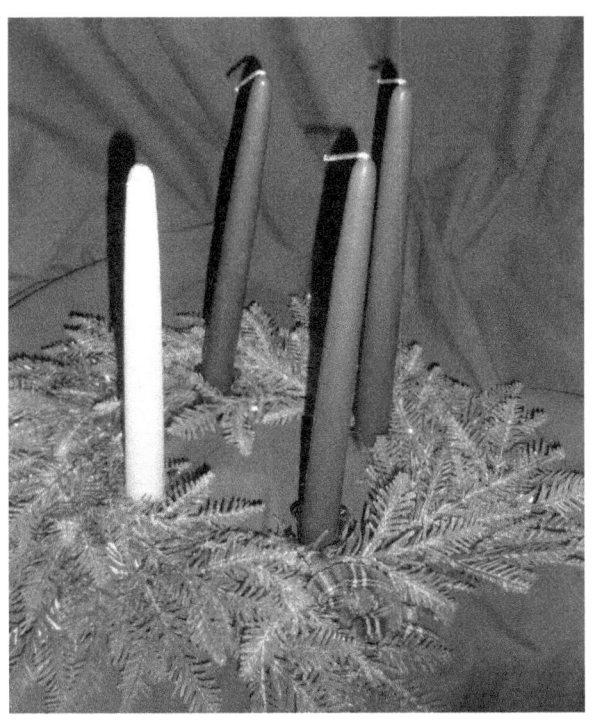

First Sunday of Advent

YEAR B

November 30, 2014

Relevant readings:
Isaiah 64:1-9
Psalm 80:1-7, 16-18
1 Corinthians 1:3-9
Mark 13:24-37

The Advent of the space age and the end times

The Ordinary season after Pentecost is now over. We begin the season of Advent today, with Advent recognized as the first season of each liturgical year.

We just finished Year A, so now we begin Year B.

Advent Sermons: First Sunday of Advent, Year B

So, HAPPY NEW YEAR!

<pause>

Sorry there is no big ball to drop or no white squirrels[1] to toss confetti about; but we do have the Gospel of Mark!

<applaud>

The Advent season takes us up to Christmas, and begins after Thanksgiving, so some might mistake this as the season that puts the rush in Christmas shopping.

While there certainly is a message of urgency in the Advent season, that message has nothing to do with impressing friends and relatives with fancifully wrapped presents. It has nothing to do with trees and lights, or the pressures of funding such madness.

The word "advent" is defined as, "The coming or arrival, especially of something extremely important." It is derived from the Old French infinitive "*advenir*," which means, "to come to." Thus, the ecclesiastical naming of this season, as "Advent," refers to the "coming to" us of Jesus.

Of course, that means the coming of Christmas, when we recognize baby Jesus was born. That day is when we remember his birth into the world.

I remember when I was a child, being driven by my mother to and from church three nights a week. After the time

---

[1] The church my wife was rector for had an issue with squirrels inside the church, and the town was known for its white squirrels.

changed and after Thanksgiving it was dark by 6:00 PM. During the Advent season, a church we passed along our route always put out a large wreath, with four large candles at the angles, and with large white flame-shaped lights atop each. Before Advent began, the wreath was not lit. Then, as each Sunday marked a full week into the Advent season, a new light would be lit. At the last Sunday of Advent, marking the last days before Christmas, all four candles would be shining brightly. They remained lit through the twelve days of Christmas.

In a way, those lights marked a count-down (or count-up) to when Jesus would be born … to when Christ would come into the world one more time.

Still, the more serious symbolism of the count-down of Advent is the Second Coming of Jesus, representing when Christ will return at the end of the world. You might have noticed from the readings that an apocalyptic theme was clearly present.

Before I get deeper into the lessons presented today, let me just mention that I know there are many people, especially Episcopalians, who are uncomfortable with themes focusing on the End Times. If you are one of those, I only ask that you come to the realization that everyone here today is mortal. That means we are each born into life, possessing a life-filled body of flesh that will eventually – for whatever cause or reason – END. We are all going to die. We all recognize that limit of time on earth. So, that end, whether we go out with others at the same time, or whether we go out alone and privately, will find us each experiencing our own personal Judgment Day waiting. That End Time is always relevant, and should not be ignored.

Advent Sermons: First Sunday of Advent, Year B

With that understood, we must also realize that death is nothing new to consider, especially given the average age of this audience. We have all been around the block a few times. The church calendar year 2014-2015 will not be our "first rodeo."

That is what makes a New Year important, where New Year's resolutions are a way of trying to motivate ourselves to make wanted, if not needed changes in our lives. A new church year is then more important than a new calendar year, because it marks a time for us to live up to newly set goals, as atonement for past failures.

In Advent we see the urgency of change. At Christmas we want to realize that change with Christ born within us, so we become a reborn Jesus. With Jesus our model, we become ordained as disciples. Then we test our commitment to growing into Jesus through Lent. At Easter, we crucify our egos and are resurrected as Apostles in training. At Pentecost we become filled with the Holy Spirit and begin our own personal ministry, as priests for the One God, ordained to serve others over self.

If you just completed a year of dedication to Christ and God, then Advent is when you lend a hand bringing others into this cycle, while renewing your commitment to God, through Christ.

If you have forever been "kicking the tires" of Christianity, waiting for the day when you will finally buy in completely, we want this New Year to be your awakening to the Advent of that goal.

With all that said, let the lessons begin.

In the Gospel reading today, Mark remembered how Jesus said, "Beware, keep alert; for you do not know when the time will come." Jesus then repeated, "Therefore, keep awake – for you do not know when the master of the house will come."

You do not know when that Advent will be. So, in order to stay alert and awake, you have to first wake up from your slumber, and then you need to fill your lamp with oil – the "living" kind of oil that never runs out, which is the Holy Spirit.

If you remember the parable told as the season of Pentecost was winding to an end, about the ten bridesmaids with oil lamps – you can then connect that symbolism to the early Pentecost story of Jesus meeting the woman at the well. The two are telling the same thing, differently of course, but for as often as we hear those stories read aloud and for as many times as we have heard sermons preached about those themes (with many other lessons that point to a NEED for the Holy Spirit), people keep going back to the water well with dry buckets and running out to buy physical oil for empty lamps, simply because they think all those lessons apply to other people.

For the most part, those of us gathered here today are well beyond our youth. We are in the "Fall" of life. We have produced our fruit and new leaves long ago; and, now we are slowing down, preparing for winter.

When you can see yourself in this "seasonal" setting, regardless of how "young in mind" you are, you can begin to

Advent Sermons: First Sunday of Advent, Year B

see how the cycle of life projects onto everything earthly. This includes all religions, of which Christianity is one.

When Jesus said to his disciples, "In those days," which was referring to the future, he said those future days would be identified as when "the sun will be darkened." More than a statement that is limited to some celestial event, like an eclipse, which is momentary in time (only lasting an hour or so), that statement actually is powerful when you hear it say, "When the light of the earth will become dim and weak."

In the song of Isaiah, a lamentation verse sings, "We all fade like a leaf, and our iniquities, like the wind, take us away."

Can you see those statements as talking about the seasonal "Fall of Faith," where the sun is no longer rising high into the sky, like it does in the spring, into summer – when the "branch becomes tender and puts forth its leaves"?

This is how Christianity will also have had such a "Spring" and growth season, lasting nearly two thousand years; but when that growth ceases, that is the point in time when the "sun will be darkened," setting sooner, lower in its path across the sky, and weaker in its ability to bring warmth to the lands.

We are living in those days now ... literally and figuratively. It is now Fall, headed towards the Winter Solstice in late December (around Christmas). But, more importantly is seeing how the Church (of all denominations) has become filled with old folks, like ourselves. The Church is in Fall.

That reflects how we feel too slow to be filling ourselves with the Holy Spirit, because that is for the younger folk … the younger members, many of whom have left and why so many pews here, now are filled with emptiness. This decline began way back when (as Elton John sang), "The New York Times said God was dead, and the war's begun." The "Fall" of Christianity began when we were young, when we … never taught to be miracle workers, like Jesus and the Apostles … let our children wander away from religion, while we did little to bring back Spring to the Church.

In the news this past week was how NASA had landed a small spacecraft on a meteor. Such tricks are made possible due to a great expansion of mental capacity within mankind. Science and technology has abounded since 1969, when we first landed a man on the moon.

"and the moon will not give its light," said Jesus. Landing on the moon has not enlightened our souls, it has led us to place faith on the minds of Man.

The reason NASA is interested in landing a small spacecraft on a meteor is because the big brains of science have had their eyes opened to the danger of a meteor, comet, or asteroid crashing into the earth, making life, as we know it, become extinct. They see the Advent of Death, so science and technology want to play god and figure out how they can protect the earth with missiles and rockets and weapons that could destroy meteors.

So, landing that little spacecraft was a another "small step for man," perceived by NASA to be another "giant leap for science ruling over mankind."

Advent Sermons: First Sunday of Advent, Year B

However, just as when Samuel said to his Lord, "The people want a king," and God replied, "I am their King," we get more thrilled thinking NASA can protect us from meteors better than can true faith in our God.

Jesus said, "and the stars will be falling from heaven, and the powers in the heavens will be shaken."

Isaiah sang, "O that you would tear open the heavens and come down, so that the mountains would quake in your presence – as when fire kindles brushwood and the fire causes water to boil."

Does any of that sound like a giant fireball of matter meeting the friction of earth's atmosphere, burning the land and boiling the seas?

Is that not what science and technology are afraid could happen, ending life on earth … as we know it?

David was afraid what would happen if mankind stopped looking to God for salvation, singing, "Restore us, O LORD God of hosts; show the light of your countenance, and we shall be saved."

Paul added, "The grace of God that has been given to you in Christ Jesus, for in every way you have been enriched in him, in speech and knowledge of every kind – so that you are not lacking in any spiritual gift as you wait for the revealing of our Lord Jesus Christ."

To which Jesus foretold, "Then they will see 'the Son of Man coming in the clouds' with great power and glory.

Robert Tippett

WAKE UP! BE ALERT!

There is still time, "But about that day or hour no one knows, neither the angels in heaven, nor the Son, but only the Father." So, "Keep awake."

You do that by receiving the Spirit; and we all need that Advent within us, especially in this "Fall" of our lives. Let Christmas symbolically signal YOU being born anew as a newborn Jesus.

Amen

Advent Sermons: First Sunday of Advent, Year B

Second Sunday of Advent

YEAR B

December 7, 2014

Relevant readings:
Isaiah 40:1-11
Psalm 85:1-2, 8-13
2 Peter 3:8-15a
Mark 1:1-8

Prepare a way of the Lord and make it a straight path

Last week the lessons read pointed out a need to understand how important it is to change ourselves … to not be caught during the End Times, when the sun will be darkened.

Advent Sermons: Second Sunday of Advent, Year B

It was like a warning not to be caught without oil in your lamp, unable to bring forth the light of Christ when the end comes. Our mortality means each life faces a personal End Time.

Thus, the season of Advent acts as a warning to have ourselves be reborn as baby Jesus ... a new Christmas for each new budding Apostle ... and not be caught napping, with no way to light a lamp quick enough to save a soul.

As long as there are no ICBM's or unannounced meteors streaking towards us at this very moment ... there is still time. Act now, before it is too late.

That is the continuing message of Advent.

Today, in effect, we read what the first step towards salvation is. It is repentance.

Now, everyone here knows that repentance is the way to wash away our sins, putting us back on God's good list, the "go to Heaven" list. We feel comfortable as Christians, with Episcopalians (minimally) making sure we do not forget that vital step. Shortly, we will make a public confession of our sins and once again beg God to forgive us.

Cleansed of sin ... and then next week we will say it all again.

While it is true that we repent when we say those preprinted words from the Book of Common Prayer, it helps to see our public proclamation as "for demonstration purposes only." We can never forget just how important it is to personally, and privately, have a deeper, more sin specific conversation with God. It should be done regularly, as a personal dialogue with God and Christ, as a way to help us stay sin-free.

While repentance is the first step, staying sin-free is a most important statement about the sincerity of one's request to be forgiven.

This maintenance of righteousness, once forgiven, is the meaning behind Mark repeating the words of Isaiah, as he began his book telling the Gospel of Jesus Christ. Mark wrote, "Prepare the way of the Lord, make his paths straight." Isaiah wrote, "In the wilderness prepare the way of the LORD, make straight in the desert a highway for our God."

The "way of the Lord" and the "straight path" or "highway," means WE must set out paths straight. Rather than wandering in spiral roads to sin and repentance. WE must prepare to meet the LORD at the end of that journey. WE must be walking the line and not weaving like a drunk pulled over by the State Patrol.

Now, Paul wrote in his letter, "The Lord is not slow about his promise, as some think of slowness, but is patient with you, not wanting any to perish, but all to come to repentance." The Greek word translated as "slow" is "*bradynei*," which means "to retard, to be slow, to tarry."

Thus, when Peter said, "as some think of slowness," ("*bradyteta*") he meant God is not "slack" or forgetful of his promise, while also not being quick to turn his back on the promise to be the God of His servants.

Advent Sermons: Second Sunday of Advent, Year B

So, God is smart enough to know when you falsely beg for forgiveness – when you don't really mean what you say in repentance – and God is not quick to stop forgiving you, even when you are not being completely truthful.

As Christians, we are baptized with water in a ceremonial ritual. We can call ourselves Christians by that symbolic act, just like we can call ourselves forgiven because we repeat aloud a confession of sins. However, as Mark pointed out, there was no need for Jesus to come into the world IF being sprinkled or dunked in water would wash all our sins away – past, present, and future.

Mark told how John the Baptist admitted, "The one who is more powerful than I is coming after me; I am not worthy to stoop down and untie the thong of his sandals. I have baptized you with water; but he will baptize you with the Holy Spirit."

This is not hard to understand, but it may be unwanted to realize, being baptized with water by a church (an institution like was John the Baptist) is NOT as powerful as is being truly baptized by the Holy Spirit, through BECOMING Jesus, as advocated by faith in CHRIST.

We all wander in and out of sin and righteousness because we know who Jesus is and because we believe in baptism … BUT, we have a most difficult time receiving that Holy Spirit, which is the only way to walk that straight path, which prepares us for the End Time we all must eventually reach.

Repentance is the first step to receiving the Holy Spirit, but receiving the Holy Spirit requires a demonstration of commitment. Thanks be to God that He is patient with us and lets us make mistake after mistake, hearing our pleas for forgiveness from time to time.

Isaiah wrote in his song, "All the people are grass, their constancy is like a flower of the field. The grass withers, the flower fades."

David sang, "You have forgiven the iniquity of your people and blotted out all their sins."

Still, this circular path is the danger. We do not know when our time will come.

In chapter three of Peter's second letter, before he wrote, "the day of the Lord will come like a thief," some Bibles list this chapter as "The Day of the Lord."

We read part of what Peter said about the Lord being patient with us, but when we read, "the heavens will be set ablaze and dissolved, and the elements will melt with fire," that is reference to the End Times, when the Day of the Lord comes for many souls at once.

In the first seven verses, Peter told the reader, "You must understand that in the last days scoffers will come, scoffing and following their own evil desires. They will say, "Where is this 'coming' he promised? Ever since our ancestors died, everything goes on as it has since the beginning of creation."

That attitude will have developed over a long period of time ... waiting for the return of Christ, before the End.

Advent Sermons: Second Sunday of Advent, Year B

Waiting ...

... and waiting ...

... and waiting ...

... until people stop believing there is a God ... that there ever was a Christ ... that there really is a Holy Spirit ... and that all this praying for forgiveness stuff is a waste of time.

However, Peter said, "The present heavens and earth are reserved for fire, being kept for **the day of judgment** and destruction of the ungodly." Remember last week and the meteor that was said to be coming?

Well, Peter begins our reading today by saying, "Do not ignore this one fact, beloved, that with the Lord one day is like a thousand years, and a thousand years are like one day."

People have been waiting so long because Jesus said, "Truly I say to you, this generation will not pass away until all things take place. Heaven and earth will pass away, but My words will not pass away." They expected him to come back soon.

But their expectations were based on human clocks and solar days. According to what Peter wrote, the year 2014 is only about two God days past the times Jesus walked the earth.

But, look around ... and what do you see in the news? Changes that are showing a crumbling of our patience, our society becoming too weary to stay awake waiting for the

Master to come.

The only way we can stay alert is to repent, and then be diligent towards receiving the spirit of God within. That acts like a time change. We stop worrying about solar says and ninety-year life spans, because we get on God time.

Everything slows down. Patience is a way of life. Preparing a straight path is accomplished.

We have fulfilled the Advent of Jesus Christ when we have truly repented and been prepared.

May God be with you.

Amen

Advent Sermons: Second Sunday of Advent, Year B

Third Sunday of Advent

YEAR B

December 14, 2014

Relevant readings:
Isaiah 61:1-4, 8-11
Psalm 126
 or Canticle 15 (or 3)
1 Thessalonians 5:16-24
John 1:6-8,19-28

People are always going to have inquiring minds

We live in the historical times called the Age of Reason. That age was born when human beings began cutting the heads off of kings and queens and placing the crowns of leadership on common men. That marked the "Advent" of human philosophies as justification for evils ... as long as the majority accepted that.

After a little over two hundred years, we have come upon the Information Age, where we put technology in the hands of everyone above the age of three. The "spirit" of knowledge is upon us.

The only problem with all this intelligence about is it can make people ... to use a simple phrase ... "too big for their britches." I like to call this Big Brain Syndrome.

Too often, we **THINK** we have everything figured out, when we really haven't a clue. Simply because we have become so advanced in the capabilities of enhancing our minds ... at the touch of a screen ... it is an illusion to think we are any better than those countless souls who walked the earth prior to us.

What I am saying is we are roughly two thousand years beyond the times of Jesus and the Apostles. We are as far as six thousand years after the times of Genesis, when we read from that book, and the lineage before the Great Flood. Because we have access to I-phones and computers, we think we are the smartest humans ever to walk the planet.

But that is where the Big Brain blinds us from the reality of it all.

Imagine just how stupid we would look, using that narrow-minded perspective, to someone living in the year 3,500 AD or even 7,500 AD. Imagine what advancements will exist then ... if you can. Surely, we would seem like idiots and morons, with no grasp of what is to come.

In reality, we are always what we are, as smart as the times allow; and, that is how we need to approach the readings of ancient times each week.

We need to imagine what it would be like back then, knowing that people back then were not the complete idiots we can so quickly write them off to be. To write them off that way is to see oneself as just as lost mentally, because history acts like a mirror of time.

For example, put yourself in the situation where John the Baptist has been called before the temple authorities – the priests and Levites – because they want to know, "What's up with this baptism thing?"

Imagine how it would be today, if you went to a Baptist church one Sunday and it happened to be when they dunked some new members in their large pool. You would see a line of children and adults, all wearing white robes, entering a pool where the preacher in standing in waist deep water, ready to dunk them, to completely submerge each in the water. In times past, preachers would go down to the river to do these dunkings ... before technology allowed for indoor pools with heated water.

Compare that to the sprinkling of water on an infant's forehead, which other denominations see as symbolically appropriate enough to cleanse the sins of would-be-believers. The two events are drastically different.

Would you not want to ask a Baptist preacher (or at least a

member of the Baptist Church) to explain, "What's up with that?" Regardless of where on the world's timeline man is, as the ad used to say, "Inquiring minds want to know."

Regardless of how much technology one has in his coat pocket or purse, people still need to question what their religion is about. We need to stop assuming it is a sign of weakness to ask a question, to clear up something we know "everybody does," but no one ever adequately explained why.

When we hear some people claiming to be messengers from God, we need to hear what they say the message is, don't we? Unless we hear what someone has to say, how can we make sure we are not missing out on something important ... **FROM GOD!?**

In our modern society, we tend to love change. The older people tend to not adapt with the new times. Questions have to be an ongoing procedure, simply so that inappropriate desires for change do not get accepted as normal ... without someone taking the time to question the rightfulness of a new way taken.

After all, when John the Baptist was dunking Jews in the Jordan River the Jews had certain cleansing rituals already in place. They would also release a scapegoat once a year, where the sins of everyone happily rode off into the wilderness sunset, resting on a beast of burden.

The Levites were responsible for ritualistic cleansing ceremonies in the temple. The priests would assist in them. So, it was natural for them to question John as to his authority to do baptism in the Jordan River.

According to John the Beloved, they asked John the Baptist, "Who are you?" He told them what he was not.

John the baptizer said, "I am not the Messiah." He also admitted he was not the reincarnation of Elijah … who left in a whirlwind, riding in a chariot of fire. Thus, since he did not die, Elijah was expected to return one day …

"So," they asked, "John, is that you?"

"Nope, not Elijah," said John the Baptist. He was not a prophet either. He was just a Jew who knew the prophecy of Isaiah … answering, as we read last week, "I am the voice of one crying out in the wilderness. Make straight the way of the Lord."

So, John the Baptist was then approached by some Pharisees. The Pharisees are still around today, going by different names, in all the various denominations of Christianity. They are the preachers, priests, ministers, and church elders that study the Holy Bible. They are also the Rabbis of Judaism today, who still study the Torah and other relative documents. It is the job of a "Pharisee" to know the written word, backwards and forward, to make sure any new interpretations pass their tests and approval.

"What is your purpose for baptizing with water?" the Pharisees asked John the Baptist. "What are you getting out of this act?"

He said, in effect, "It is symbolism, man. Pure symbolism. It is symbolic of what this dude who is coming after me will do. None of you know any of what he is going to bring to the table. I don't know either, so I could never pretend to be like him."

The symbolism was not the use of water to wash away sins. The temple priests were all over that, because it was written in the Law. The Pharisees knew all about it, so they made sure all Jews knew what rituals and procedures needed to take place. So, John the Baptist was not symbolizing the washing away of sin.

What he symbolized was how the temple priests and Levites, as well as the Pharisees and rabbis, were putting way too much emphasis on words on paper, while doing nothing to teach anyone how to go through life without sin.

They could heap the sin on, but they could never wash any of it off.

Just recently in the news, the comedic institution that is Bill Cosby has been accused of raping multiple women over the past thirty-plus years. One woman told a reported that after her rape she went home and took a hot shower to tried to scrub herself clean.

I remember her saying, "It was something one shower cannot wash away."

Sin has that effect on people who do not want to sin. They do not want to sin because they believe in God and know sin is wrong. Religions are designed to bring people's awareness to good deeds, with Judaism and Christianity rooted in beliefs that the one God demands righteousness in believers.

So, if you listen carefully to what John the Beloved wrote, as to what John the Baptist said, when he had him say, "Among you stands one whom you do not know," if you tweak your ear just a little, you can hear how that "one" was God.

John the Baptizer said, "Among you stands God, whom you do not know."

The priests, Levites, and Pharisees knew the Torah, they knew **of** Moses, Elijah, and the prophets, because of their words left behind, but among all those scrolls was the one presence Moses, Elijah, and the prophets knew, which those new leaders did not.

The modern guys ... the latest, greatest, biggest brained leaders ... did not have God in their hearts.

Today, there are those who are just like the temple priests and Levites, like the Pharisees, who also stand among God, while not truly knowing what standing **with** God means. It is not about a sermon read from teleprompters or handheld devices, where you give the impression, "I know some things."

When one finishes preaching and the people listening still do not know how to scrub the sin off them, then everyone is still unknowing of God within.

Now, in the short reading from Paul's first letter to the Thessalonians, he wrote, "Rejoice always, pray without ceasing, give thanks in all circumstances; for this is the will of God in Christ Jesus for you."

Advent Sermons: Third Sunday of Advent, Year B

Paul was saying, "Through being born anew with Christ Jesus, you know God. You know God through the Holy Spirit." He then added, "Do not put that fire out. Do not fail to let the prophets make perfect sense to you."

<u>Write this down and memorize it:</u> Paul said, "**Test everything**; hold fast to what is **good**; abstain from every form of **evil**."

What that means is this: Do not be like a priest of the temple, a Levite who serves the temple, or a Pharisee who teaches at the temple – none of who know God. **UNDERSTAND EVERYTHING!**

You must understand what the prophets said, because God has spoken through the prophets. God only speaks the truth. So, if ever there is some guy like John the Baptist running around making up stuff that maybe was written down by a prophet, but everyone else missed it – **DO NOT JUST LET IT GO UNTESTED!**

When you have God in your heart, meaning you **know** God and feel certain that God will lead you to the truth, you then **know** that God will lead you to expose evil, so you can avoid it and tell others to avoid it too. Listen to what people say. Ask questions, as the people we read about today asked John the Baptist ... roughly two thousand years ago.

However, if your only response to someone telling you, "I am just a voice in the wilderness telling you that you are not making a straight way for the Lord," then hear that as your failure. Isaiah was a prophet made aware of the failures of nations, saying, "Guys, you are not walking a straight path to the LORD." John the Baptist said the same thing to the people running Jerusalem, hundreds of years later. We read it today because the same prophecy fits our nation, our churches. It is not "outdated."

There are so many attacks upon Christianity right now; it is hard to list them all. By drawing a line in the sand and casting out blind condemnations on others, you are winding down a path that will crucify Jesus … from your ignorance and lack of true faith. To watch Jesus be born, as we will on the 25th, and then to watch him die, as we will during Easter week, but to not know him resurrected in us, it to stand as a group of know-it-alls, not knowing God.

In Isaiah's reading today, we hear him say, "The spirit of the Lord GOD is upon me, because the LORD has anointed me; he has sent me to bring good news to the oppressed, to bind up the brokenhearted, to proclaim liberty to the captives, and to release the prisoners."

In short, when the Spirit of the LORD is upon you, then you embrace all who need help. Perhaps they need help by sensing that God and can answer every question, so they go to a church for an answer. They come, just like the Jews went to Jerusalem and the temple there, to ask "How can I ever feel clean from sin, when no one ever tells me how not to sin?"

Sin has tested God. Those who know God know what is good and what needs to be held fast onto – which means understanding from one's own past sins and the experience of seeing the value of not sinning. Those who know God also know what is evil, from past failures to sin. With the help of God, their experience can then tell others how to abstain from those sins. Otherwise, you do not know any answers.

When God is **known** by someone, fear of sin ceases. All one has to do is stand up and reach out to those who question. Simply by opening one's mouth, in response to a question ... as John the Baptist did ... one lets the Holy Spirit flow through.

It is that simple, but it might require saying goodbye to smart phones and other gadgets of technology and modern advancements. John the Baptist lived like a wild man, eating insects and honey, wearing animal skins. In a modern world, that translates as "simple living, within one's means."

In this third week of Advent, we read the song of Mary, who praised the Lord, singing, "My spirit rejoices in God my Savior, for he has looked with favor on his lowly servant."

We now have three candles lit on the Advent wreath. We should not be waiting for Jesus to be born again in Bethlehem. We should be "with child" right now, just as was Mary then. We should be anticipating the birth of Jesus within each one of us, so that on Christmas Day the world will have brought forth countless new extensions of the Savior, through newborn babes ... Apostles-in-training.

If we open our hearts to the Lord, "then were we like those who dream. Then will be our mouths filled with laughter, and our tongues with shouts of joy."

Amen

Fourth Sunday of Advent

YEAR B

December 21, 2014

Relevant readings:
2 Samuel 7:1-11, 16
Canticle 3
  or Canticle 15
  or Psalm 89:1-4, 19-26
Romans 16:25-27
Luke 1:26-38

It is a big decision to make, when one is ready to be a parent to a baby

Not long ago the Bishop was here for a confirmation service. The Old Testament read that evening was from the book of Jeremiah, chapter 31. In verses 31 & 32, this is what was read aloud:

> "The days are coming," declares the Lord, "when I will make a new **covenant** with the people of Israel and with the people of Judah. It will not be like the **covenant** I made with their ancestors when I took them by the hand to lead them out of Egypt, because they broke my **covenant**, though I was a husband to them," declares the Lord.
>
> "This is the **covenant** I will make with the people of Israel after that time," declares the Lord. "I will put my law in their minds and write it on their hearts. I will be their God, and they will be my people."

You might have noticed the word "covenant" was repeated. It appears four times, referring to the Covenant of Moses and the New Covenant of Jesus, so this reading is important. It states why newly confirmed Episcopalians must realize the meaning of this new covenant, as that determines who are true Christians.

For today's readings, and in order to fully grasp how the first covenant and the new covenant differ, you have to see how that ties in with the Second Samuel reading, where it tells of the "ark of God."

That means the Ark of the Covenant, where "the **covenant**" was the physical stone tablets brought down by Moses. An ark was built to hold that holy document. Still, instead of having an external **covenant** chiseled in stone by the finger of God, Jeremiah prophesied that Jesus would be coming to announce that he was fulfilling that prophecy, when God would "put [His] law in their minds and write it on their hearts."

In Second Samuel, prior to today's reading, in chapters five and six, David had been anointed King of Israel, he had captured Jerusalem, and he had defeated the Philistines. He then ordered the Ark of the Covenant to be moved from its place in Judah (*Ba'alam*) to Jerusalem. As it enters the city, David danced wildly before the ark, barely dressed. All the people are given fruit cakes to commemorate the event.

It is then, from understanding this state of joy and excitement in David, that we can best grasp why he talked to the prophet Nathan, telling him it is not right to have such a powerful relic inside a tent, while he has a fixed house of cedar to reside in.

Nathan told David, "Go, do all that you have in mind; for the LORD is with you."

Then we read how God came to Nathan at night and wanted to know why David would think His presence in the Ark of the Covenant was not fine where it was … in a tent or tabernacle. When this conversation with Nathan was finished, God told Nathan to go tell David, "Moreover the LORD declares to you that the LORD will make you a house."

Remember how Nathan said, "Do all that you have in mind; for the LORD is with you"?

God had already put His law in David's mind.

When God said, "I will make you a house," he was not say-

Advent Sermons: Fourth Sunday of Advent, Year B

ing, "Tell David I'm sorry if all the hammering wakes him up, because I will be making him another cedar house."

No, God meant David ... himself ... would be a home for God; where God would write His law on his heart."

In the reading from Jeremiah, which was read the night of the confirmation, the word covenant was repeated four times because that external THING, where God resided to be with the people, was a law broken ... over, and over, and over again.

The problem with external things is they are so easy to forget about. As holy as the covenant was, it was hidden away inside a tent, regardless of how portable tents can be.

As the saying goes, "Out of sight, out of mind."

Since you can't see God (and be alive), then His law is not on your mind all those times you are caught up in thought over sins.

Now, in the Jeremiah reading we heard God say, "I was a husband to them." I don't know if anyone who was here when the Bishop visited caught that; but I will ask you now, "Do you understand what a husband is? What a husband does?"

It can be defined as a "married man, especially when considered in relation to his wife." That is an important gender determination that is being made by God the Father.

When God is your husband, in a relationship of marriage, the Israelites were His brides. To put it bluntly, all of them held the status of wife to God, regardless of their human sex biology.

As such, the traditional role of a wife is to follow the lead of her husband. God leads. We follow. We follow God's lead by knowing His law. Our minds are set on the husband's lead.

The only problem with that model is nobody likes to be given orders. We get used to saying, "Yes sir. Whatever you say sir," when the Father is looking at us. That is the understood unequal relationship of father to child. However, that relationship between husband and wife is no longer so clear.

Wives, today especially, loathe the thought of playing second fiddle to a husband. The system of ownership, of dominance and submission, is not the same as it is with adults and minors. Husbands no longer command wives to do anything.

It was not like that back in the day, when women and children were seen but never heard. Everybody wears the pants in today's families. With no sure head of a household, with no lion of the pride, God gets seen in the same light.

To relate our relationship with God to a modern marriage, there is another saying to consider: "When the cat's away the mice will play."

Us human "wives" will do what we please, thank you very much. And, God gave us "wives" that freedom of self-will: to obey our husband or to disobey Him.

Advent Sermons: Fourth Sunday of Advent, Year B

Still, this husband relationship aspect is important to grasp when we see Mary having her conversation with Gabriel. While she was betrothed to Joseph, she was pregnant with the Son of God. God was her husband, thus the Father of her child.

Jesus was the Son of God, born of a woman. Joseph was part of the Most High overshadowing a single girl having a baby, apparently out of wedlock.

While I have no doubts that everyone here today grasps the distinction of the Virgin Mother and Jesus divinely conceived. The Immaculate Conception is essential to believe during this Advent season, as we prepare for "The Coming" of the Christ child. It is important that we see how all of these readings today are pointing to **you** being Mary, to **you** being David, to **you** being the wife of God … males and females … and letting the angel Gabriel tell **you** that you are pregnant, with the Son of God in **you**.

You need to hear Nathan telling **you**, "The LORD said He will make **you** a house" where the love child of God, wed to **you**, can be born and raised.

It is too easy to stay a virgin and suggest, "Can't you just keep your presence in the holy relic that we go to once a week, on Sunday, for about two hours?"

After all, Mary "was much perplexed," with Gabriel sensing her fear. She asked, "How can this be?"

It is a major step of maturity when a young couple decides to have a baby. They have to have all the answers to the questions: How can we afford it? How can we handle work and caring for a baby? How can we sacrifice being children and become adults?

Most don't put that much thought into it. They just find out, "You're pregnant." Then they are forced to let faith in God do the rest.

Pregnancy will change your figure. A mother has to eat for two, but a wife eating makes the husband eat more too, so they both grow in preparation for the baby.

Pregnancy will make you stop doing some things that were harming you … like quitting vices. That means being serious about parenthood forces you to know that when a baby is on the way you have to change and become responsible for your actions.

The first pregnancy will make you prepare for the Advent of a new you … from child to adult, from girl to mother, from child to parent.

The first pregnancy as the wife of God will change your life, because that means, "The Holy Spirit is upon you, and the power of the Most High has overshadowed you."

It makes you an Apostle waiting to be born. When that birth arrives, it becomes like Paul wrote to the Christians of Rome.

He said, "It is God who is able to strengthen you according to my gospel and the proclamation of Jesus Christ."

That means that God has put the same mind in you that he put in David, and Jesus, and Paul. It is the mind of Christ, so you understand Paul's gospel and his proclamation that his abilities mean Jesus Christ has been born in him.

Paul was the wife of God. He opened his heart and received the Holy Spirit. His mind was given all the knowledge of Christ.

Paul explained further, saying, "According to the revelation of the mystery that was kept secret for long ages but now is disclosed." That means the mystery of God's presence … that unseen presence that had for long ages been out of sight and out of mind … that was within him and felt strongly.

It was revealing God, through the Holy Spirit, as the rebirth of the Son of God … regardless of what sex one is.

Paul then added, "Through the prophetic writings made known to all the Gentiles, according to the command of the eternal God, to bring about the obedience of faith."

BRILLIANT!

We understand how all the prophets foretold of Jesus Christ and it all took place exactly as written, but could not be understood without the missing link … the mind of God with you, with His law written on your hearts.

This brings out the need to understand the importance of order. God told Jeremiah, "1.) I will put my law in their minds; and, 2.) I will write my law on their hearts. One is as natural coming before the other as is pregnancy naturally coming before childbirth.

This order is why Jesus first broke the blessed bread and said, "Take this and eat it, for this is my body."

Before you can understand anything, you have to consume the body of work that prophesied his coming. You have to read this. You have to study and ponder this. You have to discuss this. You have to share this with others. You have to feed your mind with the law of God before you can understand the first covenant, and how Jesus became the new covenant.

Then, once you have fed the Christ child within your mind, your eyes will begin to see the words growing in meaning, until the heart of the Holy Spirit begins to beat strongly. This is then the second stage. It is the new covenant, where the heart beats and the blood of Christ circulates through you. It spreads through you like new wine in the bloodstream. You remember Christ, because you have become Christ reborn.

Christmas is our day set aside to remember the birth of the baby Jesus, in a manger in Bethlehem, about two thousand fourteen years ago. But Jesus does not want us to see him like the Israelites of David's day saw the Ark of the Covenant … as something to place on a stand in a temple or on the wall of a church, enclosed in a fixed location.

Jesus does not want to be a mystery, unseen, in need of being called down from heaven to become one with wafers and wine. Jesus does not wish to be eaten physically, so his memory can go into our bellies.

God did not build a house for Jesus made out of cedar. He made the Church of Christ out of the flesh and blood of his faithful.

When you understand that, you can begin to see that we are here today … in this repeating of the Advent season … not because Jesus has been nailed to a tree and reproduced as an image of that scene, hung on a wall in a church.

Jesus has been reborn countless time over the past two millennium … or we would not be here today. That means we owe it to our predecessors and we owe it to our progeny to become pregnant with baby Jesus inside us. We owe it to God and Christ to be reborn as Jesus this Christmas.

Only then can the new covenant be in your mind all the day long, because it is written in your hearts forever.

Amen

Christmas

YEAR B

First Sunday after Christmas

YEAR B

December 28, 2014

Relevant readings:
Isaiah 61:10-62:3
Psalm 147 or 147:13-21
Galatians 3:23-25; 4:4-7
John 1:1-18

Celebrating the gift of a new Jesus in the world

The Lord be with you.

We have just experienced Christmas, opened all our presents, played with our new toys, and gone around the neighborhood showing off what we got, while seeing what all our friends got.

Merry Christmas!

Raise your hand if your gift was the Holy Spirit and you are a newly born baby Jesus.

<look for raised hands>

I want to take our memories back to the Gospel reading last week, to the first verse in the Luke selection (Luke 1:26), which states, "In the **sixth month** the angel Gabriel was sent by God to a town in Galilee called Nazareth, to a virgin engaged to a man whose name was Joseph, of the house of David."

Since none of us here uses the Hebrew calendar, the "sixth month" is named *Elul*. It is a summer month, similar to the Gregorian calendar's sixth month of June. Whereas the summer begins in late June for us, *Elul* aligns between the Gregorian calendar months of August and September.

Now, this means the angel Gabriel came to Mary and announced she was pregnant. She was instantly pregnant with Jesus. We know that because when Gabriel left Mary, telling her that the previously barren Elizabeth was **six months** pregnant, Mary ran to see Elizabeth. Elizabeth's baby, John the Baptist, leapt inside Elizabeth's womb and Elizabeth spoke the Word of the Holy Spirit, saying Mary was special among all women.

So, in the month of *Elul*, Mary became pregnant with Jesus.

If you do the math, figuring that Mary would carry baby Jesus for nine months, his actual birth would have been at the end of the second month (*Iyar*), or the first of the third month (*Sivan*). That is around the end of May, first of June, on the Gregorian calendar.

Now, if one sees that Jesus was an important extension of God – as all Christians avow – then the birth of the Son of God would have been on a day that was significant to God. God would have it no other way. If God instantly made Mary pregnant when Gabriel appeared to her, God would have chosen that time for a reason. God would know when the baby would be born, with that chosen time a day of significance. Realizing that, then one can see how the 6th of Sivan is the first day of Shavuot, or the Day of Pentecost.

That "Fiftieth Day" was when Moses brought down the Covenant between God and the Israelites. That day was ordered to be remembered forever, such that as Jews gathered in Jerusalem to maintain that command, the disciples of Jesus were filled with the Holy Spirit. What better time for the Son of God to be born?

If you recall, Jesus would ascend on Pentecost Eve, meaning his entire life completed a cycle. He would come from Heaven on Pentecost and return to Heaven on the day before Pentecost. It becomes an amazing way to "read between the lines" of the Holy Bible and see the depth that comes out.

On the real birthday of Jesus, the Day of Pentecost after Jesus ascended, each follower of Jesus was reborn as Jesus, through the presence of the Holy Spirit sent by God. We read that in the Book of the Acts of the Apostles. "All of them were filled with the Holy Spirit and began to speak in other tongues as the Spirit enabled them." (Acts 2:4)

God did not send Himself upon those disciples simply because twelve men believed Jesus was a good man and a prophet of the Lord. The Holy Spirit suddenly came upon them because those twelve followers had **studied** under the resurrected Christ for forty days, **preparing** themselves and **dedicating** their souls to God. Jesus Christ advocated on their behalf, knowing their hearts, so he would ask the Father to fill those followers with His Spirit, so they could become twelve Jesus's.

One became exponentially increased in body. After Peter spoke to the crowd that was attracted to those Apostles, "about three thousand were added to their number that day." (Acts 2:41)

That was a true Merry Christmas, because they all, individually, became <u>bodies</u> for Christ, filled with the <u>blood</u> of the Holy Spirit. They embodied the truest meaning of Christ Mass.

During the Christmas Eve service, we read about the shepherds seeing angels, who gave them the good news that the Savior had been born in Bethlehem. They went and found Mary and Joseph with baby Jesus. When they left to return to their flocks, we read, "The shepherds returned, glorifying and praising God for all they had heard and seen."

Merry Christmas children! The Father has given you the gift of Salvation!

While the shepherds were simple people, young boys, teens

or pre-teens, symbolizing how all the new editions of baby Jesus will be shepherds to the flock of God's sheep, we too often push aside the shepherd boys' part in the Christmas play.

The commercialism of Christmas, which has concretely set upon this generation of Christians, loves to focus on three kings coming with fine gifts. We have replaced baby Jesus and the news of angels with Santa Claus and elves. The gifts of Magi are replaced with ads on TV for fancy cars, diamonds, and the latest electronic gadgets, none of which comes free of charge. You must have access to a king's ransom of wealth (or good credit) to afford such lavish tastes.

This projection of Christmas in December, rather than on *6 Sivan*, also becomes a competition with other faiths, where Christians are more able to afford gift giving, due to the blessings of Christ. We take over the news during the season of Hanukkah, or the Jewish *Festival of Lights*, which is not a gift-giving recognition. The commercialization of Christmas has led atheists to complain about manger scenes on public grounds; and, it has led to equal attention being paid to the creation of Kwanzaa in the United States.

One possible reason for why Christians celebrate Christmas in December is that the Hebrew month *Elul* is the twelfth month of the Hebrew civil year (the sixth month ecclesiastically). December is our twelfth month now, although it was the tenth month in the Julian calendar. Regardless of the month number or month name, there is a celestial event that occurs at this time for all the Northern Hemisphere.

That event was recognized by many religions around the

world; so, recognizing that time of festival became a way for the Roman Church to get pagans into the sheep fold. The event already celebrated was that of the Winter Solstice, which happens around the 22nd of December each year. Therefore, to have the birth of Christ coincide with that timing was a way of appeasing believers and non-believers alike.

One has to then see that the Winter Solstice as when the light of the Sun is lowest in the Northern Hemisphere sky. It is when there is less light. The weather turns colder.

The sun is said to be motionless for three days, before it begins to slowly ascend to the Vernal Equinox (Spring) and the Summer Solstice.

From that symbolism, the light three days dead (the death and burial of Jesus), then the light rising anew (the Resurrection of Christ), one can see how the Gospel of John speaks of the light of Christ.

Jesus was "The true light, which enlightens everyone." Jesus is "the light that shines in the darkness" of winter; and although it was a dim light for a period of time, "the darkness did not overcome it."

That dimness was because the apparent death of Jesus left no one capable of replacing that light. Despite his having followers and believers that Jesus – one human being – was the Savior for the world (in particular the Jewish world) – he died without heirs that could become the torches of his light, once Jesus was placed in a tomb.

Those believers and followers were not filled with the Holy

Spirit at that time, because they were not then ready. Although some residual spark still burned within them, it was hidden from plain view – behind locked door, fearing their own deaths. They were not ready; and, Jesus would not be overcome by death. He would rise again to light the way for his disciple to take up his light and keep the world free from darkness.

The lives of the eleven disciples (plus the replacement for Judas, chosen by lot before Pentecost) would change on the Day of Pentecost, after Jesus had risen. The Holy Spirit passed the light of Christ to them, as his Apostles. They would then immediately pass the light onto others.

The Apostles were not named Peter, Matthew, Mark, James and John any more. Although they were called by those names, they became the rebirth of Jesus. Christmas is all about the rebirth of baby Jesus in his followers and believers … when they have done the required preparation, training, and learning.

Christmas is all about the gifts of God to His shepherds, so from having been brought the news of a child born in Bethlehem one can "return, glorifying and praising God for all" one has seen and heard from angels of the Lord. Christmas is about receiving the gift of God, before you can ever think about giving that gift to someone else.

The gift is one that truly keeps on giving. It is given free of charge … as far as money and credit limits are concerned … but you still have to pay. You pay with your egos. You must die of self-importance first, in order to be reborn as baby Jesus.

Christmas Sermons: First Sunday after Christmas, Year B

Paul wrote words of encouragement to the Christians of Galatia, saying, "Christ came, so that we might be justified by faith." Our faith becomes "justified" by our validation of Jesus as the Son of God, as a continuation of the Christ mind. We validate that by ceasing to put all our eggs into the "**ME**" basket. We sacrifice [your name here] to become Jesus, through the Holy Spirit.

We must receive that mind on our Day of Pentecost, which comes from our works based on faith – learning the <u>Word</u> of the prophets, and the <u>Word</u> of Jesus, the Son of God. We must learn the law so we can demonstrate our willingness to live by that law, "so that we might receive adoption as children" of God; and so that we might receive the Holy Spirit and be reborn as the child of God, as baby Jesus.

A truly Merry Christmas is when we wake up and find that "God has sent the Spirit of his Son into our hearts," causing us to cry out, "Abba! Father!" That joy can only come from knowing we have become heirs of that birth.

On a true Christmas dawning, "I will greatly rejoice in the LORD, my whole being shall exult in my God; for he has clothed me with the garments of salvation, he had covered me with the robe of righteousness."

"Hallelujah! How good it is to sing praises to our God! How pleasant it is to honor him with praise!"

Amen

Second Sunday after Christmas

YEAR B

January 4, 2015

> **Relevant readings:**
> Jeremiah 31:7-14
> Psalm 84 or 84:1-8
> Ephesians 1:3-6,15-19a
> Matthew 2:13-15,19-23
>   or Luke 2:41-52
>   or Matthew 2:1-12

Parenthood is an epiphany that begins dedication to learning what it takes to change from child to adult

This is the last week of the Advent-Christmas seasons, the

Christmas Sermons: Second Sunday after Christmas, Year B

second Sunday after Christmas.

Thus, the anticipation of Jesus being born again has happened. Our pregnancy has gone full term and we have delivered the baby Jesus.

Today is also the tenth day of Christmas, so it is time to take down the tree and decorations on Tuesday. (You can leave the lights along the rooftop and in the shrubs, if you want, but just know it is tacky to turn them on before next Thanksgiving ... or whenever the advertisers decide when to first show the Santa of a Norelco shaver in the snow commercial, or the "Oh Christmas Tree" – Corona beer on a palm tree on the Mexican coast commercial, since that lets us know when to start redecorating.)

After today, we will enter into the season of Epiphany.

The word "epiphany" means, "A revelatory manifestation of a divine being," or "A sudden insight or intuitive understanding." Ecclesiastically, it is, "A Christian feast celebrating the manifestation of the divine nature of Jesus to the Gentiles as represented by the Magi, traditionally observed on January 6."

For that reason (partially) we have the option of reading from Matthew about the Magi, or "wise men from the east," either when they met Herod and then the baby Jesus, or when they left the baby Jesus and returned home. Both are from Matthew's second chapter, but we only read the last parts aloud (verses 13-15 and 19-23).

Let's set aside the festival part of Epiphany for now, and focus on "a sudden manifestation of a divine being," and look especially at how that is accompanied by "a sudden insight or intuitive understanding." That is what the readings focus on today, such that the central theme is on wisdom, as reflected in the "wise men."

Throughout the season of Advent, where we prepared for the coming of Christ, born again as the baby Jesus within each of us, and these last two weeks of Christmas – the Twelve days of Christmas – we have given birth to a new self.

We hope to have been reborn as Jesus. That should be our goal in the seasons of Advent and Christmas. But the work does not end there, as there is a newborn to raise.

If you have children of your own, then you know the work is just beginning when the baby enters the scene.

That is an epiphany, because the child that became pregnant has forever gone upon delivery of a baby, bringing about an adult … a parent … a caregiver.

In the song from Jeremiah today, we hear God tell the prophet, "I have become a father to Israel, and Ephraim is my firstborn."

In the Book of Genesis, the person named Ephraim was actually the second child of Joseph and his Egyptian wife, Asenath. Joseph was the favorite son of Jacob, whose name was changed to become Israel. All of those biblical characters lived long before Jeremiah, so when God said that to Jeremiah, there was nothing about Israel or Ephraim that was a current event. Still, for that remembrance to be prophetic, the meaning has to be seen as more than a history lesson.

The name Ephraim means, "Two-fold Increase," or "Doubly Fruitful." It is a combination name, where the number "two" is combined with the root meaning of "fruitful." Thus, God was not talking so much about a baby named Ephraim, as much as He had then fathered a nation of people ... Israel ... only to have them become scattered, so God would have that fallen nation reborn ... a second exercise in fruitfulness.

God would be Doubly Fruitful with His flock. Thus, God led the Israelites out of Egypt through Moses the first time; but after Israel became scattered, God called Joseph, the father of baby Jesus out of Egypt to fulfill the original prophecy that had failed.

Twice, God's gift to mankind ... His own set of priests for the world to be led by ... would come from Egypt.

Now in one of the alternate readings from Matthew, chapter two, the first twelve verses have us hear God tell this to Joseph. He said, "Out of Egypt I have called my son."

That is a reference to the prophet Hosea, from the eleventh chapter of his book. However, if you read the whole chapter you cannot easily see how there was a prophecy that needed to be fulfilled. It appears to tell of how Israel had fallen away from God, to the point of being scattered.

BUT ... in the Book of Hosea, in chapter eleven, God mentions his son Israel and then refers to Israel as Ephraim.

Or, does He? For a prophecy to be fulfilled by Joseph taking baby Jesus back to Galilee, from Egypt, the fulfillment of prophecy was doubly fulfilled.

Now this brings up the point of prophecy not being easy to understand. It was <u>impossible</u> to see the words of Hosea as a <u>prophecy</u> of Jesus, until after Jesus was born **AND** after God had to let Joseph know how the meaning of Hosea's words were prophetic.

This means two things, stated symbolically and not as a clear instruction written into a document approved to be in the Holy Bible:

> 1.) The Holy Bible is a collection of books (a library or "*biblios*") that are holy, thereby prophetic.
>
> 2.) You need God coming to you and telling you what deeper meaning is – that which is hidden, unseen, and there; but you can't understand it without help.

In the reading from Matthew today [first alternate selection – Matthew 2:13-23], after the Lord told Joseph to take baby Jesus to Egypt, to fulfill a prophecy, we then read:

> "There [in the district of Galilee, Joseph, Mary and Jesus] made his (Jesus') home in a town called Nazareth, so that what had been spoken by the prophets might be fulfilled, "He will be called a Nazarene.""

When you read this, it makes inquiring minds want to look up which prophets said that. Therefore, I did a search of the Internet and entered the question, "Which prophets said "He will be called a Nazarene"?

The answer was clearly, "Only Matthew said that. No prophets said the Messiah would be called a Nazarene."

I found one blog site where some man seemed perturbed that not only did no prophet (in the singular number) utter that prophecy, but Matthew stating "prophets" in the plural number was doubly wrong. How dare he be so wrong!?!?

His point was, "Wrong means less reason to believe anything."

That is "human wisdom" speaking.[1]

Then it became so clear to me. The prophets never said the Messiah would come from Nazareth. They said he would be born in Bethlehem [the alternate reading from Matthew 2:1-12 states this, quoting from Micah 5:2 and 5:4]. Those prophets would have their prophecy fulfilled because Jesus would be born in Bethlehem. However, he would be called a Nazarene by everyone who would later come to know he lived in Nazareth. Had he been called a Bethlehemite, then he would have been killed by Herod's orders, keeping the prophecy from being fulfilled.

It is so clear … once one has been led to awareness … from a higher power … because we read with human minds first and foremost, so that we can only understand with human

---

[1] In my research done as I wrote the book The Star of Bethlehem: The Timing of the Life of Jesus (2020), I found the word is mistranslated as Nazarene. It should be read as "Nazarite," which becomes reference to Exodus, and one devoted to serving God. The Nazarite sect, during Jesus' time was called the Essenes, who had a temple on Mount Carmel, which was only ten miles from Nazareth. Thus, Nazareth was a place for Nazarites and Jesus would be known as one of that sect.

minds ... initially. Our human mindset limits us from seeing the parts that require a divine mind.

In the alternate reading from Luke 2:41-52, where Joseph and Mary leave Jerusalem after the Passover festival, headed back to Nazareth, only to realize they had left Jesus – then a twelve-year-old – behind, we read in verse 52, "And Jesus increased in wisdom and in years, and in divine and human favor."

This is stating how there are two ways to read and understand what we sense from Scripture. We understand some that is written, due to human minds receiving favor from God. Still, there is more, which requires divine favor.

Joseph and Mary found Jesus in the temple among rabbis ... or teachers ... after they had searched all of Jerusalem looking for him, for three days. When they finally found Jesus, he was "sitting among the teachers, listening to them and asking them questions. And all who heard him were amazed at his understanding and his answers."

Jesus was taking the time to be schooled (or educated, intellectually increased in awareness) about what was written about his faith and religion. The teachers holding "class" were reading aloud the passages of the Torah and then discussing their meanings. One can imagine Jesus was in the temple, doing that for up to five days, after the Passover festival ended and up until his parents found him.

Jesus, the young boy who was still learning things, said to Mary, "Why were you searching for me? Did you not know that I must be in my father's house?"

Christmas Sermons: Second Sunday after Christmas, Year B

Where else was a student of God's written relationship with Israelites supposed to be?

If you have been pregnant with the baby Jesus inside you, and if you were born anew as Jesus on Christmas Day, then you need to put yourself in the place of young Jesus. You need to hear Mary be the voice of God telling you, "I have been searching for you in great anxiety!"

Then, your answer should be, "I'm here Lord, studying your Word, trying to understand divinely what I have only seen with human eyes before. You know I **must be** in your house."

In the alternate reading from Matthew 2:1-12, we read how the wise men appeared before Herod, asking, "Where is the child who has been born king of the Jews?" We translate "Magi" as "wise men," which fits a theme of "wisdom," and we assume some divinely enlightened wisdom has led those men to ask that question.

This is true, but can you see how Matthew, writing as a prophet inspired by God, had the Magi say, "We observed his star rising" because that was an **astrological** statement?

Can you see how the Magi were "wise" in astrology and the "star" was a major planet, a light seen brighter in the night sky, which was moving into aspect with the chart of Jerusalem, or the Second Temple, or the freedom from Babylon?[2]

Can you see their astrological interest in a "king of the Jews" was because they themselves were Jews, lifelong

---

2   The star of Bethlehem, I have realized, is the sun and not a planet or other phenomena of outer space. It is the earth's only star.

students and priests of the Kabbala?

Can you see them going to Herod because he was the king of Judea (also Jewish), and they thought perhaps he was the one who had sired a baby?

Can you see the place in the East, from which the Magi came, as being Babylon, with them the descendants of Jews who remained scattered there?

Can you see their trip to Jerusalem coinciding with a festival that made a pilgrimage to Jerusalem a doubly good excuse to go pay homage to a new baby king expected to be born at that time?

Do you think if this reading were discussed by teachers in Bible Studies, the teachers would hear those questions with amazement and understanding, as if someone who should not know such things was speaking not from human wisdom, but from divine favor?

In the quote from Micah that prophesied the Messiah was to be born in Bethlehem, not Jerusalem, Micah actually said, "But you, Bethlehem <u>Ephrathah,</u> though you are small among the clans of Judah, out of you will come for me one who will be ruler over Israel, whose origins are from of old, from ancient times."

The word "Ephrathah" is the root for Ephraim, meaning "Fruitful." Bethlehem would be fruitful, bringing forth the Savior, who would later flee to Egypt and then return … as Ephraim … Doubly Fruitful … the Two-fold Increase from God.

Christmas Sermons: Second Sunday after Christmas, Year B

This is how each of us is "small among the" whole "clan" of Christianity, so we flee from our religious responsibility, as it should be. If we do not experience the world as humans, gaining human wisdom, then how can we experience the divine as different? How would we be able to **know** which favor is better?

However, once we are called to return, once we feel in our hearts the touch of Christ and sense the call of God to serve Him, then we too must be reborn into a new life, as a Twofold Increase as Christians led by Christ the king.

We must know to travel a different path than the one that took us to that day of paying homage, just as the three Magi listened to their dream and followed that divine recommendation.

We must be able to see the symbolism of "gold" as the metal of Christ, as King. Gold is a metal that shines and gloriously reflects light. We must see the burning of frankincense as the transformation our lives must take, just as we see service to God's house means burning away an adherence to the worldly and becoming the essence of spirituality that scented smoke represents. We must be able to recognize how myrrh is the perfumed embalming ointment that we must cover our flesh with, burying the old self, so we can become the new self, devoted to God and Christ.

The readings today [including all of the Gospel alternative readings] point to there being two types of wisdom – one of human understanding and one of divine understanding. Our mind needs to grow through years of dedicated study and devotion, so that the Christ child within us can bring us to a divine state of awareness.

We are just babes in swaddling clothes now, newborns with years of dedicated devotion still before us. We must develop basic knowledge of what it is we profess to believe in. We must be educated, as symbolic seminarians listening to our teachers, led to ask amazing questions, and produce amazing revelations, before we can fully become ministers of Christ for the world, becoming true priests for the One God.

This is what Paul wrote to the Ephesians, when he stated, "I pray that the God of our Lord Jesus Christ, the Father of glory, may give you a **spirit of wisdom and revelation** as you come **to know him**, so that, with the eyes of **your heart enlightened**, you may know what is the hope to which **he has called you**, what are the riches of his glorious inheritance **among the saints**, and what is the immeasurable greatness of his power for us **who believe**."

Now, that is a huge chunk of Spiritual meat to swallow without mentally chewing first. It is the bread of Christ, which must be consumed for us to have remembrance of Jesus the Son of God. It is the food of prophecy that foretold of Jesus, which nourishes us to feel the blood of Christ cursing within our veins.

Let's review all that Paul said:

"The spirit of wisdom" means an understanding from divine favor.

"Revelation" is an epiphany, as a sudden understanding of something not seen before.

"The eyes of your heart enlightened" speaks of the emotions that link to God and Christ, bringing the baby Jesus into your being so you can be enlightened in ways never known before, through the human mind's wisdom.

"The hope that he has called to you," means hearing God ask, "Child, why has it taken you so long to be found?" It is a call to be Ephraim, as Doubly Fruitful as a Christian … to become hope for others.

"The riches of his glorious inheritance" becomes your own symbolic gifts of gold, frankincense and myrrh, because you have replaced the human you with the divine baby Jesus, inheriting him within, to properly display without.

"Among the saints" means you forever more going without sin, **not** because you <u>will</u> yourself to abstain from sin, but from your love of the Holy Spirit keeps you from being attracted to anything other than God. It means you become an Apostle to Christ.

"The immeasurable greatness of his power for us who believe" says the full ability to understand everything comes to us from our dedication. God's power has brought us to see, through the presence of God's Holy Spirit, adopting us as His own, sending us the mind of Christ, through which to serve Him.

Let us each see these last two-plus days of Christmas have us led to an Epiphany where this greatness of God's power begins to develop inside <u>everyone</u> of us.

Let today be the first day towards our new education, a new dedication to learning what is behind our faith, through reading, listening and asking questions ... and praying for answers.

Let us begin to be obedient to the Father, so we may increase in wisdom and in years, and in divine and human favor.

Amen

Christmas Sermons: Second Sunday after Christmas, Year B

Epiphany

YEAR B

First Sunday after the Epiphany

YEAR B

January 11, 2015

Relevant readings:
Genesis 1:1-5
Psalm 29
Acts 19:1-7
Mark 1:4-11

When did Jesus have an epiphany?

Last Tuesday was the day recognized as the day of Epiphany, January 6, 2015. To many of the Episcopal – Lutheran – Catholic branches of Christianity that day marks the end of the Christmas season. That concludes the "Twelve Days

Epiphany Sermons: First Sunday after the Epiphany, Year B

of Christmas," which fall between December 25th and January 6th.

So, in one way it means it is now time to take down the Christmas tree and put away all the decorations. We should now turn out the festive lights trimming the house and lawn and start making King Cakes.

While marking all the seasons of the ecclesiastic year with little fun things to do … happily busying ourselves from one seasonal color on the altar to another, from having drapes on the cross outside and not … so on and so forth … all that procedural hustle and bustle takes away from the "<u>reasons</u> for the seasons."

Last week I mentioned Epiphany was upcoming and I gave some definitions for the word "epiphany." I said the word itself means, "A revelatory manifestation of a divine being," and/or "A sudden insight or intuitive understanding."

Did anyone have a "revelatory manifestation of a divine being" or "a sudden insight of understanding" last Tuesday … that you would like to share with us now? Raise your hand if so.

<look for raised hands>

In the readings today, we have a Creation story and a song of praise for the Lord, paired up with an Acts story of Paul basically repeating what we read in Mark's Gospel – about John the baptizer using water, whereas Jesus used the Holy Spirit.

In actuality, every reading today tells of the Holy Spirit.

Further, the Christian day of Epiphany **IS like** the Day of Pentecost (as far as Christians understand the meaning of that day), because "a sudden insight of understanding" and "a revelation of the presence of a divine being" **IS ALL ABOUT** being filled with the Holy Spirit.

Now I know none of you sitting here today are unfamiliar with the words, "Father, Son, and Holy Spirit" (or "Holy Ghost"). That is the Trinity; and, it is what we all profess aloud, in unison, avowing what we believe.

We recite, "We believe in the Holy Spirit, the Lord, the giver of life."

Some know that as the Nicene Creed, because the Council of Nicaea began to hammer together this profession of faith … **BUT** … (despite some pronoun usage differences) that which we state is actually is The Apostle's Creed.

An **Apostle** is someone who has had a real Epiphany, not someone who has just changed into different color robes because a manual says that is proper.

If you notice in the Acts of **the Apostles** reading, it tells how Paul "found some disciples." What isn't written is how those "disciples" identified themselves as Christians. They were disciples of Jesus, because they professed belief in Jesus as their Messiah.

Most likely, they were converted Jews, rather than Gentiles, because they said they had been baptized "Into John's baptism."

Paul, as did Mark, explained that baptism by water was

"the baptism of repentance." Jews were required to know the laws of Moses, even if they spent most of their time breaking those laws they memorized. The Jews recognized all the rules that called for admission of sins; and, they had a special day set aside each year to cast out the sins of all Jews, starting anew with a clean slate.

Repentance through baptism was not a law of the temple. Despite all the recognition of sins, and rituals of cleansing involving water, the Jews were not required to ask God for forgiveness. That left many sinners feeling empty and guilty, so John baptizing people with water, as an act of repentance, drew crowds of people wanting to have God forgive them individually, rather than collectively.

Repentance was at least a first step towards receiving the Holy Spirit. Simply by admitting, "I have a problem with sin," God knows you are saying the right words, even if you keep on sinning.

Still, being a disciple means you have not yet had an Epiphany. So, God reached out and touched the twelve lead disciples left behind by Jesus; and, we find, "the Holy Spirit came upon them, and they spoke in tongues and prophesied."

That was an Epiphany for those twelve, as they changed from disciples into Apostles.

Now, this image of twelve guys hanging out, completely unable to "speak in tongues" or to "prophesy" one minute, then suddenly being able to do it after God laid hands on them all, gives the impression that the Holy Spirit comes fast. It seems like a loud rush of wind suddenly overwhelming one, as "Wham, bam, thank you Man. I needed that."

But, while that did happen, that is the wrong impression to get.

Last week, one of the alternate readings was of Jesus as a twelve-year-old boy, having been left behind in Jerusalem by his parents. They found him in the temple, about four or five days later. The focus of that reading needs to be seen as how Jesus was still learning Judaism at the age of twelve.

He took learning his religion seriously, asking, "Where else would I be other than my Father's house?" At twelve years of age, holy Jesus ... the Son of God, born of a woman ... still had to educate himself as to what Jews believed and what laws they followed.

The Son of God was not learning religion in the temple. He was learning how lacking in knowledge the leaders of the temple really were. That was a most important lesson; and, it was why Jesus (as a boy) felt it was important to stay there and teach the old men a thing or two. However, his parents returned and snatched him by the ear, telling him, "It is not your time to teach anyone here."

If you remember the story of the "Wedding in Cana," where Jesus turned the water into wine, his mother was the one wanting that miracle to happen. Jesus actually said to Mary, "Woman, how does that involve me? My hour has not yet come."

If you also recall how Jesus was about thirty years of age

when he attended that wedding party, then when you do the math Jesus had been learning Judaism for thirty years; but his time still had not come. There was still something more he needed to gain first, before he could be totally dedicated to a ministry of salvation.

Jesus still had not had his Epiphany. As such, he probably still had a little playfulness in him, some impish pranks he still liked to pull on his brothers perhaps? Maybe, Jesus held onto a slight selfish desire to use the powers he knew were at his disposal to benefit himself, rather than someone not having enough wine on hand for a wedding.

You see, when Jesus walked into the Jordan River and was baptized by John the baptizer, Jesus was repenting his prior selfish acts. John washed Jesus clean of his sins, however minor they probably were.

And then … God tore the heavens apart "and the Spirit descended like a dove on him." That was the Epiphany of Jesus. It was **the Epiphany** that he experienced, just as like the day the Apostles were first filled with the Holy Spirit, like a loud rush of wind; but in his case like a dove lighting upon him.

A select few others witnessed his Epiphany; but not everyone in the Jordan River at that time (including John the baptizer) could clearly hear a voice come from above, saying, "You are my Son, the Beloved; with you I am well pleased."

When God is "well pleased" with your repentance, He gives you the full package of Holy Spirit gifts – seven in all. Unlike the twelve disciples Paul converted into Apostles in Ephesus, Jesus could do much more than "speak in tongues" and "prophesy."

If you remember the story of Jesus, when he was preparing for his arrest, trial and eventual death, he stopped by a fig tree to pick some fruit, because he was hungry. But, the fig tree was not producing its fruit, because it was not the season. Jesus rebuked the tree for that failure and said, "May you never bear fruit again." "Immediately the tree withered," we read.

That is not a human power. That is a power of the Holy Spirit.

Jesus explained to the disciples that the power of God can have anything you command happen.

In Psalm 29, we heard these words today: "The voice of the LORD makes the oak trees writhe and strips the forests bare." The "**voice** of the LORD" is the Holy Spirit, so when God spoke to Jesus and the Holy Spirit lit upon him like a dove, that was Jesus' Epiphany.

In the Creation reading today from Genesis, we heard, "Then God said, "Let there be light"; and there was light." That command was the voice of the LORD invoking His Holy Spirit into the "wind that swept over the face of the waters." The earth had an Epiphany when God gave it light, separating the night from the day, and made a shapeless void become transformed into a purposeful order.

In that Genesis reading, at the end it said, "And there was evening and there was morning, the first day."

Epiphany Sermons: First Sunday after the Epiphany, Year B

From that we get the impression that the creation of the heavens and the earth, followed by the lighting of the earth's star – our sun – all took place in one twenty-four-hour period.

Hello? Do you recall the analogy that a day to God is like a thousand years?

That "day" took hundreds of millions of human years, where the earth spins around in an orbit of the sun, so the sun appears to rise and set daily; but mankind wasn't there yet. So, it was like one day's **work** for God. That **work**, that **act** of God, reflects what is required for one to have an Epiphany and hear the voice of God say, "Work is good."

The point of all the readings today is about the sudden change from being an ordinary repentant disciple, until one's faith leads one to **acts** that please God, so He will set His Holy Spirit upon each of us, if we meet that requirement. However, it is only sudden at the time when we experience that wind over our face … that voice within us.

It took Jesus thirty years to stop using God's benefit for selfish purposes (as few as those might have been). It took some amount of time for the disciples in Ephesus to learn that there even was a promised Messiah, a Christ, before they had a clue what the Holy Spirit was.

They did not know they were blessed by God so they could happily **work** FOR OTHERS the rest of their lives. All of the Apostles experienced their Epiphany during their lives, when there was still time to do more **work**.

By the time most of them were tortuously murdered by

jealous believers of the same God, those who never did the work necessary to get to know God personally, upon their soul's release from their bodies the Apostles could say things like, "It's okay God. Please forgive them because they don't have a clue what they are missing."

There **will be** one Epiphany for everyone, whether you are Christian or non-Christian, whether you are filled with the Holy Spirit while a living, breathing human being or not. We believe in one Baptism for the forgiveness of sins – one baptism with the Holy Spirit is all one needs.

You can be assured that having a true Epiphany while one is still alive and still able to **work** afterwards for the Lord, leading others to their one true Baptism, is much better than having "a sudden revelation of God before your soul," after it has left your body and you are evaluated on past **works** done.

You do not want to be finding an "immediate understanding" that your life's work was only for foolish, selfish desires. Then your Epiphany will be all about coming back to this world for another chance to do it right, having to face all your past failures all over again.

Recently, I watched an HBO showing of a documentary about George Harrison, the former Beatle. His wife, Olivia, told the story about a break-in at their home, where an intruder seriously stabbed George, nearly killing him. This happened after he went downstairs to investigate the noises of breaking glass.

His wife said, "All of a sudden I heard George chanting his mantra very loudly."

George Harrison was chanting very loudly what his Hindu-Christian mixture of religious learning had taught him many years before. This chant was a way of producing the effect of a dove lighting, calming him; and, he had been practicing this for many years, solely for the purpose of being in control of his soul's exit from his body at death.

We think we can prepare for death, but unexpectedly George Harrison had been stabbed; and, he then tried to force his death mantra for a selfish desire to be in control. However, his assailant, who was high on drugs and going upstairs to do more harm, left George chanting in pain.

Olivia met the intruder with an iron bar, breaking open his head and causing much blood to flow. She thought he was dead, but then he got up and grabbed her. George Harrison, stabbed and bleeding, ceased his mantra chant and came to the aid of his wife, children, and mother-in-law. He defeated the intruder and then George was rushed to the hospital.

I tell you this story because this first Sunday after the Epiphany is **ALL ABOUT** not waiting until death is staring you in the face to panic and start trying to remember how to be in control of your soul. You are not able to control your soul without the Holy Spirit. So, don't let your "death mantra" be an "I'm sorry God" plea.

After all, just like George Harrison found out, you never know when death can interrupt you "selfish time." You do not know the time or date when it will be too late to start learning what it takes to receive the Holy Spirit. You will never know how much time you have left to do the **work** of the Lord, and to have your Epiphany in a timely fashion, with God pleased with you.

It is not as hard as it seems; but it is completely inconvenient, as it requires you to put more than one or two hours of effort per week into your faith and your religion. It demands that you do something before God to prove your beliefs.

We have programs that can help you along that path. We are here ready to reach out to you … to lay figurative hands upon you so the Holy Spirit can open your eyes, ears, and mouths to the tongue of prophetic Scripture, so you too can prophesy to others.

But, no one is going to come to your home to make it easy. We have no tapes to place under your pillow, to listen to as you sleep, so you wake up filled with the Holy Spirit. You have **work** to do; and, after six days of good labor, then you can rest in peace.

You have to want an Epiphany before you can receive God's Spirit.

Let me know when I can help.

Amen

Second Sunday after the Epiphany

YEAR B

January 18, 2015

> **Relevant readings:**
> 1 Samuel 3:1-20
> Psalm 139:1-5, 12-17
> 1 Corinthians 6:12-20
> John 1:43-51

Come and see how to properly follow

While spending three years on "The Mountain," at Sewanee, Tennessee, I became familiar with their campaign to entice future seminarians to go there. It is called the "Come and See Visitation Weekend." It is a big event for the School of Theology there; and this year's event will take place between February 13 and 15.

Epiphany Sermons: Second Sunday after the Epiphany, Year B

If you ever get a chance to visit Sewanee, you will "see" how picturesque it is. It is a small village that is an extension of the University of the South, which (according to the Wikipedia article about the school) "consists of 13,000 acres of scenic mountain property atop the Cumberland Plateau."

It truly is scenic; and, the promotion of "Come and See" means the idyllic setting was enticing – one hard to see and not want to come back to. I call it a "throwback" university setting, one that instantly reminded me of the old television show "*Dobbie Gillis*." That show became, in my childish mind's eye, how college campuses were supposed to look … where stone buildings all had ivy growing up their side walls ... of the dorms, the Greek houses and the school buildings. Stately oak trees grow around manicured courtyards with designed sidewalks, and statues and plaques here and there. It is a picture-perfect, photogenic place.

In a way, Sewanee seemed much like Disneyland to me … a perfect place to vacation for a few days, up to a week; but way too expensive to live there year-round.

I am reminded of this from my past because of the reading from John today, where Phillip told Nathanael, "Come and see." He said this to Nathanael because Phillip told him he had found the one, "about whom Moses and the prophets wrote, Jesus son of Joseph from Nazareth." Nathanael had asked in response, "Can anything good come out of Nazareth?"

"Come and see," was then an offer to see for yourself. It says, "Don't let me be the one who answers that question.

Let the proof be from your own mind, through your own eyes."

Or so it seems.

Remembering that we are now at the second Sunday after the Epiphany, where we should be expecting an "ah ha moment" from all the readings; this Sunday is no exception. It is not going to disappoint you.

To bring you to this moment of sudden revelation, let's first go to the reading from First Samuel, where Samuel is a boy, believed to be around twelve to thirteen years of age. Samuel had been dedicated to the temple in Shiloh by his parents and placed under the guidance of Eli, the last of the judges of the Israelites. Eli was also a priestly prophet caring for the temple.

If you recall not long ago, one of the optional readings was of Jesus being twelve years old and left in the temple in Jerusalem, where he was eager to learn from the elders, the rabbis, the teachers. So Samuel is, in a way, similar to Jesus in this dedication to learning what his teacher had to offer.

We are told up front, "The word of the LORD was rare in those days; visions were not widespread." When we read those words, we are not misled to think people did not talk about the Torah ["words of the LORD"] and only a few people had eyesight ["visions were not widespread"]. We clearly understand that we are being told the existing conditions surrounding the Israelites, as far as the number of true holy people then, who were guiding them as would prophets and judges. They were few and far between.

We are told, "the boy Samuel was ministering to the LORD under Eli." That means Samuel was Eli's servant, with Eli still the one officially God's "go-to guy."

We learn that Eli's eyesight was growing dim, which is a physical condition of old age; but we read, "the lamp of god had not yet gone out." This means Eli still was able to "See" divine visions, only those had slowed down considerably over some number of years.

We are also told that "Samuel did not yet know the LORD." This means Samuel had not yet learned to distinguish an auditory hallucination … which is what a disbeliever would say a prophet hears, when no one else can hear anything out of the ordinary … from a real – "physical" – sound. Sound is, after all, invisible, like sight, but both are measured by how many people similarly register the physical reception of vibratory impulses.

If you recall last week's Gospel, when Jesus was baptized by John the baptizer, one of those auditory hallucinations was heard by some, but not all, when God said, "You are my Son, the Beloved; with you I am well pleased." Today, Samuel is hearing the voice of God while he is trying to go to sleep, but he keeps thinking it is Eli calling him.

Samuel, we learn, is obedient, as each time he hears his name called he says, "Here I am!" The exclamation point lets us know his answer was emphatic, rather than weary. Jesus, we learned after his retrieval from the temple by Joseph and Mary, was "obedient to his parents." And, we are told "he increased in wisdom and in years, and in divine and human favor," due to this obedience. This is more that reflects a parallel between young Samuel and young Jesus.

It says, in essence, "If you want to hear <u>the word of the LORD</u> and you want to receive <u>visions</u> sent by God, then listen for when your name is called, respond eagerly, "Here I am!" Then obediently do what you are told."

As such, Samuel would **follow** Eli as the prophet of Israel. Others, such as Elijah, Elisha, Jeremiah, and so on, would **follow** Samuel. Jesus would then **follow** in that line of holy men of Israel.

When you can see that set up, you can then begin to go "ah ha," when you read how Jesus "found Philip and said to him, "**Follow me**."

Sure, Phillip would walk in the shadow of a great prophet of Israel, just as Samuel physically followed Eli around the temple of Shiloh and Jesus physically followed the path taken by Joseph and Mary; but the importance is not that Philip <u>walked</u> behind Jesus. The importance is Philip would become just like Jesus, because of his hearing the call of his name, of him responding eagerly, and him obediently learning how to stop being a disciple and receive the Holy Spirit, becoming the next line of prophets **after** Jesus.

Philip would not go find Nathanael and tell him the Messiah had come, if he had only heard the physical voice of a man say, "Follow me." Philip had been one of those who heard God's voice say, "Jesus is my Son, the Beloved; with you I am well pleased." After having heard **that**, Philip would then be excited about finding Nathanael and telling him who he was joining, as a servant to a master.

Epiphany Sermons: Second Sunday after the Epiphany, Year B

Thus Nathanael, as a student of the laws of Moses and the prophets, posed the question, "Can anything like the Messiah come out of Nazareth, without being written to come out of there?" That was like him asking, "Philip, are you sure this is the one?"

When Philip said, "Come and see," the ultimate reason for those words was, "Our <u>obedience</u> will show us **divine visions**." In the long run it meant, "Our time to be prophets of the LORD has **come**. We have been **chosen to follow** this path."

Now, let's look at the conversation Jesus had with Nathanael, when Nathanael asked Jesus, "Where did you get to know me?" Jesus replied, "I saw you under the fig tree."

Think about that statement for a moment and let your mind's eye picture that scene.

Do you see Nathanael in a sitting position, as if he were seeking shade from the sun? Or, do you see someone standing under a fig tree reaching up, picking ripe fruit?

Whichever you see in your mind, you are "**seeing**" in a physical sense, and not in a divinely visual way. As American Christians, long separated from any Jewish – Israelite understanding of fig trees, we simply do not understand the symbolism present in that statement by Jesus.

The symbolism is why Nathanael would exclaim, "Rabbi, you are the Son of God! You are the King of Israel!" You do not go that overboard, reacting with exclamations of wonder simply because someone saw you physically under a fig tree.

The fig tree represents the future of the religion of the **One God – YAHWEH – the LORD – the Father** of Jesus, the Messiah. A fig tree that bears fruit is like Eli, Samuel, Jesus and Paul, those who continued the line of holiness, as dedicated priests of God. Thus, Jesus said to Nathanael (in essence), "I knew you were from Jeremiah's basket of good figs – one who has obediently studied the laws of Moses and the writings of the prophets – and God has allowed me to see you in that way."

This means, when Jesus next said to Nathanael, "You will see greater things than me having this vision of you," the meaning was Nathanael would have many such visions from God in his future. Jesus, then, just prophesied that Nathanael would become an Apostle, just like Philip, as both would "follow Jesus" in that way.

This brings us to the warning of Paul, which appear to focus on a need for those like Philip, Nathanael, young Samuel, and young Jesus … all who would become prophets of the LORD … that you must be faithful to the LORD in order to divinely hear the word and see. You must be married to Jesus, becoming one united with the Holy Spirit, becoming as Jesus, such that your physical body is filled with that divine link to God.

Paul wrote, "Your bodies are members of Christ," which means anyone who seeks to "Follow Jesus," who will "Come" to be holy and "See" visions of the LORD, **you become** the physical representation of Christ – **you become** the reincarnation of Jesus in the flesh.

You cannot then just begin some adulterous love affair

with sin, while married to Christ. You cannot maintain an engagement with God, if your heart still longs for pleasures of the flesh.

Fornication is not simply some physical act with someone you are not married to, as simply the sin of adultery or as a sin that can be forgiven through repentance. The Epiphany is the realization that you are only Baptized by the Holy Spirit once, so you will never cheat on your lover, when your lover is the LORD.

Paul wrote, "Your body is a temple of the Holy Spirit within you, which you have from God, and **you are not your own**." This means, like Samuel, "you lie down in the temple of the LORD, where the ark of God is." Whenever you hear your name called, you get up and excitedly say, "Here I am!"

You have a commitment to say, "Speak, LORD, for your servant is listening."

You can no longer let your eyes, ears, nose, tongue, or fingers search out physical pleasures that lurk in the external world, once you have been united with the Holy Spirit.

"The two shall be one flesh," … the flesh that is your body has become married to God, your soul entered into permanent union with the Holy Spirit, so you become the Christ child reborn.

Paul wrote, "Every sin that a person commits is outside the body; but the fornicator sins against the body itself." This means you keep yourself from being married to Christ by continuing to sin, keeping your body from ever knowing the ultimate pleasure of the Holy Spirit.

"For you were bought with a price; therefore glorify God in your body," Paul continued. That says the dowry you pay for being married to God is submission to a higher calling, where the glory of the LORD is upon your flesh and bones, due to that obedience to the MASTER.

In this season of Epiphany, you have to have your blind eyes opened so you can truly "See." You have to have your deaf ears tuned to the inner voice, where the Word of the LORD is always spoken.

You have to come to the ultimate realization that the LORD has searched you out and known you; He is acquainted with all your ways. Still, He calls your name to come, serve Him by Following in the path of His Son.

Are you sitting under a shade tree, avoiding the heat of commitment and responsibility?

Are you feeding off the fruit of a good fig tree, but storing that only for yourself and doing nothing to share it with others?

Or, are you a good fig that is waiting for ripening, so you can be picked to serve the LORD?

The message has not changed. It is still the same song, just a different verse. It is up to you to commit yourself to God when he says, "Follow me. Come and see."

Amen

Epiphany Sermons: Second Sunday after the Epiphany, Year B

Third Sunday after the Epiphany

YEAR B

January 25, 2015

Relevant readings:
Jonah 3:1-5, 10
Psalm 62:6-14
1 Corinthians 7:29-31
Mark 1:14-20

Are you a fish out of water as a fish for people?

I don't know if I have mentioned this before, but I am psychic.

I mean that I have an ability to know what the future will

be ... up to five minutes before that future happens.

Now, this is not a controllable ability. It comes and goes. Usually, I can only understand these enlightenments that burst into my normal mental activities in hindsight.

What I mean by that is I do not have an epiphany, or an "ah ha moment." It is more like a Homer Simpson moment.

"Doh!" <slap forehead>

For example, the last time a "vision" happened to me, I was walking out of the grocery store. I went to the store with my wife, and after checking out we split up – she went to the car and I went to the pharmacy. Since it always takes a long time at the pharmacy, she went to the car and loaded up, and then she waited for me at the front door.

As I walked outside, I saw my wife sitting behind the wheel of a running car, in the "No Parking" area. At that time my psychic sense said to me, "Drive."

I heard that suggestion loud and clear; but in an instance I rattled off reasons to myself why not to "Drive."

1. My wife was sitting in the driver seat.
2. The car was in a zone that needed to be exited quickly.
3. My wife has a driver's license.

Without a pause in my steps, I walked to the passenger door and got in. Off we drove.

Then ...

As we got down the road, less than two minutes later, my wife got a call on her cell phone. It was someone she was supposed to meet at the church, at about that time. My trip to the pharmacy had taken longer than we had planned. This person calling was already at the church.

Before my wife could look over at me, I said, "Go to the church. I'll drive home and take care of the groceries. I'll come pick you up when you call, if need be."

You see, a smarter mind than me told me to **drive** because that mind knew it would be the smoothest future ahead … the route of least resistance.

But I resisted that suggestion; and, because of that, I had to get out of the car (without bumping our car door against the woman's car that was already at the church) and walk around and get in the driver's seat. Then I had to back out, drive home, and unload the groceries.

Before we arrived at the church, I told my wife, "I knew I should have taken your place as driver …."

No one understands these "premonitions" until after they have become "I shouldas."

I believe everyone here has this same ability. We all have foresight and we all have hindsight; but the question is how often do we use our insight?

The saying goes: Hindsight is 20/20.

You can add to that: You need special lenses to see the present; and, the future is clouded by conditions of vision that act as blinders.

In all of the readings today, including the lyrics of Psalm 62, the message is like that insight I had, which said to me, "Drive."

That word was not accompanied by the heavens parting, a dove of light beaming down upon me – illuminating me so all the people walking in and out of the grocery store paused and gasped. There was no loud, booming voice saying, "**DRIVE!**"

What I heard sounded like my voice. It sounded like me telling me what to do. Because it sounded so normal, and because I know so well that I have had many thoughts that have best been ignored, I did not blink an eye as I walked the wrong way.

Therefore, in my mind's eye, I can see Jonah, David, Paul, and those who heard Jesus – Simon Peter, Andrew, James and John of Zebedee – hearing a voice inside their heads that sounded like themselves speaking to themselves.

The miracle is then that they all did the right thing and went the right way.

Jonah went to the great city Nineveh.

David wrote lyrics to memorize and sing, as a practice to prepare others to go the right way.

Paul wrote a letter that explained just how easy it is to go the wrong way, thinking nothing of it.

And Mark noted how those who go the right way are specifically named, but those who don't are generalized.

While everyone went the right way in the readings of today, a keen eye sees that all of those named people had been given a second chance.

In David's song he wrote, "God has spoken once, twice I have heard it."

Jonah's chapter begins by saying, "The word of the LORD came to Jonah a second time."

We all know that Paul was writing from the perspective of an Apostle, one who first ignored God's call as he held the cloaks of those stoning Stephen to death.

And, the disciples of Jesus were all Jews who, despite knowing all the laws of Moses and all the prophecies of what to watch for, none of them had heard a call to quit their day jobs and follow a guy that happened to be walking by.

Jonah had first heard God tell him to get up and go to Nineveh and tell them they were wicked and that they were going to be destroyed, about a week or so before what we read today. In essence, he had heard God say, "Drive," and instead he immediately went to the passenger door.

We don't read that today, but we all know the story of Jonah and the whale. Jonah was running away from God telling him to go to Nineveh. He took a boat in the opposite direction and the seas got rough. The sailors on that

Epiphany Sermons: Third Sunday after the Epiphany, Year B

boat became fearful and figured out Jonah was the cause of God's wrath, so they threw him overboard. God saved Jonah by sending a big fish to swallow him.

Because Jonah was saved by the whale, he was given a second chance to go to Nineveh.

This tendency to go the wrong way is seen when Mark wrote, "And Jesus said to them, "Follow me and I will make you fish for people." He then wrote, "They left their father Zebedee in the boat with the hired men."

Have you ever been fishing?

You have to have patience. You have to enjoy the peace and quiet. For as many fish as there are in the water, you are happy when you get a bite; and, you are even happier when you catch one fish … or more.

You know you aren't going to catch all the fish. "There's plenty more fish in the sea …," as the saying goes.

But, when Jesus said, "I will make you fish for people," he was not "fishing," *per se*. He was not trolling for disciples.

In fact, it wasn't Jesus speaking … even though he probably opened his mouth and those words came out of his body. God spoke those words. The ones to whom Jesus spoke heard his message "intuitively" as a promise that came from God. Thus, the four named men heard the voice inside their head say, "Drive," and they went the right way. They followed Jesus.

Still, when we hear "fish" as a verb, we think of the potential of saving souls, where patience pays off in the long run. We see fishermen with nets to catch fish and see the analogy of fishermen with nets to catch disciples. You are "fishing," therefore you will still be "fishers."

But, think of "fish" as a noun.

When you hear that said once, in a second way … "twice I have heard it" … you see Jesus is himself a "big fish." Jesus is the epitome of the **whale** that saved Jonah, sent by God to swallow other reluctant servants of the Lord. Jesus was then himself a "big fish." A big fish saved Jonah by swallowing him, transforming him after three days inside, spitting him out as a reformed prophet. Thus, Jesus called for volunteers to "follow me," meaning become the next generation of big fish to save humans; and, in the enclosed environment of discipleship, they would be spit out into Apostleship.

Hearing "I will make you fishermen" as "I will make you fish saving men" means that those who would follow him would themselves be "made fish." They would become whales "for people," as vehicles of salvation.

If you recall the story that Jesus told the Pharisees, where he said he was the gate keeper of the sheep fold, he said that he was also the gate. "I am the gate; whoever enters through me will be saved." (John 10:9a)

As the gate through which others enter, others would become Good Shepherds to the flock. Jesus is saying he is the **whale** from which all like Jonah will exit.

The big fish, or what we commonly call the whale of Jonah,

represents the sheepfold. God then becomes the big fish that swallows a lamb, surrounding that with the Holy Spirit of God.

Jonah stopped being fearful when he spent three days in the belly of the whale. Jonah stopped running from that voice he heard inside his head and became a Good Shepherd.

Jesus said that once a lamb leaves the sheepfold, they follow the voice of their shepherd. **BUT** … some shepherds are only hired hands.

In John 10:11-13 Jesus said, "I am the good shepherd. The good shepherd lays down his life for the sheep. The hired hand is not the shepherd and does not own the sheep. So when he sees the wolf coming, he abandons the sheep and runs away. Then the wolf attacks the flock and scatters it. The man runs away because he is a hired hand and cares nothing for the sheep."

When one recalls the analogy of a "hired hand" to a bad shepherd, one can then read Mark write, "They left their father Zebedee in the boat with the hired men."

That is a profound statement, especially if one knows the Church of Rome is where the seat of the Papacy is located. Catholics refers to that seat as the "Bark of Saint Peter." A "bark" is a "boat." We sit in a "nave," which comes from the Latin word meaning "ship."

The first symbol for Christianity was the "fish" symbol (<><).

The name Zebedee means, "Yahweh Has Bestowed," or

"Gift of the Lord." From this gift came two sons who would be Good Shepherds to the flock; but Zebedee represents more than one man, one father.

Zebedee represents the remnant of Israel and Judah, which had been given a second chance. Zebedee represents Jerusalem.

Those who James and John left behind are then the hired hands of Jerusalem, or those who cannot hear when the Word of God speaks. If they do hear it, they run away. They write off the Word of God as themselves talking crazy talk to themselves.

The hired hands flee from responsibility when they hear themselves think, "Go to the great city that is three days walk across and tell them, 'The time is fulfilled, and the kingdom of God has come near; repent, and believe in the good news of a prophet."

When one can see Zebedee as representative of Jerusalem, then it is not hard to see how Jerusalem represents the rebirth of Nineveh. The hired men on that boat are the Pharisees, the Sadducees, and the Temple priests who care nothing for the sheep. They are not fish offering salvation, but fishermen seeking material food.

The result of being led by bad shepherds ... of being false leaders ... is that time is running out and the sheep will be overthrown. The wolf will attack and scatter them.

Salvation comes from hearing the word of the Lord, proclaiming a forty day fast from sin, and putting on sackcloth that represents submission to the big fish ... the Holy Spirit

Epiphany Sermons: Third Sunday after the Epiphany, Year B

sent by Christ.

In Jonah we read, "When God saw what they did, how they turned from their evil ways, God changed his mind about the calamity that he had said he would bring upon them."

Jesus refers to his ministry as a prophet as like that of Jonah, as one who speaks the word of the Lord so that people hear that voice and go the right way.

Turning from evil ways requires faith. It requires hearing the Word of God and not running away.

Paul stated how evil ways are so often found in mundane things, such as:

> Being **married** to human wives, rather than Jesus, through the Holy Spirit.

> **Mourning** those who physically die, rather than see a symbolic death as a requirement before one can come out of the whale and do as the Lord says.

> **Rejoicing** in earthly delights, rather than experiencing the euphoria of hearing God tell you which way to go.

> Hoarding material comforts, seeking **possessions**, rather than sharing with others – becoming a **fish** of salvation - finding comfort in the promise of faith.

> **Dealing** with those who buy and sell souls, rather than finding the only deal worth making is with Christ.

Paul said, "The present form of the world is passing away."

Jonah told the people of Nineveh, "Forty days more!"

David sang, "Those of high degree are but a fleeting breath."

And Jesus said, "The time is fulfilled."

We need to be able to see how we are not reading about the successes and failures people long gone from the face of the earth. We are reading the stories of our lives, in our relationship with God and Christ, while using the name of others to make it seem like we have no responsibility other than sit and do nothing.

In this season called Epiphany, the time has come to realize this message has never changed. It is now as it **once** was. It is for all times, because at all times we are only one heartbeat away from "passing away."

The characters presented today heard the voice of God **twice**, before they reacted and went the right way.

The root meaning for the word "psychic" is "soul," and we all have one of those. So, we all hear the Word of the Lord telling us to go the right way.

We all get those intuitive messages to "Drive," to "Go," "to Follow."

How many more times will we opt for the passenger seat?

Amen

Epiphany Sermons: Third Sunday after the Epiphany, Year B

Fourth Sunday after the Epiphany

YEAR B

February 1, 2015

Relevant readings:
Deuteronomy 18:15-20
Psalm 111
1 Corinthians 8:1-13
Mark 1:21-28

Who do you root for after God, family and country?

Everyone here has heard the saying: God, family & country.

Epiphany Sermons: Fourth Sunday after the Epiphany, Year B

Of course, this is a ranking that says three very important concepts are implied to be of most importance, over all other concepts of service, devotion and responsibility. God comes first, family second and country third.

In a way, everything else can be sorted to those three categories; such that life, liberty and pursuit of happiness – our inalienable rights, according to our Declaration of Independence – can be seen as a subset of "country." This accepts as 'given' that God gives us "life." As to "family," that has a way of restricting the concept of "liberty" and "pursuit of happiness," based on the needs of "family" being more important.

If one has several free hours to ponder the duties and responsibilities that preferences and rewarding opportunities are presented us in life, we could then list them all and rank them in order of personal importance. In such an exercise, where do you think your list would place:

Modes of transportation?

Modes of communication?

Places of employment?

Availability of education?

Availability of food?

One could list a plethora of "needs," on and on. But I'll stop there. I mention this way of organizing the elements of life because it is time to have another epiphany, during this season of the Epiphany.

In the reading from the Book of Deuteronomy, where God told Moses about the prophet he would send, "who shall speak to them everything I command," we know that prophet by the name of Jesus. Jesus the Messiah – the Christ.

So, when we rank "God" number one, are we doing that as Christians, where "God" means (as Paul wrote), "One God, the Father, from whom are all things and for whom we exist"?

That implies that God then expects one to also worship "one Lord Jesus Christ, through whom are all things and through whom we exist," doesn't it?

Sadly, while we might think that is the meaning of "God" being first in our ranking system, as the most important concept to be devoted to, it allows for any "god" to come into the mind of the one thinking that.

As they say, "Beauty is in the eye of the beholder."

The same can be said about the mental images one gets when stating a ranking of "God, family and country." To a Jew, "God" means Yahweh, the God of Moses. To a Muslim, "God" means Allah, the God of Mohammed.

There is nothing specified that says Jesus Christ is the Lord of "God," when we say that ranking of importance.

This makes what God told Moses more important to realize the meaning of, when He said, "Any prophet who speaks in the name of other gods, or who presumes to speak in my

Epiphany Sermons: Fourth Sunday after the Epiphany, Year B

name that I have not commanded the prophet to speak."

God told Moses there will be other "gods," with their own lords, or prophets.

This is not the epiphany I mentioned, although it is good to know that God recognized there were other gods and other lords in the world, by saying those who pretended to speak for the One God would die.

When God says they will die, that means they are mortal, and not eternal. Worship of lesser gods leads to the end of a lifespan, with no promise of spending eternity with the One God.

That can only come by placing God – Christ – Holy Spirit first on the devotion list … all tied for number one.

Paul told the Christians of Corinth, "Indeed, even though there may be so-called gods in heaven or on earth – as in fact there are many gods and many lords." That confirms gods are everywhere.

Which brings me to the epiphany for this week.

We sit in a house of worship, where this building speaks for God, as if saying "We are devoted to God, through Christ." But, do we put God number one?

In this town there are many churches that speak the same words as ours, but do we leave this building and feel a sense of superiority, thinking our style of worship is better than those in the other churches here?

Are our religious practices better than someone else's?

If ours is not the best, then do we go to all the churches around town?

If ours is the best, do we go try to get other people to realize that and stop going to their "inferior" churches and come to ours?

Do we see our branch of Christianity like we see college and university athletic programs, where we suit up and battle it out to prove who is better … at least in one game, if not over a collective of games over the years?

Has anyone here ever tailgated before a college football game?

It is a deep-rooted tradition, especially in the major universities. High school football is very similar to a religion across the South, whether or not you can see that sense of importance. Thus, sharing fellowship with school chums and football program fans before a big game has a special feeling to it.

People set up grills, fire up the coals and toss on the meats: hot dogs, hamburgers, brats, ribs, chicken breasts, steaks, roasts. The "chef" is the "keeper of the flame." There are others who tap the keg, uncork the wine, and pop the tops on beers kept cold in icy coolers.

In the reading from Paul, he wrote of "the eating of food offered to idols." When you see that scene at a college football game and compare it to a festival like the Passover, where the "fans" of Judaism crowd the place for a big event, preparing for the Temple "chefs" to fire up the altar and throw on the sacrificial lambs, there is not much difference in the activities and atmosphere of fun and celebration.

Now ask yourself this question: Is the popularity of college football waning or growing?

Before you answer that question, compare it to your answer to this question: Is the interest in Christianity in America waning or growing?

There may be a correlation there, such that a need to place "God" first has morphed into a lesser position on one's list. Perhaps a lesser "god" has moments in the top spot? Perhaps one feels a responsibility to act as a prophet who thanks God for the success of a college football program? Perhaps that prophet if reflected as the "lord" quarterback of the team, who is worshiped as a "savior"?

Don't laugh. There are plenty of people praying at sporting events, especially if the home team is losing. They think they are praying to God, as if He cares who wins a game being played.

It is a sign that priorities have become corrupted.

Paul warned of this corruption, which can be modified to read as if he was specifically talking about true Christians being seen partying in the parking lot of a major college stadium. He can be shown to warn that one's devotion must not be to some school team, but to the One God and Christ, first and always foremost.

Still, doesn't this fit like a well-worn school sweatshirt, where Paul said … "Take care that this liberty of yours does not somehow become a stumbling block to the weak. For if others see you, who possess knowledge, eating in the parking lot of an idol, might they not, since their conscience is weak, be encouraged to the point of eating food cooked on grills as a sacrifice to idols?"

Can you see how the NFL has turned Sundays into a gathering of the assembly in parking lots outside stadiums, beginning at 9:00 AM ... rather than in the local churches?

Have you ever watched ESPN and seen how much the pundits preach about how a child's game, played by young adults, should be given a high degree of importance?

Are they not promoting the sacrifice of one's devotion to sports and entertainment?

In the Gospel of Mark today we read of "a man with an unclean spirit" in the synagogue where Jesus was preaching. This man "cried out, "What have you to do with us, Jesus of Nazareth? Have you come to destroy us?"

The spirit within him knew Jesus was the prophet of which God told Moses He would send.

That is a statement that says we all know what is right and what is wrong; but we are afraid someone might actually come to us with God's words in his or her mouth, speaking what God commands.

What if that prophet knew we were all pretending to put God first, when we really love other things much more than

Epiphany Sermons: Fourth Sunday after the Epiphany, Year B

God?

Would that person be coming to destroy our way of comfortable life, of doing things the way things have been done forever and a day?

"Why are you here Jesus? Our team has a winning record this year!"

The epiphany for today comes from realizing how anyone who has such a demon spirit inside, which keeps one from really, completely, totally, without question placing God-Christ-Holy Spirit first … as proved by being an Apostle of Christ … then one is **not** promised the eternity of Heaven.

If there is not the epiphany that comes from suddenly convulsing and screaming, as the unclean spirit departs, then one sits pretending not to need that change.

The penalty is death to any who say what they think God would want them to say, while not truly speaking the word of God, from the Holy Spirit within, sent with the approval of Lord Jesus Christ.

If everyone here is truly filled with the Holy Spirit, then:

> "Hallelujah! I will give thanks to the LORD with my whole heart, in the assembly of the upright, in the congregation."

Amen

Fifth Sunday after the Epiphany

YEAR B

February 8, 2015

Relevant readings:
Isaiah 40:21-31
Psalm 147:1-12, 21c
1 Corinthians 9:16-23
Mark 1:29-39

The epiphany of witnessing an exorcism with no Hollywood special effects needed

I remember, when I was a teen, I heard a report that Billy

Epiphany Sermons: Fifth Sunday after the Epiphany, Year B

Graham limited how much his children could watch television. I heard that on the TV news.

Right about that time in my life, I quit the Boy Scouts because I would rather watch *The Munsters*, and I stopped going to church, partially because I always missed *The Ed Sullivan Show*, *My Favorite Martian*, *Combat!* and other shows on Sunday, Tuesday and Friday nights. Those were shows that other children would talk about at school the day after.

I was left out of those conversations because I was embarrassed to say, "I didn't see that show, because I was at church."

Recently, I watched a documentary on television about George Harrison, "the quiet Beatle." I recall that show presenting a news clip from about 1964 that reported, "Nine out of ten parents believe going to church was very important, but for teens and young adults the number is only four out of ten." Today, the stats are much lower than they were in 1964, for parents and children.

Not only was religion too restrictive to kids my age, it wasn't new ... like television and the latest fads were. I was caught up in "Beatlemania," just like all my peers, and I had missed their appearances on *The Ed Sullivan Show* ... although I remember claiming to be sick one Sunday, so I could watch one of the reruns that featured *The Beatles*. And ... that was before John Lennon said *The Beatles* were more popular than Jesus Christ.

He was right, in one regard ... but popularity is best measured in longevity; and *The Beatles* have another 1,900 years to go **IF** the popularity of Christianity were to die this very moment.

On that subject of the popularity of Christianity, in recent weeks, I have watched two movies on my home television set that featured Catholic priests. Television and Hollywood tend to treat religion as a foreign object, as some form of interpretation of "what it must be like being a priest."

For as much as "method acting" had led actors to live with those whose roles they will pretend to emote, it would seem priests don't merit starring roles or are not supposed to be portrayed seriously. I doubt if a young Al Pacino would have lived with a Jesuit priest for as long as he hung around with the police detective that he would portray in *Serpico* ... but then who did he learn how to play the lead in *Devil's Advocate* from? Still, with that glaring lack of attention to truthfully reflecting religion in movies, the two films I watched went against that trend, giving a sense of reality to the priesthood.

One of the movies, *Calvary*, symbolically predicted the end of the Church. This was because of people having lost their faith ... including many priests. It was set in Ireland and it placed blame on past priests who had abused their positions of trust long ago (as pedophiles), and then were never justly punished for their "sins."

The other movie, *The Rite*, was based on the true story of a Roman Catholic exorcist, who was trying to convince another priest – one who was educated as a therapist or psychologist – that demons did indeed possess human beings. The "young priest" kept saying he did not believe in crazy people needing exorcists, more than they needed a psychiatrist and prescribed drugs.

The most powerful line of the movie was when the young priest was forced to cast out a demon. A battle of words ensued, where the unclean spirit inside a man had told him, "You don't believe in God. You believe in me." The "me" was evil, eventually revealed as "Ba'al." The priest (who had a past which the demon spirit knew about) was not without the regrets of sin, thus the priest was vulnerable because of his doubts. He eventually said to the demon, "I do believe in you … which means I believe in God," at which point he cast out the demon. He stopped having doubts.

The end credits of the movie stated how the young priest was a practicing exorcist for the Catholic Church, in Chicago, having performed a number of exorcisms since then. The elder exorcist was said to still be practicing in Rome (in 2009), having then performed over two thousand exorcisms.

In both movies, dedicated priests were presented within a setting of modern conditions, where the majority of people have largely lost their faith in religion, amid dwindling attendance by professed Catholics. Those who were truly shepherding the few who still clung to the church were shown working alongside priests who were less dedicated and less faithful.

In *The Rite*, the mere presence of demons in people was a statement about having lost faith. In *Calvary*, the dedicated priest encountered his fellow priest, who was leaving. That departing priest admitted, "I'm having doubts." The good priest said, "You have no integrity. That's the worst thing you can say about anybody."

When I was in a seminary setting, I witnessed a trend away from "good priests" as depicted in *Calvary*. He was a mid-60's male, having become a priest after the death of his wife, with an adult daughter. Today the trend is towards "young priests," like the therapist-priest, who was full of doubts to overcome in *The Rite*. I saw a seminary that educated would-be priests with questionable integrity, who seemed to be looking for a stable job, more than answering a call to serve God.

All of this that I have recalled for you just now fits snugly into the readings for today, especially when we are reminded of Jesus as an exorcist, in Mark's Gospel.

You may recall how Mark said that Jesus, "cast out many demons; and Jesus would not permit the demons to speak, because they knew him." In the movie *The Rite*, both priests who performed exorcisms got into exchanges of wills, between the priests and the demon possessing someone. The demon spirit indeed said **it knew** the person who was trying to be stronger than it. Because that spirit knew the exorcist had cracks of doubt in his armor, a history of sin that was covered by a façade of faith, it fought back viciously.

In the movie *Calvary*, the "good priest" remarked that the faithful only remained faithful because they feared death. If you fear evil more than God, you believe in God only as a way to beg for forgiveness before you die, so you can avoid hell. You cannot defeat evil with faith like that.

The demons in the village of Simon-Peter's home knew

Epiphany Sermons: Fifth Sunday after the Epiphany, Year B

Jesus was without doubt, without a sinful past, and bringing the full power of God within him. That presence, of Jesus' complete faith in God, would not permit the demons a chance to fight back.

When you see how Jesus cast out demons while also "curing many who were sick with various diseases," that makes a statement that says illnesses, both mental and physical, are a result of lowered faith. Lowered faith is a condition of poor shepherding. Poor shepherding is a result of lowered faith. It is a downward spiral – a self-fulfilling prophecy of failure – that creates a force away from an inner faith in God, towards an outer belief that God is in others who will "save me from myself."

We put our faith in medical doctors and psychiatrists – physical and mental healers. We put our faith in priests and preachers, evangelists and exorcists – who will ward off the evil spirits that we allow inside us. We put our faith in things, as a sign of how well God loves us.

This condition today is no different than the conditions in the days of Jesus' ministry. When Simon found Jesus and said, "Everyone is searching for you," Jesus said, "Let us go on to the neighboring towns."

That was not a statement of avoidance, as if Jesus had doubts. You see, Jesus was not in that village seeking to be the one those people could put their faith in – as their healer, as their teacher and confessor, as their good luck charm – because Jesus was not there to glorify himself. He was there to give a message to everyone; and, even though they might not know it, **everyone was indeed searching for the Messiah and his message**.

The message said, "Those who serve the LORD shall renew their strength. They shall mount up with wings like eagles. They shall run and not be weary. They shall walk and not be faint." (As Isaiah's song sings.)

In short, Jesus came to show **everyone**, in that village and throughout Galilee and Judea, that they have the power to heal themselves by allowing God to become one with them. They simply need to serve God, and not self. Serving self only allows for one's self to become possessed with evil spirits that cause illnesses.

It was not a new message, as Jesus did not come with a caravan of clanging cymbals and trumpets blaring to announce, "New for you! Must see what has never been seen before!" The coming of Jesus was not like a circus coming to town.

Instead, the message of Jesus was, "Have you not known? Have you not heard?" (As Isaiah's song begins and refrains.)

Jesus sang, "The LORD lifts up the lowly, but casts the wicked to the ground." (As David's psalm sings.) "The LORD has pleasure in those who fear him, in those who await his gracious favor." (As Isaiah's song sings.)

When you all claim to be faithful to God, "Have you not known? Have you not heard?"

Now Paul was doing the same thing Jesus was doing. We know this because Paul was an Apostle, so he was a model of Jesus. Paul was not coming as a sideshow, but as one bearing the same message that Jesus took to the village of Simon.

Paul said, "If I proclaim the gospel, this gives me no grounds for boasting, for an obligation is laid on me, and woe to me if I do not proclaim the gospel!"

Jesus could have said the same thing!

Because we call the four books that tell of Jesus the man "the Gospels," realizing the word "gospel" means "good news," we begin to think the "good news" was Jesus has come; and he is that external idol we should all now pray to for health, sanity and prosperity. That misses the point of Jesus also "proclaiming the gospel."

God is who Jesus prayed to early in the morning. Jesus quietly, without fanfare, went to a solitary place to thank God for allowing him to present the message that God is all-powerful, as the source of good health and humane life. Paul modeled that; and the message says for all of us to model Jesus too.

Paul added that the message was "free of charge" to all. So, as Jesus told Simon, "Let us go on to the neighboring towns, so that I may proclaim the message there also; for that is what I came to do," the message cannot stop and be set upon a pedestal in a museum that then charges admission, just to maintain a building's upkeep and management. The message is living and not stagnant.

God sent Jesus to tell the world to be like Christ, while showing the world what rewards came from being like Christ. Paul, and all the Apostles, and all the Saints thereafter, were multiplications of Jesus, exponentially spreading that message, so that Christianity grew because there were so many more Jesus models in the world.

In that vein of thought, Paul said, "I have made myself a slave to all, so that I might win more of them." He said, "I have become all things to all people, that I might **by all means** save some."

In that regard, Paul meant respecting the values of all people, rather than meet people as if stating, "I have God within me, and you don't. So, listen to me if you want a better life." That is threatening and scares people away.

Still, Paul did not "become all things to all people" because he was like some person who has a sign in the front yard proclaiming "Psychic Reader." He was not adept in reading people's facial expressions and then telling them what they wanted to hear … for a fee. Neither did Jesus go from town to town doing such parlor tricks.

Paul, like Jesus, was filled with the Holy Spirit, possessing the mind of God – which like the demon spirit knew … that Holy Spirit was God in Jesus – the Holy Spirit knows all people, as well as all spirits. Jesus knew those whom he healed through the mind of God, so the mind of God worked miracles through Jesus. Likewise, Paul was led to act in the ways of those he encountered, so they were put at ease and not defensive and guarded.

By being all things to all people, all the people Paul encountered were open to receiving the message that God would save them, as long as they became dedicated to being the reincarnation of Jesus, believing Jesus worked

Epiphany Sermons: Fifth Sunday after the Epiphany, Year B

miracles as an extension of God.

Like the people of Israel, who wanted a king to rule over them, a king who could be trusted to be connected to God – like David – the people of Galilee and Judea had been trained to have no true faith that God would work miracles within themselves. They waited for the Messiah to come and be that external protection again.

It does not work that way. The people of Simon's village were ill in body and spirit because they did not know how to face God … and become His child, reincarnated.

We are no different today, after centuries of Saints and Kings spreading the message of Christ, that message has slowly been lost. That has taken away the light, and in the darkness we have stumbled back to a repeating of the times when the people fall ill and seek external salvation.

More people get their "religion fix" from watching television – either CBN, TBN (the PTL Club), or movies that enter the eyes and leave seeds of thought behind that grow into doubt. We watch cable news networks that repeatedly tell us how much evil there is in the world, with no message how to exorcise those demons.

Most people would rather do anything, other than come to church, pray, discuss the Bible, and go spread the message of God's healing love. We watch the television news and wonder why someone doesn't go stop all the insanity that permeates the world?

That "someone" is never us. We are too weak. We are but one person in a sea of evil. We have no faith in our ability to act alone, because we fear our death.

Paul said, "To the weak I became weak, so that I might win the weak." That says, "Everyone is strong enough to heal the world if you stop thinking in terms of one frail, weak, sick human being, and start thinking in terms of one who has been touched by God and healed, with the abilities of Jesus, and willing to spread the message of God's power to a world filled with demons."

The unclean spirits of this world know that Holy Spirit; and, they know they cannot fight against it. With you and the Holy Spirit, the rest of the world is outmatched.

Amen

Epiphany Sermons: Fifth Sunday after the Epiphany, Year B

Last Sunday after the Epiphany

YEAR B

February 15, 2015

Relevant readings:
2 Kings 2:1-12
Psalm 50:1-6
2 Corinthians 4:3-6
Mark 9:2-9

The epiphany of Scripture transfiguring before your eyes

I remember watching a television program about the lost civilization of Atlantis, a long time ago. It might have been a story based on some of Edgar Cayce' trances and the

Epiphany Sermons: Last Sunday after the Epiphany, Year B

information he gave about those ancient times. Or, maybe it was based on the writings of Plato, who also wrote about that ancient place.

Whatever the source, the image that program placed in my mind's eye was of a large arena where many people had gathered to be informed about the latest news. This was not only news "broadcast" to that arena, but simultaneously to many places around the world. Instead of murmur and noise filling that arena, where a featured speaker would be expected to "speak" words that were amplified by large speakers to all who were there, it was a scene of complete silence.

No words were expressed, as we recognize "audible speech" today. Everything was communicated through what we call ESP. Extrasensory perception.

Because silence is a central theme in the readings today, I will now THINK of a sermon, and it will be up to you to pick up on it.

Remember to, "keep silent" and "listen to him," the voice of God who connects all of our minds.

<make face like thinking hard>

Is everyone able to hear well enough?

<listen for responses>

<repeat squeezing out thoughts>

How about now? No?

Well, this doesn't seem to be working very well. Maybe we should work on our ESP a little longer and try this again another Sunday.

In the meantime, I'll vocalize a sermon about the readings today.

Over the past year, we have read the Second Kings reading before (albeit without the last two verses) and we have read of the same account told of in Mark's Gospel, as that told by Matthew. So, these messages are not new to us.

And, then again, the messages I will convey today **are different** from the last two times I talked about those readings.

They are different because, as we read from Paul today, "our gospel is veiled." That means it is difficult to understand clearly what everything we read aloud means, simply from reading … without reflection.

The gospel is like a cloud. We can see it look like one thing now, but give it time and it can change and look like something else. Same cloud, different shapes.

Paul wrote about those who have the hardest time understanding what the Holy Bible says and means. He said they are "those who are perishing."

He said, "In their case the god of the world has blinded the minds of the unbelievers," where "god" is spelled with a lower "g."

That use of "*theos*" has to be seen as intending to project a

Epiphany Sermons: Last Sunday after the Epiphany, Year B

lesser deity than the Father who art in heaven. Unbelievers tend to worship material gods, or "the god of the world."

Thus, when we believers read the Holy Bible, we have to read through the veil; and, we are just like the unbelievers except "we proclaim Jesus Christ as Lord and ourselves as your slaves for Jesus' sake."

We stop being unbelievers when we start being slaves for Jesus' sake.

That means Jesus has to whisper in my ear what the readings mean, so I can then tell you … so I can "lift up the veil" and let you see … to "Let light shine out of darkness."

So, you can understand, I have to first be shone in my heart the light of knowledge, so I can then become the face of Jesus Christ. Only as a slave can I wear that face.

That means that I am not standing alone before you, as one leader speaking audibly to followers of Christ. The fact that I have to talk out loud means I am teaching in a worldly way. If we could be doing the Atlantis thing … telepathically communicating ... it would be like Jesus, Peter, James and John did on the high mountain.

If that be the case, you might be able to see Jesus standing beside me, telling me what to say.

If I am able to tell you something about the readings that makes you marvel, to see something clearly that you had never seen before in the scriptures, then you might feel like exclaiming, "It is good for us to be here in this building, dedicated to the worship of Jesus Christ as Lord."

However, that is when God speaks, saying, "Jesus is my son, the Beloved; listen to him!"

Jesus speaks here, but also on high mountains, on Interstate highways, and even in the Walmart ... if you listen close enough.

God spoke that message to three frightened disciples from a cloud. The cloud is the veil surrounding the gospel, making it change shapes from one reading to the next. Jesus is the one who whispers the hidden meaning of those veiled words ... to each of us believers who are willing to listen.

So, like in that arena the television program depicted, of a meeting in Atlantis ... shut up and listen for the inner whispers.

<tap on the podium >

<whispering like an Atlantean announcer> "Attention. Attention. Can I have your attention please? The gathering is about to start having meaning."

In the Second Kings reading, where Elijah is making his farewell tour through the Northern Kingdom of Israel, also known as "Samaria," the stops he made were to places where a "company of prophets" came out in each place to meet him.

In each of those places (Bethel and Jericho), the prophets came out to ask Elisha, "Do you know that today the LORD will take your master away from you?"

Epiphany Sermons: Last Sunday after the Epiphany, Year B

In the veil of those words, one can become confused and think something happened that informed them of that information … such as a messenger arriving beforehand with that news, or Elijah holding a meeting with the prophets that announced that … but the reality is they had that collective ESP thing working for them. They listened to the whispers and they had this light of knowledge.

When you understand that, then when Elisha responded to each question, "Yes, I know; keep silent," he was not telling the company of prophet to shut up and listen. They had done that, so they knew.

The companies of prophets were asking Elisha, "Do **you** know?" He was then confirming to them, saying what he said, that **he knew**. Elisha understood that by being silent one is able to receive valuable information from God.

In essence, Elisha responded, "Gotcha. I have to listen to the whispers. I need to use my ESP."

Now, the purpose of having these three readings, and Psalm 50, all together to ponder today … to receive the messages that are sent by God to us believers … is for us to see ourselves in each of these readings.

We are Elisha, who wants to "inherit" the abilities of a high priest, a true prophet of the Lord. We want to be able to listen and hear what God sends to us.

We are the unbelievers, who want to believe. We want to be able to see through the veil and wear the face of Jesus Christ. We want the light to shine from us to those in darkness.

We are the disciples of Jesus who are too busy trying to understand the meaning of visions we have ... those that are projected to us through the messages held in the Torah (Moses), the Prophets (Elijah), and the New Testament (Jesus).

We are the Israelites who "gather as loyal followers, those who have made a covenant with God and sealed it with sacrifice."

David told **us**, "Our God will come and will not keep silence."

He comes to **us** in a cloud, as veiled words, and as a whirlwind.

We want a "double share." We want to be able to be a social butterfly, doing as we please, while also being a servant to the Lord ... <u>on Sunday mornings</u>; but "that is a hard thing to ask for."

The clothes we wear cannot serve two gods, one of this <u>world</u> and one of heaven. If we can see Heaven, we can rest assured we have served the same God, both on earth and in Heaven.

However, if we can only see "a chariot of fire and horses of fire separating us from heaven," and if we lose sight of Jesus as he ascends, we are forced to choose who we serve.

Do we serve the God of Christ and Israel?

Or, do we serve the god of this world?

As loyal followers of Christ, with the new covenant with God, through Christ, we still must seal that choice with a sacrifice.

We must tear our clothes in two and pick up the mantle of Apostleship.

We have to live by what we have been taught … "keep silent" … "listen" to the Father, through the Son.

We are called to wear the face of Jesus Christ and shine light to the world.

Amen

Advent, Christmas and Epiphany Sermons

YEAR C

Advent

YEAR C

First Sunday of Advent

YEAR C

November 29, 2015

Relevant readings:
Jeremiah 33:14-16
Psalm 25:1-9
1 Thessalonians 3:9-13
Luke 21:25-36

Being called "The LORD is our righteousness"

Another beginning is upon us. We have almost begun December and the Advent season lets us know that Christmas is coming.

As I mentioned last Sunday, when I talked about the cy-

Advent Sermons: First Sunday of Advent, Year C

cling and re-cycling of time, here is another consideration: December is the last month of our calendar year, yet it represents the first month of our liturgical year.

The last month of our secular calendar year is then when we celebrate the "New Year" liturgically.

You may notice how the same theme is seen in the readings today, where much of the text focuses on the end of times, while we are preparing for the beginning of Jesus.

That "*Genesis*" story of baby Jesus is presented now as the prophecy of Jesus telling of signs to look for, "in the sun, the moon, and the stars." That is like the signs of *The Revelation*, so we flow from the first to the last and then from the last to the first. The Alpha and the Omega stated symbolically.

That is how a circle is. The one point designated as the first leads around to the point designated as the 360th, which joins both the first and the last together. However, when the circle is seen from the side, as the shape of a threaded screw, the place where the two appeared to join are actually where the two are aligned – one above and one below.

All of the points in the circle between the first and last are either ascending or descending. This is the natural circular path between two ends that come together and align.

In this cycle of growth, we can learn that the principle stating "As above, so below" is demonstrating how what seems to be the end is merely a reflection of a cycle before, with another cycle still to come.

As such, the prophecy of Jeremiah, the wishes of Paul to the Thessalonians, and the signs that are to come told of by Jesus are not limited to any one time, past or future. These readings [as with all scheduled readings from Biblical liturgy] have bearing at all times.

The <u>Advent</u> is thus not limited to any one time: past, present or future. **Everything** in the readings today that is seen as focusing on the times that are apart from ours now can equally be seen as reflective of **Our Times**, as models of **Our Lives** now.

The Advent then reflects a time for <u>beginning</u> to see ourselves in the words sent to us through Scripture, as all Christians need their own Advent, in order to find the truth of Salvation.

In Jeremiah we read how the promise made to the houses of Israel and Judah by the LORD would be fulfilled, with that fulfillment being "a righteous Branch to spring up from David."

That new growth should be seen as a spiral upward, to a new higher level. Likewise, we should hear the parable of the fig tree [and all trees] as symbolizing this upward growth in one's quest to fulfill our Covenant with God, where we "will be called, "The LORD is **my** righteousness.""

Since history tells us the house of Israel was scattered to the four corners of the world, as the tribes lost through captivity and interbreeding, they represent the past. Israel, as the Northern Kingdom (with its ten tribes), represents those who were given opportunity but squandered it. Through neglect, they reverted to Gentile status.

The Jews, who represent the house of Judah, are still around. They call themselves and are referred to by others as Jews. However, by calling themselves Jews and not Christians, they are locked down in the present, not secured of any future promise. They still await God's promise being fulfilled, which means God still awaits their commitment to Jesus as their Christ.

Jeremiah then prophesied, "And this is the name by which it will be called: "The LORD is our righteousness."" That means, instead of Jews not being righteous, they are equally as flawed as Gentiles. While still claiming a lost Covenant makes them special – so special they deny the promise having been fulfilled by Jesus of Nazareth – the Jews have no claim to righteousness, which is always their end of that bargain.

Thus, **Christianity** represents the totality of a <u>future</u> where Salvation is possible.

Unfortunately, just as the Israelites mostly lost out on the promise that was Jesus of Nazareth, so too can Christians miss out on Salvation. That loss comes by doing what one wants, rather than doing what is required to **receive righteousness**.

Now, Paul wrote in his letter to the Thessalonians, "May he so strengthen your hearts in holiness that you may be blameless before our God and Father <u>at the coming of our Lord Jesus</u> with all his saints."

That was not a recommendation for the Christian apostles

of Thessaly to wait for the end of the world, as if that was when our Lord Jesus was going to be seen <u>coming</u>.

Add what Jesus said in the Gospel of Luke to what John wrote in *The Revelation* [read last Sunday], where both John and Jesus quoted from Daniel, saying: "the Son of Man coming in a cloud," **and** one could conclude that implies a not yet seen occurrence. We believe no one has yet seen Jesus Christ coming from the sky; and because of that <u>we await his return</u>.

That view keeps the "coming" of Jesus an event that keeps getting "kicked on down the road," into the future. It projects in our minds the End Times.

The problem with that mindset is that Christianity would have died long ago if we all had to wait forever to see Jesus Christ returning from heaven in a cloud. Therefore, Paul did not intend anyone to wait for that "coming." He had already seen it, along with his fellow apostles, including some of the Thessalonians.

Every **true** Christian has experienced the coming of Christ, when the Holy Spirit has "happened" upon them, transforming each into Jesus Christ reborn.

When that happens "our hearts are strengthened" from that holy presence. We become "blameless before our God," as God sits upon the throne of our hearts. The Holy Spirit of our Father brings about the Christ Mind within us, just as was the Holy Spirit in Jesus of Nazareth. That is itself a circle path that repeats, because that way happens "with **<u>all</u>** God's saints."

Advent Sermons: First Sunday of Advent, Year C

When you can see this is an ever-present "NOW" call to be a saint, as every Christian's Advent, it is not hard to see Jesus saying, "People will faint from fear and foreboding of what is coming upon the world, for the powers of heaven will be shaken." That is a statement about all times, ever since those words were spoken, because a world without Christ's presence will always be as lost as were the houses of Israel and Judah. We can look at the news today and see fear and foreboding all around.

This need to fear a loss of God in one's heart makes the "suggestion" of Paul forever relevant in the NOW, and only when fear and foreboding sets into one's heart … a fear of not having God within … can one pray for "our hearts to be strengthened" by God's rescue.

Jesus said, "Be on guard so that your hearts are not weighed down with dissipation and drunkenness and the worries of this life, and that each day catch you unexpectedly, like a trap."

He then said how we should be "praying that [we] may have the strength to escape all these things that will take place, **and to stand before the Son of Man**."

We stand before the Son of Man **NOW**, when the Son of Man is set inside our being by God, via the Holy Spirit bringing us the Mind of Christ. We stand **before** that which is behind our strengthened hearts.

When Jesus told the parable, stating, "Look at the fig tree and all the trees; as soon as they sprout leaves you can see for yourselves and know that summer is already near." **That** is a "sign in the sun," our life star.

We are like trees that sprout shoots of new growth, as the Advent of warmth and comfort that comes from the Sun – our **light** of truth – brings forth that new beginning. The Advent is then when we "know that the kingdom of God is near." The "sun" that is Christ brings the warmth of peace.

All generations begin the same way, thus "this generation will not pass away until all things have taken place." We are but one link in the spiraling course of humanity over time. Therefore, "Heaven and earth will pass away," as a cycle of beginning and end, *Genesis* and *The Revelation*. It reflects a transformation from the spiritual to the physical … as life to death, which is assured to all mortals.

Still, the words spoken by Jesus "will not pass away," as the cycle that breaks the chain of soul reincarnations, back into the earthly plane, comes when our hearts are strengthened in holiness and we stand before our God – just as we stand before the Son of Man, as the Son of Man reborn.

We then share the same Father as Jesus of Nazareth, as we do "at the coming of our Lord Jesus" into us, we become righteous. We change the cycle of growth from life to death to a higher level. We sprout the leaves of eternal rebirth and everlasting life, once we join the ranks of God's saints.

May this Advent mark your beginning on this path to righteousness … to a Happy New You!

Amen

Advent Sermons: First Sunday of Advent, Year C

Second Sunday of Advent

YEAR C

December 6, 2015

Relevant readings:
Baruch 5:1-9
  or Malachi 3:1-4
Canticle 4
  or Canticle 16
Philippians 1:3-11
Luke 3:1-6

Christ coming into one's own

A definition of "advent" is: "The coming or arrival of something or someone that is important or worthy of note."

Advent Sermons: Second Sunday of Advent, Year C

The Christian definition is: "A period of time before Christmas, marking preparation for the coming of Christ."

Christians – since "Christ" is the root of the name – see Jesus as that "someone who is important" AND as that "someone worthy of noting" as "coming."

The word "advent" comes from the Latin word "*adventus*," via the Old French word "*advenir*," meaning, "to happen, to come to pass, to befall, to chance, and to betide."

As such, we read during the Advent season of prophecies that tell what will happen and who will come to pass.

While we sit almost 2,015 years after the birth of Jesus of Nazareth, thinking we need to remember "the coming or arrival of something or someone that is important or worthy of note," as if we are so glad Jesus came, went, and left us a religion in his name, the truth of prophecy is it tells us what will happen, what will come to pass, and what will befall all who listen, as well as all who fail to heed prophecy.

Prophecy is thus a double-edge sword, where it tells the good that will come to pass for those who do heed, while also telling the unfortunate consequences those who do not listen can expect.

Today's readings have reminded me of natural disasters that have occurred close to areas I have lived. Most recently, there was a tornado that cut a path of destruction across the city in which I live; but prior to that was the path of destruction that came from Hurricane Katrina, which included the place I was living.

In a sense, both were "prophesied" to happen, although the exact places and times were unknown. Those who listened to the warnings were prepared to act properly, lessening the impact of harm. Those who did not prepare for the worse lost more than they had imagined.

Still, the specifics of those two storm cells that were seen on weather radar screens and projected to be potentially very dangerous are just two of many similar storms that come and go. Before Hurricane Katrina was Hurricane Camille, in basically the same place. After the tornado in that city, long-time residents remarked how all tornadoes that strike the town somehow track over the same general path.

That means the warning of the past will always apply to the future; and the same aspect is connected to the Advent readings today.

Christ was prophesied to come. Because Jesus was born, lived and died does not mean that Christ is not still a potential coming in our future.

This means the danger comes when we sit here listening to readings prophesying the coming of Christ and then fail to heed that prophetic message as directed specifically at us ...

<pointing randomly> At **YOU** ... and **YOU** ... and **YOU** too.

We hear how Baruch (who was the scribe for Jeremiah) spoke of the "sorrow and affliction" of Jerusalem. The Jews had lost something dear to them, which caused them pain and suffering.

Advent Sermons: Second Sunday of Advent, Year C

In an alternative reading for today, from Malachi, we are asked, "Who can endure the day of his coming, and who can stand when he appears?" Malachi then stated, "For he is like a refiner's fire and like fuller's soap," where such treatment of the unrefined and dirty will certainly bring about "sorrow and affliction."

In the Canticle 16 song, the "subtitle" is the "Song of Zechariah." This song is recalled by Luke, in his first chapter, verses 68-79. While it is easy to overlook where today's reading says, "John son of Zechariah," we need to realize that reference is to John the Baptist and that he was not the son of an ancient prophet of Judah. We learn from Luke 1:67 (not read today) that Zechariah was a priest in Jerusalem (rather than one of the "Minor" prophets), who was the father of John the Baptist.

Verse 67 says, "His father Zechariah was filled with the Holy Spirit and prophesied." Thus, the prophecy of John's father said later (read from Luke1:78-79), "In the tender compassion of our God the dawn from on high shall break upon us, to shine on those who dwell in darkness and the shadow of death, and to guide our feet into the way of peace."

Once again, a prophecy inspired by God's Holy Spirit tells of the good times that will come to the righteous, but the trying times that will come to those with less dedication to God. Sorrow and affliction, being tested by fire until one's sins dissolve away, those will be the emotions of human who live in darkness, hiding from the light of salvation, clinging to mortal lives that will always hide in the shadow of death.

Then, from the Gospel of Luke we read how John the Baptist fulfilled the prophecy of Isaiah, another of Judah's prophets who foretold of both coming glory and pain. John the Baptist was another "one crying out in the wilderness," repeating the warning of Advent that Isaiah prophesied.

They both cried out, "Prepare the way of the Lord, make his paths straight." Then they added, "The crooked shall be made straight, and the rough ways made smooth; and all flesh shall see the salvation of God."

John went out, "into all the region around the Jordan, proclaiming a baptism of repentance for the forgiveness of sins," which was based on the prophecy of Isaiah. Because Isaiah had done the same as John, who foreshadowed what Jesus of Nazareth would do, and more of the same would follow with the disciples who were elevated to Apostleship – the continuation of this proclamation becomes our Advent.

All of those prophecies read today that foretold of the Advent of a promised Messiah, who would be known in the body of Jesus, as the Christ, remain valid. As such, all of the prophecies say how the Messiah comes to correct the broken and reward the holy.

Jesus did not come-happen-betide when he did: to keep things from breaking, to prevent people from taking a crooked path, to stop the lost from wallowing in the darkness of sin, and to cease guilt to those making them so ashamed they seek the shadow of mortal death. The ways of the world will always be an ever-present danger. There is a never-ending need for Jesus to come-happen-betide.

Advent Sermons: Second Sunday of Advent, Year C

The influence of evil has strength in the material realm, but only when surrounding the weak and hopeless souls of humanity. Therefore, the same prophecies marking the Advent of Christ continue to foretell of that same Coming to Pass, forever more.

A new storm is always forming on the horizon and messengers will always be sent to warn of the harm that will happen to those who do not seek safety, to those who ignore the warnings to find shelter beforehand.

Those who never think that prophecy involves them, and never hear the words of Scripture as a personal warning that requires them to prepare a path for the Lord … into one's heart … they are the most prone to suffer sorrow and affliction. Those who have eyes but cannot see, or ears that cannot hear, they imagine how hard it is to take a straight path. A crooked road seems more gratifying to those who have not yet experienced a personal Advent.

I boarded in a home that had survived Hurricane Camille. After Hurricane Katrina, that house and countless others were swept off their foundations and piled as rubble, one on top of another. All possessions were forever lost. Hurricane Katrina became the Advent of long-term sorrow and affliction for many people … most who heeded the warnings and came back to find destruction; but to some – those who ignored the warnings - they found their shadow of death a reality that was much closer that they were prepared to face.

A life saved from natural disaster is a life that can give glory and praise to the Lord, recognizing Him for having sent messengers of warning. A life cannot be replaced as can houses and furniture, cars and clothes.

You can buy natural disaster insurance that will replace things lost, although one-of-a-kind possessions are irreplaceable. But, for a body giving shelter to a soul, the message of a storm warning is to keep God alive in one's life.

Rather than a paper policy of promise, the only assurance that comes from a covenant with God and Christ is felt within. One's emotions become uplifted from heeding the call to hear what is coming.

As Jesus Christ said to his followers after he was risen, "Receive the spirit." That is the Advent step. You have to love God in order to desire for yourself to be reborn as Jesus, so you can follow the will of Christ and walk in the same footsteps of Jesus, in service to God.

We know that the Advent is an <u>ongoing</u> prophecy of the Coming of Christ, because of the letter written by Paul to the Philippians. Paul was encouraging Christians seeking the Holy Spirit to keep working towards "**the day of Jesus Christ**."

The "day" of Jesus Christ means the birthday of one's self as Jesus's duplicate. It is that memorable event when wanting to be Christ-like is fulfilled.

Happy birthday of Jesus Christ in **you**!!!

Paul wrote to them saying, "I long for all of you <u>with the compassion of Jesus Christ</u>." Paul had already had his "day of Jesus Christ," so he felt the depth of "compassion" that

Advent Sermons: Second Sunday of Advent, Year C

Jesus felt for others who sought to receive the spirit and serve God.

At the same time, Paul prophesied to the Philippians – AND TO US HERE TODAY – that his longing was "for all of you [to also be] <u>with the compassion of Jesus Christ</u>."

Paul made it clear to the Philippians (and to us) that "in the day of Christ you may be pure and blameless, having produced the harvest of righteousness that comes through Jesus Christ." We can only "produce the harvest of righteousness" when we are an extension of the Good Vine of Christ … as another "Jesus Grape" full of the sweet moisture that is the emotion from the Holy Spirit.

That is the blood of our Savior flowing through our veins.

We become another Advent of Jesus as the Christ, fulfilling the prophecies, just as John the Baptist fulfilled his priestly father's speaking as Isaiah, through the Holy Spirit. We become a repeating of that voice in the wilderness, crying out for all to heed a warning, while giving praise for a promise to be fulfilled.

Everything we are to do, in order to be clothed in the robes of righteousness that Jesus of Nazareth wore, is done for the glory and praise of God. To be so pure as to offer yourself to the LORD in righteousness, there can be no glory or praise for yourself.

You become a lightning rod through Christ, grounded in the earth, with arms raised in praise to God.

Picture yourself as a Y, with all that is YOU at the convergence of three straight paths. The Trinity then surrounds your being.

When the refining fire strikes, as like a lightning bolt from God, you cease being raw ore and start being purified silver. You become transformed into Jesus, as another Son of Man subservient to the Christ Mind. You become a physical receptacle for the Father's spiritual outpouring.

Thus, we say, because we ARE the ADVENT of:

> "Glory to the Father, and to the Son, and to the Holy Spirit: as it was in the beginning, is now, and will be forever."

Amen

Advent Sermons: Second Sunday of Advent, Year C

Third Sunday of Advent

YEAR C

December 13, 2015

Relevant readings:
Zephaniah 3:14-20
Canticle 9
Philippians 4:4-7
Luke 3:7-18

See Christianity as a crip course that is fun and rewarding

When I was a senior in college, I needed an elective course to meet the graduation requirements. Due to a full course load, I sought a course that would not require much work.

Advent Sermons: Third Sunday of Advent, Year C

A classmate recommended I take "Hand Molding," saying it was "a crip course." So, I signed up for that course my last quarter at school.

Hand molding was a class offered by the School of Art. I had never taken any art courses where I had to actually produce works of art. I had only taken (and enjoyed) one Art History class. I was worried that I might be expected to know preliminary basics of hand molding, which I knew nothing of. That inexperience made me worry that it might be difficult to get a good grade and maintain my honor status. I was worried that I might have to drop the class and find another to replace it, at the last possible moment.

At that time in my life, having returned to complete my degree in my early forties, I was under a lot of stress. I had made many sacrifices so I could go back to school. I changed from one full-time job to two part-time jobs, which allowed time for class and homework; but that schedule had me working seven days a week. I had taken from my savings to subsidize my income, so I could continue to support my family financially.

My well-planned path to the future, via a bachelor's degree course scheduled and mapped out over two and a half years (at two colleges), had hit a major road block: my marriage fell apart as I began my senior year and divorce was a fork in the road that I could not ignore. On the verge of graduating with honors, I was suddenly struggling to concentrate on my studies.

On the first day of my Hand Molding class, the teacher alleviated all my fears about needing to have any experience. She said it was a beginner's class, it would be fun, and the grade would be based on turning in five projects. Each project would be based on different hand molding styles. She assured us that no one who completed those tasks would fail.

After going out and buying a twenty-five-pound square chunk of river clay, a plastic tool box, and some assorted gadgets for working with clay, I was ready for the first assigned project. It was called a pinch pot.

The assignment was easy. Take a piece of clay, ball it up, push your thumb into the ball and then make it make it look like an ashtray. It took me five minutes.

"That's it?" I asked the teacher.

"Yep. That's it," she said.

I loaded up my books and walked past all the others in the class who were still working on their projects. Getting out of class early let me do some textbook reading and note taking. I liked that crip course.

The next art class, a couple of days later, had me back looking at my puny ashtray and comparing it to all the other works of art my classmates were creating. Everyone else had made elaborate variations on that basic theme, with some still adding delicate details to theirs.

The teacher told us to leave our finished project out to dry when we were done. Otherwise, we were to spray it with a mist of water and keep it covered with plastic so it would remain pliable. That way we could keep working as long

Advent Sermons: Third Sunday of Advent, Year C

as we needed. However, the project had to be completely dry before we could paint our work with glaze and then fire it later.

I don't know if any of you are familiar with pottery glaze, but it is painted on dried clay, so both the clay and glaze yield any luster or shine to a piece of work. The pinch pot would be painted with glaze the art school supplied, because that project would be fired in a simple kiln - Raku style. We were instructed to buy small bottles of regular glaze for use on our future projects. Either way, glazes don't go on looking like what they will look like after being heated, especially the Raku glazes. Once the glaze is applied to dry clay it dries to a dull, flat state, almost void of color.

Due to the style kiln our first project would be fired in, and the special type of glaze used for that process, there were no guarantees what the finished glaze would look like. We were told to experiment. Often, the teacher told us, the finished work often yields surprising colors.

The firing process used for the pinch pot projects was outside, with propane torches shooting flames into a long, low brick oven. All of the class' works of art were placed inside that, via the top having a removable lid. After the projects were set inside the oven, one set on top of another, the lid was put in its place.

After a number of hours of flames being forced into the oven, from both ends, the torches were turned off and the top lid was removed. The projects glowed with a translucent appearance. Wads of newspaper had been placed in large metal drums and the glowing works picked up with large tongs and then set into the drums with care, igniting the paper. That got a lower level burn going to activate some chemical process in the glaze. Finally, using the metal tongs, goggles and heavy gloves, the pots were carefully picked out and set it into a shallow pool of water, for the works to cool. Cooling only took a few minutes.

My simple little ashtray was transformed into a beautiful rimmed dish that had an array of bright, shiny colors, making it appear to have had much more effort put into it than it really had.

Something that was small and less artistic than any of the other works of art in the cooling pool had morphed into a feature of remarkable colors that made it sparkle with beauty. For some reason (unknown to me), my combination of glaze colors worked so well that the results made my other classmates envious. Their glazes had not produced that same radiance.

This firing part of hand molding was exciting. It made me committed to putting more effort into the other projects that were to come. Seeing the result of that changed state made me elated and anxious to do another project.

The days of the week my art class fell was scheduled such that I did not have another class until several hours later. Hand Molding officially started at 11:00 AM and lasted until 1:00 PM, with my next scheduled class at 5:30 PM. Still, art classes are only set up with schedules to satisfy school needs, as art students work on projects whenever they feel like it. That feeling can go well beyond a two-hour scheduled window. For that reason, the art building where the kilns were located had a coded entry, so all art students could choose when they needed to work on projects, anytime of day.

The hand molding class was indeed for newbies. We were set up in a loft that overlooked where the wheel throwing work was done. That was where the real art students would work towards becoming true potters. We walked past entire sets of china that were stored along walls and under the wooden stairs leading to our loft. Those pieces were the degree projects of dedicated artisans. As I would go to my bench to work on my projects, I could see all the "master potter" works that were set carefully around the workroom, in various states of drying, glazing, and finished ceramics.

I began coming in early and staying late. I became mesmerized by working with my clay. It was truly therapeutic for me and just the feel of the clay had a healing and uplifting effect. All of the weight on my shoulders felt lifted away, as I got lost in my projects.

All of our remaining projects were fired in one of the large oven-type kilns, which were inside, in a kiln room. Different types of glazes were required for that type of firing, which were truer to the color shown on the glaze bottles.

I made a bell pepper that was bigger than a pumpkin, with variations of greens and black. I made a highly symbolic bust that depicted my personality, trying to mimic a veined gray marble; and, I made an Old English cottage, with brown, gray, yellow, white and green colors giving it a realistic look.

I got A's for all those projects, with my final grade also an A, primarily because the teacher saw how much effort and enjoyment I got from the class. Regardless of how artistic my projects were – and the other classmates would remark about my work, along with the teacher – the reward went far beyond grades and recognition from others. I felt so much personal enjoyment that I never wanted my Hand Molding class to end.

I remember more about that one art class than I remember learning from almost all other classes I took in college. I was emotionally moved by that experience.

I tell you this story now because this Advent season we should all see how we are like raw, unshaped clay. We are all like twenty-five-pound bags of river clay, sold in pottery stores as raw material waiting for caring hands to mold into something functional … something remarkable … and something beautiful.

Therefore, when I read Zephaniah say, "Sing aloud, O daughter Zion … Rejoice and exult with all your heart!" those words remind me of my experience with hand molding.

You see, "Zion" means "Dry Place" and "Very Dry," with another meaning seen as "Fortress." This aspect of drying relates to a finished state of pottery, where if a master potter makes a flawed piece that is dried and gets fired, it cannot be reshaped so the flaws get corrected. Thus, we read it said, "[God] will break them with a rod of iron; [God] will dash them to pieces like pottery." (Psalm 2:9)

We are meant to be kept moist, like clay, such that our emotions towards our religion keep us pliable. From that state of faith, we are also meant to be shaped by the hand of the master potter, who is Jesus Christ. The hands controlled by the Christ Mind are our own, but the Holy Spirit moves them so the finished project is each of us being molded into another Jesus.

When that project is assigned and when we respond with a desire to see beautiful changes come upon our raw states, we "sing aloud" and "rejoice and exult with all our hearts" because "the king of Israel, the LORD, is in our midst. When we have received the Holy Spirit, our own "hands" begin molding us into shape, as we follow the insights of the Mind of Christ.

We then act and see the unexpected results that we never thought were possible from our hands. From human beings going through the motions of basic requirements, always seeking the easy way … the "crip course" of life … we take a new delight in doing more and seeing what else is still to come.

We enter into a personal Advent when we want to see ourselves do more. We want to see more beautiful results.

When Paul wrote to the Philippians, saying, "The Lord is near," he meant "the LORD, your God, is in your midst." So, what if you have no experience making pottery projects? "Do not worry about anything," Paul said.

Making one's self into a project for Jesus Christ brings about "the peace of God." What you do not know is moot. The Mind of Christ feeds your brain in ways that "surpasses all understanding." Just by **doing** … **ACTING** … "your hearts and your minds" are duplicating that of Jesus Christ.

In the Gospel reading, it is easy to picture John the Baptist standing in the River Jordan, with a line of people on the shore waiting their turn to be baptized with water. I can imagine him standing on a rock that is under the water, for stability and balance. Perhaps, near where the people wait to wade out to John is where the master potters would find river clay.

When John said, "God is able from these stones to raise up children to Abraham," he was referring to the hard earth that had long dried as rock. Water flowed over stones. John stood on sand and stone rubbed smooth by the water's flow. However, John saw the "vipers" as lifeless, like a stone.

Rock can be quarried and cut into blocks for building temples, or it can be chiseled and smoothed into monuments as "Very Dry" reminders of what was; but it is lifeless. Stone cannot be molded and formed into purposeful vessels.

The "vipers" who John saw waiting to be baptized were (according to Matthew) Pharisees and Sadducees. They were supposed to be molded by the hand of God, as useful tools that would serve the people, showing others how to also become clay in the hands of God.

Thus, when John told the people he was not the Messiah they hoped for, because there would come one who "will baptize you with the Holy Spirit and fire," he was saying, "all I am doing is spraying moisture on you to keep you from drying out and becoming too hard to become shaped as God wishes."

Jesus would come to be the model of a perfectly shaped

piece of fine china, made by God, and from that form would all others be made. While still pliable clay, once in hands moved by the Mind of Christ, one could take that same form and transform new clay into another righteous servant to God. Perfection being consistently reproduced over and over.

Then, when one has shown to be without blemish AND "Very Dry," as a "Zion" made by God, **then** one can be glazed by the Holy Spirit and fired by Christ. One becomes a "Fortress" for God and Christ, as a vessel that is no longer shaped by external influences. It becomes one that is capable of being filled with the wine of Christ, as a holy chalice from which others can drink.

Just as the Jesus used the analogy of a winnowing fork being used to separate the grain from the chaff, done on the threshing floor of a granary, the same effort goes into changing raw clay into a useful container, with the glazing and firing done in the potter's shop. The raw state of clay is refined into usefulness.

We cannot claim to be saved because of the works and deeds of others before us. Just as John called out the pretenders who claimed, "We have Abraham as our ancestor," we have no right to claim favor as descendants of Jesus Christ. We must produce our own works.

My hand molding teacher gave me a C for my Raku ashtray, even though it had remarkable colors. I got a passing grade because I turned in a finished project; but she knew how little work I had put into that project. I got an A for the course because I did more than the minimum from then on; and, God, likewise, knows our works and our heart's desires.

Being an ancestor of Abraham is like spending five minutes to make a crappy ashtray. Being an heir of Christ is like losing all sense of time in a potter's workshop, because you feel God holding the clay with your hands, while talking to you like a loving Father. An heir to Christ longs to start another project, never wanting the fun and reward to stop.

The Advent message is today telling us that there is "one who is more powerful than I coming," and that none of us blocks of river clay are "worthy to untie the thong of his sandals." There is work shaping still to do … but the work will be fun and all worries will be lifted away.

Christianity is a "crip course" in the sense that everyone can make an A grade, but only **IF** Christians can see the beauty of early results and then take delight in doing more.

Amen

Advent Sermons: Third Sunday of Advent, Year C

Fourth Sunday of Advent

YEAR C

December 20, 2015

Relevant readings:
Micah 5:2-5a
Canticle 15
  or Canticle 3
  or Psalm 80:1-7
Hebrews 10:5-10
Luke 1:39-55

The birth of a son who will be called Jesus

Here we are on the fourth Sunday of Advent. All four candles are lit on the Advent wreath and we are five days away from Christmas.

Anticipation is officially high now.

Today, we read the Song of Mary Magnificat, which she sang to Elizabeth. It is a song that came to her from the Holy Spirit's presence within her.

We read the first line of that song as saying, "My soul **magnifies** the Lord," where that translation is the New International Version, found in Luke 1:46. In Canticle 15 [and in Canticle 3], the words sung are presented differently, as "My soul proclaims the greatness of the Lord."

In the Greek words written, "***Megalynei** hē psychē mou ton Kyrion*," the literal translation says, "Magnifies the soul of me the Lord."

Again, realizing that Mary had burst into song while visiting her pregnant cousin Elizabeth, due to the Holy Spirit, Mary was singing words placed in her mouth by God. While the words she would sing did present God as "Mighty" and "holy," the purest intent of the words written is not read aloud.

What she said, in essence, was, "I have a soul as a living, breathing human being ["the soul of me"]; but my soul is now on a much higher level, because of God ["The Lord Magnifies the soul of me"]."

Mary had a magnified soul because of the Lord … not because a sixteen-year-old Jewish girl wanted to please anyone or make herself seem special in the eyes of others.

Thus, thinking delightful thoughts … like those I used to think as Christmas neared and anticipation made my little heart beat rapidly … did not make Mary suddenly "proclaim the greatness of the Lord." Her exclamation was not because of a <u>momentary</u> uplifting of emotional spirit, brought on by anxious thoughts.

Still, Mary did nothing out of the ordinary. The Holy Spirit of the Lord did everything that became unique to Mary, the mother of Christ.

Based on what Luke wrote [not read today] of the angel Gabriel appearing before Mary, telling her she would become pregnant with a baby to be named Jesus, we now see that she "set out and went with haste" to see Elizabeth. If put in Mary's place, the "ordinary" thing for a young girl to do is seek some reassurance of mature themes … to find someone who could confirm that she had not just dreamed a wild dream.

Instead of visions of sugar plums dancing in her head, Mary was told she would conceive a child and her cousin would also give birth. Such wild thoughts of anticipation for a virgin girl **and** a barren relative said to be pregnant too!

Gabriel told Mary that her cousin Elizabeth was six months pregnant, at an old age; presumably well beyond the "ordinary" years of childbearing. Could that be another miracle birth, like Sarah conceiving Isaac? Certainly, Elizabeth being pregnant would be proof of an angel's visit, because no one would ever expect an old woman to be with child.

Mary did not even get a chance to ask Elizabeth anything after she said, "Hello Elizabeth, it is I, Mary, your cousin."

Advent Sermons: Fourth Sunday of Advent, Year C

Elizabeth did all the talking … until Mary began singing.

Now in the part of the story not read, where Gabriel visited Mary, the angel told her, "You will conceive and give birth to a son." When we read, "<u>In those days</u> Mary set out and went with haste," one can imagine how some time passed after that holy apparition occurred. However, the words written by Luke paint a better picture of how the visit by Gabriel did take place in a dream Mary had.

When you see that possibility, the literal translation says, "Having risen up next, Mary, in the daylight hours after this dream, went into the hill country with haste to a town of Judah." From that reading, one can see how Mary was immediately affected by the dream and its **vivid reality**, to the point that as soon as she woke up she had to go visit Elizabeth … at least to tell her what she had dreamed … because Elizabeth had no children, as a barren wife.

So, the dream might have been meant for Elizabeth to know too. Mary would have wanted to share that news of knowing that miracle, as well as telling Elizabeth what was going to happen to her.

When we see how Elizabeth immediately knew Mary was "with child," Mary's pregnancy began sometime between the dreaming of her sleep and getting to Elizabeth's house after the sun had risen. There was no time for any "hanky-panky" in between.

This miracle birth becomes the primary focus of these readings and the Song of Mary Magnificat, which in Latin says "Mary the Glorified." The Advent of Christ had been presented to Mary, the would-be mother, who was a virgin girl. Mary experienced a sudden need to share her Good News.

Mary sang out to Elizabeth, "Surely, from now on all generations will call me blessed; for the Mighty One has done great things for me, and holy is his name."

Mary was blessed because she had Jesus growing within her womb. God, the Mighty One, had placed Jesus within Mary as a great changing event in her life. The change in her, more than a miracle fetus beginning to grow at the hand of God, was accompanied by the presence of God's Holy Spirit surrounding her, enveloping her soul.

That Holy Spirit spread from Mary to Elizabeth. We read, "When Elizabeth heard Mary's greeting, [baby John] leaped in her womb. And Elizabeth was filled with the Holy Spirit" too.

Ladies and gentlemen, boys and girls, we are called today to become Mary. The Advent of Christ within Mary becomes a reminder for us that the Advent season calls to us like Gabriel appearing in a dream, sent by God.

We are called to become pregnant with holiness, to have our souls **magnified** to a righteous level. We are called to **feel** the beginning of ourselves slowly transforming into the maturity of Jesus's ministry. We are called to **leap** with joy at the nearness of that gift, which God offers all His faithful priests.

The prophet Micah sang, while also in a state of spiritual movement by the Holy Spirit, "Therefore he shall give them up until the time when she who is in labor has brought forth." That means God lets us do as we please, to be "given up" to our own decisions about worldly matters, until we individually become pregnant with <u>desire</u> to marry God and submit **all** of ourselves to His will. Submission unto God allows one to receive the spirit, as a holy pregnancy.

Giving birth to a reborn Jesus does not come without some pains, as any mother will tell you. "Labor" is not a walk in the park. However, what "labor has brought forth" makes **all** the pain be worthwhile.

Thus, Mary sang, "[God] has looked with favor on the lowliness of his servant."

We must come to the dawning that the universe does not revolve around us. It is the ego that makes it seem that way. To have God "look with favor" upon us, we have to recognize our "lowliness" before God and commit our whole being to God, as "his servant."

This is the only sacrifice that attracts God's blessings. In Paul's epistle to the Hebrew-speaking Jews of Rome he reminded them of Jesus, quoting Psalm 40:6-7, which said God was not pleased by the ritual burning of animal flesh.

Jesus said, "These are offered according to the law," as reminders that sins need to be atoned, by God. Atonement is to be meted individually, and not *en masse*, through public ceremonies and collective feasts. Neither the killing of animals or the releasing of goats into the wilderness does anything to get God's attention.

Burnt offerings or sin offering are designed to get **your** attention. Every year **you** need a wake-up call to get right with the Lord. Or, as some wryly say, "Have a 'come to Jesus' meeting."

Jesus added, according to Paul, "See, I have come to do **your** will." He did not come to do God's will, but **yours** and **mine**. Jesus came to be the sacrificial lamb for **all** those individuals who, for so long, were too weak-minded to make themselves sacrifices unto the Lord. They lacked the **will** to atone for their own sins, so Jesus had to come to do it for them.

Paul said, "[Jesus] abolishes the first in order to establish the second."

We, of course, think that means the law in the **Old** Testament has been eliminated by the birth of Jesus, so no more animal sacrifices are required. Being favored by God is no longer just for the Jews, as Jesus came to allow Gentiles into the club called "The Children of God."

All that legal stuff has long since been replaced by the **New** teachings of Jesus Christ. We Christians do not have to memorize all 613 of the laws of Moses. The outdated laws can assuredly be tossed away, some **do** think.

However, that misses the point of our call to be impregnated with Jesus within **us**.

The reminder of scheduled recognitions – which now includes Advent and Christmas – is that they represent the **first** demands of God. The **first** assumes that we see the reasoning behind the laws and move beyond external orders that force us to comply with God's will, or face punishments. The **second** step is then to own the law, to have it

Advent Sermons: Fourth Sunday of Advent, Year C

be a part of our being, so we <u>desire</u> to comply with God's will, where the only punishment is the loss of self-ego.

Jesus was sent so we can have an "aha moment": Ooooohhhh!

We have to do both: one and then two. That means doing part two assumes the first part has already been secured!

That means it is not our schemes to avoid the law that gets us to heaven, but "by God's will that we have been sanctified through the offering of the body."

That "offering" means **OUR BODIES, INDIVIDUALLY**.

Through sacrifice of self we can become "the body of Jesus," through the advocating of Christ. That transformation only takes place "once," lasting forever. Thus, "all" must duplicate this two-step process, as Jesus demonstrated for us.

When we see the need to prepare ourselves as sacrifices before God, we can get the feel of that anticipation by singing the Song of Mary Magnificat.

Glory to the Father, and to the Son (within us), and to the Holy Spirit: as it was in the beginning, is now, and will be forever.

Amen

Christmas

YEAR C

First Sunday after Christmas

YEAR C

December 27, 2015

Relevant readings:
Isaiah 61:10-62:3
Psalm 147 or 147:13-21
Galatians 3:23-25; 4:4-7
John 1:1-18

My true love gave to me two turtle doves

Merry Christmas everyone! I hope there were lots of presents under your tree and happiness abounds.

Christmas Sermons: First Sunday after Christmas, Year C

This is the season of giving and the giving does not stop with Christmas Day. It begins then, as we are asked to open daily presents during the Twelve Days of Christmas. The first day of Christmas was Christmas Day!

<singing> On the first day of Christmas (Friday) my true love gave to me …

<motion to the bus stop bench for responses>

<singing again> A partridge in a pear tree!

Right!

Saturday was the second day of Christmas, so …

<singing once more> On the second day of Christmas my true love gave to me ... **two** ... **turtle doves**.

<applaud> Great!

Today is the third day of Christmas, so …

<still singing> On the third day of Christmas my true love gave to me ... three French hens.

We will stop there and talk about the gifts that come after Christmas, but only up to today … the First Sunday after Christmas.

A partridge in a pear tree symbolizes Jesus Christ. In fact, God is "our true love," who presents us with his son so he can be born **in us** on Christmas Day. Jesus Christ speaks the truth. Jesus Christ comes from the love of God.

Jesus Christ is represented by a partridge because they are known for their willingness to sacrifice their lives while protecting their young. A willing sacrifice brought about the end of Jesus's life, but that symbolizes how **we** must sacrifice our self-egos, in order to save ourselves and receive Christ ... to open up that present of a partridge in a pear tree.

A pear tree symbolizes the tree of life that bears fruit. Some say a pear tree represents "Salvation," which is the greatest gift of all; and, that comes from us becoming the fruit of Christ. We are then the fruit of the tree in which Jesus Christ grows, as Christian pears.

As far as a pair of turtle doves is concerned, it is good to know that was the offering made in sacrifice by Mary, for her purification and the circumcision of baby Jesus. In Luke 2:24 we read, "And to offer a sacrifice in keeping with what is said in the Law of the Lord: "a pair of doves or two young pigeons."" This ritual in the Temple of Jerusalem was done eight days after Mary had given birth to Jesus.

As such, the gift of personal Salvation (being the fruit of Christianity) is followed by the gift that recognizes one's sacrifices for the purification of one's sins. That comes from offering a sacrifice to the LORD ... the sacrifice of ourselves ... after we have given birth to Jesus Christ within us.

Some say that December 26th represents, as the second day of Christmas, the two natures in Jesus: human and divine. Still, others say the number reflects the two Testaments,

Old and New. Likewise, it reflects our two self-choices ... the old me or a new me.

Today's three French hens represent the present of faith, hope and charity. Our choice of sacrifice displays our faith, which gives one hope and leads one to charity towards others.

The number three can also represent Father, Son, and the Holy Spirit - as the Trinity - but that is less a gift and more of a required presence for opening all of the gifts that follow Christmas. It is a presence that separates you from the **you** God calls **you** to be. That takes us back to yesterday and the meaning of our true love's second gift to us. So, let's look at how we need to progress from a personal birth of Christ within us, to a sacrifice of cleansing, in order to gain full benefit of faith, hope and charity.

The second day of Christmas represents the principle of duality. It says that <u>Salvation</u> through Christ is a gift offered to us, but just like a present under the Christmas tree ... if we never open it ... if we do not like it and never use it ... if we stick it in a closet and try to give it away to someone else some other time ... we can lose that gift.

Thus, duality means we are given the choice of <u>remaining human</u> or <u>becoming divine</u>. We are allowed to decide if we prefer the old ways, before God proposed his love for us through His gift of Jesus Christ, or if we would rather "say yes," and take a new path of life.

That choice ... that "say yes" choice ... is the theme of the readings today.

For instance, we read a song of Isaiah that sings:

> "I will greatly **rejoice** in the LORD,
>
> my whole being shall **exult** in my God;
>
> for he has clothed me with the garments of **salvation**,
>
> he has covered me with the robe of **righteousness**,
>
> as a **bridegroom** decks himself with a garland,
>
> and as a **bride** adorns herself with her jewels."

Isaiah said "Yes!" He said that at a time when the people of Judah had said the opposite, losing their land, being taken as slaves into exile, and then returning to raise an empty idol of remembrance.

Isaiah rejoiced because he was given Salvation and chose to be married to God … to be purified of his unrighteous past … and to become a pear on the Tree of Life (as garland). Isaiah became the fruit of the LORD, bearing seeds (as jewels) through which others would likewise be reborn.

In David's song of praise, he metaphorically sang of the works of God, through His children. They are the ones who say, "Yes!" to the gift of life.

When he sang, "The Lord rebuilds Jerusalem, he gathers the exiles of Israel," this is meant to mean more than the buildings of a city, in a land of hills and valleys. Cities and terrain are like organs in a body: they must have **life** to be more than just relics in a corpse.

Christmas Sermons: First Sunday after Christmas, Year C

God gives the gift of **eternal life** through His Son, Jesus Christ. Through that Son being reborn in us, we become <u>another partridge</u> on the pear tree … reborn with the Christ Mind ... <u>another pear</u> like all those before and after. We are saved so God can give salvation to others. We continue the gifts of Christmas as God's children.

"He heals the brokenhearted and binds up their wounds," sang David. We are rebuilt with eternal life, because we choose not to die as uncommitted mortals.

Thus, we sing along, "The LORD has pleasure in those who fear him, in those who await his gracious favor."

Merry Christmas! I hope you love His gift of Jesus Christ!

When we read Paul's words to the Christians of Galatia, saying: "Therefore the law was our disciplinarian until Christ came, so that we might be justified by faith," we see the gift of Jesus Christ within us being how we incorporate the duality of the human and the divine, as well as the Old Testament and the New Testament. Sacrifice is founded in faith, but then faith is compounded through hope.

What was external, as a text that judged us as sinners, just as a biological father punishes his children for not doing as told, Jesus Christ within becomes the gift of the law being written in our hearts. Our choice to receive the Spirit makes us compliant with our faith, voluntarily. We act new, based on the internalization of that faith. We can then house the divine in a human body, just as Jesus did.

We become reborn Jesus's. We are redeemed under the

law. We are received as adoptive children of God … brothers and sisters of Jesus … all becoming the outward reflection of Christ, in new bodies.

Thus, with God in our hearts … with the law written on the walls of the chambers that regularly pumps so our bodies are filled with life blood ... we cry out, "Father!"

We are no longer slaves to sin, but children of God, as reborn Sons of God (regardless of what mortal gender our body says we are).

This brings us to John's Gospel, where the first line sums the duality of the second day of Christmas up perfectly.

On Christmas Day Jesus is reborn within us. The first day of Christmas is the beginning of a new us. Through the Holy Spirit we receive Christ. Like the transformation of the disciples to Apostles on the Day of Pentecost, we have tongues of fire settle within us.

<u>In the beginning comes the Word</u>. We begin speaking in the tongues of truth, which we had never known before.

This power to speak in tongues does not come alone, as a single unit of human brain power. No, it comes joining the human **with the divine**, once we have received the Holy Spirit of God.

The Word we speak is then because we are <u>with God,</u> and God is with us.

When we realize the Word is not our thoughts, but those spoken through us, then comes the ultimate dawning that

Christmas Sermons: First Sunday after Christmas, Year C

the source of the Word is God.

The Word is God.

God speaks through our mouths. That is the gift of two turtle doves. We sacrifice ourselves so God can use our bodies - the duality of presence within and without. God takes what only has death (as a mortal) and gives it life (heaven beyond death).

John wrote in his Gospel, "There was a man sent from God." He added, "He came as a witness to testify to the light, so that all might believe through him."

"John," whom John the gospel writer named, means, "YAHWEH is Gracious" or "The LORD Graciously Gave." Thus, **all** witnesses who testify to the light do "so that all we might believe" and gleefully open up the gift of Jesus Christ, which **is** the gift of two turtle doves.

In the story of Mary, told in the Gospel of Luke, we read how she and Joseph purchased two turtle doves for her purification ritual <u>and</u> to present baby Jesus to the priest to be circumcised. That purification ritual took place on the eighth day after his birth. The presentation in the Temple of a firstborn male [called the *pidyon haben*] must be thirty days after birth (unless that is a Sabbath, then the thirty-first day).

But, more importantly than two living creatures being offered in ritual sacrifice to God, as instruments cleansing one of the "sins" of childbirth, the two **true** turtle doves were human beings that Mary remembered.

Luke recounted two witnesses that Mary and Joseph met. One was named Simeon (a man of Jerusalem) and the other Anna (a widow prophet from the tribe of Asher).

They both witnessed to the parents of Jesus, in what I would smile and say were spiritually synchronistic events. They were both filled with the Holy Spirit; and they both presented to Mary and Joseph **the Word**. Mary told Luke of the sacrifices Simeon and Anna had made in their lives, which had them both in the Temple, waiting for Jesus to come and give them fulfillment, knowing that Jerusalem and Israel would find Salvation.

Remember me saying that David wrote, "The LORD rebuilds Jerusalem; he gathers the exiles of Israel"? That is a duality, just as are Simeon (male) and Anna (female). They are another pair of turtle dove given by the LORD.

When you can see this (and I recommend you read Luke 1:21-38 to meet Simeon and Anna again), I want you to look at how John wrote, "He was in the world, and the world came into being through him; yet the world did not know him."

Can you read those words and see how on Christmas Day Jesus Christ was born in you, such that it is you who is presently "in the world" and you who had previously lived to serve yourself, "in the world" of you?

Can you **know** that "He will come again in glory" means in you and Jesus Christ has been reborn in countless Apostles ever since ... with none of them being recognized as Jesus of Nazareth?

Christmas Sermons: First Sunday after Christmas, Year C

The world does not know him. Only individuals filled with the Holy Spirit **know** that presence.

What do **you** want for Christmas little child?

Can you read those words and realize that Jesus Christ, as a spiritual presence from the Holy Spirit, is offering to come into a worldly being through **you** … just as Christ came into being through baby Jesus?

And, can you understand from reading those words **why** the world did not know Jesus Christ, because he was reborn looking like **you**?

Once you see and hear the witnesses speaking **the Word**, you change so that "your own people will not accept" **you** as having "become a child of God, who was born, not of blood or of the will of the flesh or of your own will of man, but of God"?

The Word still becomes flesh and lives among us, through the resurrection of Christ in all of his Apostles.

When one is a **true** Apostle, one has "seen the glory, the glory as of a father's only son, full of grace and truth." There is only one son, but the same one son is given by God to those who seek salvation. Ask and you shall receive.

That is the "true love" of the Father, who on the first day of Christmas gives to us the opportunity of joining the Tree of Life, by accepting God into our hearts and Christ in our minds, with us each becoming a newborn baby Jesus.

On the second day of Christmas we testify to **the Word**.

On the third day of Christmas we see how **the Word** spreads faith, hope and charity from our mouths to others.

In the beginning was **the Word** - Our Father ... Faith -

and **the Word** was with God - The Son ... Hope -

and **the Word** was God - The Holy Spirit ... Charity.

Between now and next Sunday, we are to open a new gift of God each day, seeing daily how our faith, hope and charity grows ... up to the tenth day of Christmas and the gift of ten lords a-leaping: "the Ten Commandments." The gifts of days four, five, six, seven, eight, nine and ten are all wrapped up, hanging from the pear tree of Salvation, waiting for us to unwrap them, one at a time.

Take a look at the symbolic meaning of the Twelve Days of Christmas over the next week and listen to what **the Word** has to say to you about their meaning in your life. How do they testify towards making your choice more heartfelt?

Maybe you can witness for us next Sunday.

Amen

Christmas Sermons: First Sunday after Christmas, Year C

Second Sunday after Christmas

YEAR C

January 3, 2016

Relevant readings:
Jeremiah 31:7-14
Psalm 84 or 84:1-8
Ephesians 1:3-6,15-19a
Matthew 2:13-15,19-23
  or Luke 2:41-52
  or Matthew 2:1-12

Born to take a leap of faith

<singing> hmmmmmmm On the tenth day of Christmas my true love gave to me … ten lords a-leaping.

So far, we have already received:

Nine ladies dancing,

Eight maids a-milking,

Seven swans a-swimming,

Six geese a-laying,

Five golden rings,

Four calling birds,

Three French hens,

Two turtle doves,

And a partridge in a pear tree.

Those symbolize:

The nine fruits of the Holy Spirit – Charity, Joy, Peace, Patience [Forbearance], Goodness [Kindness], Mildness, Fidelity, Modesty, Continency [Chastity].

The eight beatitudes – the blessing of Jesus' Sermon on the Mount for: the poor in spirit, mourners, the meek, those hungering and thirsting for righteousness, the merciful, the pure of heart, the peacemakers, and those persecuted for being righteous.

The seven gifts of the Holy Spirit - Prophesy, Serving, Teaching, Exhortation, Contribution, Leadership, and Mercy.

The six days of Creation, where work is required six days each week, in order to deserve rest on the Sabbath.

The five books of the Torah, which lay out the map from blissful ignorance, to lost purpose, to being chosen and shown the way to the Promised Land of Salvation.

The four Gospels that become the four cornerstones from which a square and true temple to the Lord can be built.

The trinity of faith, hope and love.

The duality of two testaments, where what is Old is first required, before a New covenant can be added.

And Jesus, the one who sacrificed himself so we could receive him and be saved.

All gifts come from our **true love** – God and begin when Jesus is reborn within us on our personal Christmas Day.

Today's gift – the ten lords a-leaping – represent the Ten Commandments. While those are the first ten of six hundred thirteen total laws passed down by God through Moses, all laws are for God's **priests**. Others can call them the foundations for their civil laws, but the laws of Moses represent a contract between God and those who will truly be His children.

Today the gift is a "diploma" dressed as a stone tablet,

etched by the finger of God. It surpasses any document produced by all seminaries (and governments) and gives you a degree to practice the ministry of Jesus Christ.

Over the next two days we will open the gifts of eleven pipers piping (the eleven faithful Apostles), and the twelve drummers drumming (the twelve points of the Apostle's Creed).

All of these gifts are all preparing us for a personal Epiphany.

More than a Christian feast of celebration for the visit of the Magi, recognizing the divine nature of Jesus to Gentiles, we must each have "a revelatory manifestation of a divine being" **suddenly** come upon us. That makes it possible for us **individually** to experience "sudden insight or intuitive understanding" – the true definitions of "epiphany."

Two weeks back, we read about Mary going to see Elizabeth because she had been told by Gabriel that she would have a son who was to be called Jesus. Her delivery of baby Jesus symbolizes the beginning of worldly growth and development of God's presence - an outward sign of inner grace for all to share. When Mary went to see Elizabeth, she was preparing for that worldly appearance, while Jesus was developing in her womb.

The birth of baby Jesus then demonstrates how something inside our being … as a newborn **priest to the One God** … cannot forever stay in the safety of self. We must enter the world and affect others. As a reborn baby Jesus, embarking on the path of a new way of living our lives, God knows we will need His help. That help is reflected in the gifts unwrapped during the twelve days of Christmas.

Epiphany is then when we are born as a new adult Jesus; but to reach that point of preparedness, we must first learn to trust that the spirit within will always be true to our needs, for fulfilling God's work. We have to go through a <u>labor</u> of love presenting ourselves as did young Jesus.

Jeremiah wrote in his song read today, "Among them the blind and the lame, those with child and those in labor, together." He sang of all who truly serve the LORD.

The blind and lame represent those who are virgins to the Holy Spirit, as everyone is crippled spiritually before losing that virginity. People need to be led by God's priests to have their own personal Christmas Day. As our new lives in that holy priesthood go along, we may find resistance, ridicule, and testing, as well as support and encouragement. That is the labor of faith that is required to have a personal Epiphany … when we meet others like us and then bring others into our ranks.

When David wrote his song of happiness and praise to the LORD, he pointed out some stages of that development. They can be seen as parallel to the gifts of God during the twelve days of Christmas.

"How dear to me is your dwelling, O LORD of hosts!" David exclaimed. We should do the same rejoicing on Christmas Day. We must feel the happiness of the LORD dwelling within our bodies.

David sang how he was, "longing for the courts of the

Christmas Sermons: Second Sunday after Christmas, Year C

LORD," where those courts can be seen as the four chambers of the heart, lined with the Laws of Moses and the four Gospels.

David also used a bird theme, paralleling the partridge, turtle doves, hens and calling birds of the twelve days of Christmas, saying "The sparrow has found her a house." Our body is the house. The sparrow is the Christ spirit.

Just as Mary AND Elizabeth shouted with glee about their new state of being with child, David sang, "Happy are they who dwell in your house!" We must feel that **JOY** of the twelve days of Christmas.

<singing loudly> **Joy** to the World, the Lord is come!

Let earth **receive** her King;

Let every **heart** prepare Him room,

And Heaven and nature **sing**.

When heaven is seated in one's natural body, then one cannot keep from singing!

Paul wrote to tell us how God "destined us for adoption as his children through Jesus Christ." That means our receipt of the Christ mind makes us just like Jesus; but for a while we will not quite be ready to minister as a saint. Through that adopted state, we take steps towards that advanced condition of life experience, by demonstrating the strength of our faith, our promoting hope and our extending charity to those in need.

When Paul wrote, "I pray that the God of our Lord Jesus Christ, the Father of glory, may give you a <u>spirit of wisdom and revelation</u> as you come to know him," this is a talent given by the master for his servant to grow and magnify. The gifts of wisdom and revelation are those coming during the twelve days of Christmas.

Now there are three possible reading from the Gospels today … two of which are from Matthew's chapter two and one from Luke's. The Matthew readings focus on events before and after the Magi gave their **gifts** to baby Jesus. The Luke reading focuses on an event when Jesus was a twelve-year-old boy.

Regardless of which reading one chooses, they all show how fear overcomes people, making them consider doing the wrong things. However, those who put their trust in the LORD are protected.

Herod feared the birth of a king that would threaten his power and control.

Joseph was afraid that Herod Archelaus – the son of Herod the Great and the initial ruler of Judea after his father's death – would still be a danger to baby Jesus.

Mary and Joseph were afraid they had lost boy Jesus in Jerusalem, in the confusion after the Passover festival had ended.

An angel of the Lord appeared to Joseph three times, warning him to take his family to Egypt, advising him to return to the land of Israel, and then warning him to bypass Judea and move to Galilee. God protected His servant Joseph.

Christmas Sermons: Second Sunday after Christmas, Year C

The wise men were warned in a dream not to return to Herod, but to take another route home. Again, God protected His servants.

Boy Jesus was found safe in the temple, sitting with the rabbis … protected by the Lord.

On this second Sunday after Christmas, the gift we must hold onto the most is trust. Once we are reborn as baby Jesus, we enter the realm of a new world … just like when all babies are born. We come out kicking and screaming … but there can be no return to the warmth and comfort we knew before.

In a practice of divination called the "Sacred Tarot," there are seventy-eight cards of different suits and importance. Each card symbolically depicts one of the multiple events of normal life, with those most important events in a separate class of cards, called the "Major Arcana."

There are Twenty-two cards in the Major Arcana, with twenty-one having some numerical value, from one to twenty-one. One lone card has a value of zero. It acts much like an Ace in a regular deck of playing cards, where it can be played as either a one or an eleven, such that the zero has no value or it has the highest value, as twenty-two. That Tarot card is named "The Fool."

The symbolism of The Fool card is that of a boy exiting a cave, in mid-step on a rocky ledge outside the cave's entrance. He has one foot on solid ground and the other suspended over the edge of a cliff. He has a happy little dog bounding along with him, with both boy and dog looking up at the sky above. They cannot see they are the edge of danger, appearing quite ready to walk off into a great abyss.

As a card of zero value, The Fool card depicts the foolish steps people take in their lives, which significantly change their lives for the worse. They failed to look ahead. They did not watch their step. They dove headlong into disaster.

Still, as a twenty-two valued card, The Fool represents complete faith in God, knowing that the cave [a symbol of the mother's womb] no longer holds any purpose in their future life development. They look to God for protection and every step they take is a leap of faith. Whatever pitfalls lie ahead, an angel will be there to soften their falls.

I tell you this because many of our major life events are forks in the road where we took the wrong path. We have experienced more zero valued, foolish life changing events, than we have demonstrated our faith in God. The history of zeroes leads us to be overly cautious and even fearful … paranoid.

We cannot be fearful and become a reflection of Herod, trying to kill that spirit of faith and trust, thinking it threatens one's livelihood, position, and stability. Fear of change makes one act as did Herod, justifying a decision to abort that growing child within, because Herod reflects saving self above all others.

Instead, we must take a leap of faith and go where God's protective hand moves us to go. The wise men traveled west, well before the time of a significant birth, so they could be at the right place, at the right time, to give thanks. They did not wait until Jesus was born to embark upon their journey.

Joseph always was led to move one step before those who would try to catch him. The foolish rulers who would try to stand against prophecy would die or become banished. By the time twelve years had passed, Jerusalem was a safe place for Joseph, Mary and Jesus to pilgrimage during holy days.

On that day Mary recalled to Luke, remembering when they finally found the boy Jesus, he asked his parents, "Why were you searching for me? Did you not know that I must be in my Father's house?"

Think about how a boy of twelve years was speaking from a firm position of trust and confidence. Luke wrote that Jesus was "sitting among the teachers, listening to them and asking them questions." How was it possible that such a young child had that level of effect on learned men? How could it be that they "who heard [Jesus] were amazed at his understanding and his answers"?

Jesus was not preaching down at the rabbis, as if he had spent twelve years 'learning a thing or two'. Neither was he sitting obediently and being told what to memorize, quietly, like it or leave it.

No, he was **listening** to what the holy leaders said, and then he was **questioning** their meaning and their understanding of what they professed to know. After he heard them speak confusion, Jesus was then **teaching** the teachers about what they had missed and what they saw incompletely or incorrectly.

When you have that level of trust that you have no need to search for any answers outside the Father's house, nor worry over how you should accept half-truths and falsehoods as "Gospel," you open your mouth and let the Holy Spirit speak up. Trust in the Lord means you can go about being the newest copy of Jesus born into this world, sitting with those who share your love of God. In company like that it is easy to **listen**, **question**, and let God **speak** through you.

God will "give you a spirit of wisdom and revelation as you come to know him."

With the new *Star Wars* movie out and once again drawing huge crowds, let me use a line from that series' original script … "Use the force." The "force" is God's Holy Spirit, which appears to us in dreams and speaks to us like an angel of the Lord. The call of Obi-Wan was to trust and have faith.

We are called to do the exact same thing, because that is how one acts without any fear, with complete trust in the Lord. We cannot sit on that rocky ledge forever. We can't re-enter our mother's womb, so the only way to go is over the edge, to places we have never gone before.

The key symbol of The Fool card is the boy looking up to the sky. That symbolizes prayer, which is how we initiate our conversations with God. God answers those prayers.

A few weeks back I told you about my return to complete my college degree, when I was forty years of age. I told you I took on a second job, in order to provide for my family. My previous main job had become a weekend job (by plan), with my new main job being a school bus driver for the county. It was only 25 hours a week, but it qualified as full-time; so I could get healthcare through the county, at a significant savings from what I had been paying. I had it all planned out and the plan fell perfectly into place.

Still … **a school bus driver**!!! That was a job for wives and old people, not a forty-year-old white American male!

To tell you the truth, I was embarrassed to tell anyone who asked me, "What do you do for a living," that I drove a school bus for the county. I was afraid someone would eventually ask that question.

I prayed to God for guidance: "God, please tell me if I am doing the right thing by completely changing my life, jeopardizing my family's security, going back to school at an age when I should be making the most money of my adult life." "**PLEASE** send me a sign," I pleaded.

After I had been driving a school but for about a month, I made an appointment with a doctor to get prescriptions filled, since my county insurance would not begin before a few months on the job. I went into the doctor's waiting room, signed in and then picked up a sports magazine, as much to protect my face from any passing germs that might be in the air than to keep up with the latest sporting news from three months past.

There was only one other person in the waiting room, and he was far away, on the other end of the room from where I sat. But then that person got up and walked past me, going to ask the receptionist a whispered question. I held the magazine up to my face, only a couple of inches away; but I would be able to tell when the man had gone back to his seat. Then I planned to lower the magazine.

His question to the receptionist answered, the sliding glass window closed. The man began walking back to his seat ... but ... his motion then stopped right in front of me. "What?" I asked myself privately, "Did he drop something?"

I slowly lowered the magazine to find an elderly, yet fit, white-haired man standing slightly bent over to me, looking at me … smiling. He asked if we could talk, and after I said, "Okay," he sat down in the chair to my left, on the other side of the small table that held the old magazines that was beside my chair.

Rather than tell you everything that the man and I conversed about, just let me tell you he asked **that** question, "What do you do for a living?" I sheepishly told him, "I drive a school bus." He smiled and said that he did the same thing once ... when he was about forty ... back when he changed jobs and went back to school to get his college degree ... to provide a better life for his family. Plus, he said, "My next door-neighbor drives a school bus now. He parks his in the yard" of their rural property.

That man even knew some of my family relatives and bits of their history I did not know. He gave me a very warm glow as he talked to me, because I knew as I listened to him talk that God was answering my prayer. The man then leaned in close to me and said, "You are making the right decision. You will thank yourself for doing it years from now."

I was so happy! I wanted to invite him home and have

him tell my wife what he had just told me. But then the nurse called my name and it was time to see the doctor. By the time I was done, the man was no longer in the waiting room.

Some call that serendipity, some call it synchronicity; but whatever it is called, it was an angel of the Lord coming to tell me what to do.

It was a gift that had nothing to do with me being born as a new baby Jesus, in need of special talents that a new priest would need; but it sent me down the path that led me to where my life has needed to be now ... writing sermons about being The Fool.

I was assured that God can be trusted.

Today's gift under the tree of life for new priests is ten lords a-leaping. They represent the Ten Commandments, which are the agreement we make with God that shape the parameters of our worldly being.

Tomorrow's gift is that of eleven pipers piping, who represent the faithful disciples that transformed into Apostles. A new priest of God is asked to go beyond faithful discipleship and receive that same calling and make that same commitment as did Jesus.

Tuesday's gift will be twelve drummers drumming, which represent the twelve points of the Apostles Creed:

> 1. I believe in God, the Father almighty, creator of heaven and earth.

2. I believe in Jesus Christ, God's only Son, our Lord,

3. who was conceived by the Holy Spirit, born of the Virgin Mary,

4. suffered under Pontius Pilate, was crucified, died, and was buried;

5. he descended into hell. On the third day he rose again;

6. he ascended into heaven, he is seated at the right hand of the Father,

7. and he will come to judge the living and the dead.

8. I believe in the Holy Spirit,

9. the holy catholic Church, the communion of saints,

10. the forgiveness of sins,

11. the resurrection of the body,

12. and the life everlasting.

Can you see the progression in those twelve points of faith?

Can you see how they are similar to the progression we find in the gifts given during these holy days of Christmas?

Your true love has **His** hand out to you. God is who **gives** during Christmas, not us. For us to give, we must be prepared and pass some laborious tests. For now, all you have to do is receive His Spirit … trusting that wherever you go and whatever you do, you will be safe and protected.

Amen

Epiphany

YEAR C

First Sunday after the Epiphany

YEAR C

January 10, 2016

Relevant readings:
Isaiah 43:1-7
Psalm 29
Acts 8:14-17
Luke 3:15-17, 21-22

Baptized by the Holy Spirit and fire

I hope everyone had a memorable Epiphany this past Wednesday.

I also hope it meant more to you than "time to take down

Epiphany Sermons: First Sunday after the Epiphany, Year C

the Christmas decorations!"

It should mean more because we have now entered into the church's part of the calendar that is between the birth of Jesus and the time when he went into the wilderness for forty days – the period that we call Lent.

Epiphany means more than getting fat on king cake before we decide what one sinful thing we will give up for the same number of days as Jesus sacrificed. We totally miss the point that the **only** <u>one</u> thing that matters is <u>our sinful self</u>. Give that up!

In that vein of thought, the central theme this week is baptism, where we all have to get clean before we can serve God. In that regard, there is a clear difference stated in the Epistle and Gospel readings, between baptism by water and baptism by the Holy Spirit.

One is physical.

The other is spiritual, with the spiritual <u>baptism</u> having much greater value.

One of the <u>less clear</u> aspects in the readings (which I feel are important to point out) is how physical baptism needs to be in holy water, not normal shower or tub-filled tap water.

Another aspect worth realizing is that spiritual baptism needs to be done alone. There is nobody that can make us serve God.

In the first verse of Isaiah's song we are told, "this is what the Lord says — he who created you, Jacob, he who formed you, Israel: "Do not fear, for I have redeemed you; I have summoned you by name; you are mine."

We miss the point, when we read of a creation by the LORD, which is then later formed by the LORD. That means we are born into physical bodies, but we must be shaped into righteousness.

Just as "Jacob" is a name that recalls the reality of "holding the heel" of a twin at birth, we are created to be "supplanted" (another meaning of "Jacob"), to take the place of (definition of "to supplant") a higher destiny.

We are created to become one who is truly deserving of a birthright from God. That requires God's redemption and a ceremonious renaming.

That means we must **change** to receive that birthright. That change comes via a willingness to receive the Holy Spirit. Still, that is easier said than done.

We must wrestle with an angel and become Israel, "formed, crafted, fashioned, and ordained" to become a body made by the LORD, which transforms into a temple where "God strives" … the meaning of "Israel."

Epiphany is about that "sudden manifestation of the divine" within **one**, where that one experiences that which had never before been known to **one**. Epiphany is revelation, insight, and intuitive understanding. Epiphany is that point between having been born a mortal human being in this world and when one is forever **changed** into a faithful servant of the LORD

Epiphany Sermons: First Sunday after the Epiphany, Year C

While not one of the readings today, I am reminded of the story from 2nd Kings, where Naaman is cured of his leprosy. He was healed because he followed Elisha's instructions to bathe seven times in the Jordan River.

We read today from the Gospel of Luke how John baptized in the Jordan River; but we do not ordinarily see how John chose that water source because of its healing <u>history</u> ... a history related to a Gentile's skin lesions being cured in its waters.

To Jews, imperfections like leprosy were signs of sins, as God's punishment for what one had done wrong. Visible marks were believed to be from the divine, pointing out the sinners.

Because the Jews of John's and Jesus's time were lost **<u>spiritually</u>**, they felt like they had an invisible leprosy covering them. Their lost way was like a mark of blindness, a lesion of vision that needed to be washed away in the holy waters of the Jordan. They believed it was best cured by a holy wild-man named John the Baptizer, who might be their Messiah or another Elisha-like prophet.

The Jews lined up on the shore waiting for their turn. The guilt of sin made them do it. The guilt of sin made them **want** to be clean.

We are no different today. As Christians we wear the guilt of sin. We confess our sins in church, faithfully, <u>each and every</u> Sunday. Therefore, we incorporate baptism into our lives, as part of our religious faith.

Baptism by water is a common ritual that connects all

Christian denominations; although baptism rituals do differ. Episcopalians most often see baptism done to babies, where a priest pours blessed water from a baptismal font over the baby's head.

Some denominations have robed pastors walking into industrially manufactured and installed baptismal pools, like a walk-in tub. There they dunk robed children and adults … I presume in water that has been blessed by prayer.

Some preachers, in some churches, still lead their congregations out to a nearby stream or river, where ceremonial robes are worn by the preacher and those who wade out into the water. Like John and the Jews, one gets dunked in the muddy waters of one's home land. I imagine a prayer blesses those waters before such events.

Physical water in large rivers is holy water in many ways, as water is a necessity for mortal life – plant and animal. Remember, Naaman commented (after being told to bathe in the Jordan River), "Are not Abana and Pharpar, the rivers of Damascus, better than all the waters of Israel? Couldn't I wash in them and be cleansed?" (2 Kings 5:12)

I guess, as Forrest Gump's momma might say, physical water can be summed as; "Holy water is as holy people do."

John the Baptizer said, "I baptize you with water; but one who is more powerful than I is coming; I am not worthy to untie the thong of his sandals. He will baptize you with the Holy Spirit and fire."

We <u>assume</u> John was referring to Jesus; but then Jesus let John baptize him and he was still like all the other Jews who were baptized by John. It was **afterwards**, while Jesus was praying, that he was baptized with the Holy Spirit.

The symbolism of that is <u>people</u> pour physical water over <u>people</u>, in the physical realm. Someone does it to us; but ask yourself, "Where was Elisha when Naaman's sin fell from his body?" Ask, "Where was the one who is more powerful" than John, who he said "will come after"?

When the Holy Spirit descended from heaven upon Jesus, "in bodily form like a dove," was it Jesus filling himself with the Holy Spirit?

No. God is the one more powerful who baptizes in the Holy Spirit and winnows the grain from the chaff. God is the one who brings fire and burns the sinners ... not Jesus.

Jesus was just a holy man like John, until he became the Son of God, through the Holy Spirit remaining upon him, when God said, "You are my **son**; with you I am well pleased."

Elisha sent a messenger to meet Naaman, basically telling him, "You have to go and baptize yourself. Do it seven times." There was no holy man present in the waters of the River Jordan when Naaman's own acts washed away his sin.

Elisha touched Naaman via a message - the Word of instruction - to get him to act for his own good. Elisha was not about to let someone think he (a man) was a cure-all that could be bought or manipulated. Jesus was a teacher, like Elisha ... in that regard.

Remember how God would tell Peter, James and John, atop Mount Hermon, "Listen to him!" God, in essence, said, "Take notes boy, he is giving you important instructions."

Naaman went back to see Elisha after he was cured, telling him, "Now I know that there is no God in all the world except in Israel." (2 Kings 5:15b)

Doing things for yourself will let you know things like that.

Episcopalians say, "We believe in one baptism for the forgiveness of sins." But, ask yourself, "Since when do newborn babies have sin?"

That should be an epiphany for you, if you had not realized that yet. A <u>Christening</u> is not truly a baptism for sin, as much as it is anointing an infant as a promised disciple of Christ.

The **one baptism for the forgiveness of sins** cannot come from a spoonful of holy water, just as it cannot be given by the touch of a magic wand. When we read in Acts that Peter and John were going to help in Samaria and lay hands on those seeking the Holy Spirit, their hands passed on instructions ... the Word.

John the Baptist baptized Jesus, along with all the others who went to the Jordan River that day; but what sins did Jesus have to be washed away? Why did he stand in line with the others?

As far as we know from the Biblical record, Jesus was like a baby being anointed by John, as a disciple of Christ ... the coming Messiah.

Epiphany Sermons: First Sunday after the Epiphany, Year C

It is actually more important to see how Jesus was <u>praying</u> after he had been ceremoniously anointed with all the others?

It was prayer that led to the heaven opening and the Holy Spirit descending upon him in bodily form **like** a dove.

When the famous Day of Pentecost came, after Jesus's Ascension, it is written, "Suddenly a sound like the <u>blowing</u> of a **violent wind** came <u>from heaven</u> and filled the whole house where they were sitting. They saw what seemed to be **tongues of fire** that separated and came to rest on each of them. All of them were <u>filled with the Holy Spirit</u> and began to speak in other tongues as the Spirit enabled them."

In that scene, we do not quite see the same image as that of a dove gently forming to Jesus's body. Still, both versions match how Isaiah wrote that God would **form** Israel upon one's body.

"Do not fear, for I have redeemed you," God said. "I have called you by name, you are mine." Together, you and I, we will "Strive for God" … the meaning of "Israel.

Maybe the difference between "in bodily form like a dove" and "like a blowing of a violent wind" bringing what seemed to be "tongues of fire" is an indication of how much sin just got washed away by the Holy Spirit?

Jesus just a little sin? The disciples significantly more past mistakes wiped clean?

Jesus was practically sin-free; but still he prayed for forgiveness **after** ceremoniously being anointed as ready for God's service. Thus, the Father said, "With you I am well pleased."

"**With you**" means I have molded you to strive for God, so we can be one together.

This "with you" epiphany makes it possible to see how Jesus could die, be resurrected, and then go sit in heaven at the right hand of the Father, where he advocates for Christians, so the Father's Holy Spirit can be "with you" too.

That is how the disciples, created in bodies, were **formed** into Saints. God was one "**with them**," individually. So, the Book of Acts tells us the stories of how Jesus was duplicated in the first Apostles. The same stories apply to each of us.

Today we read a short excerpt from Acts chapter eight, where we see Peter and John of Zebedee going to Samaria to help Philip lay hands on newly baptized-with-water Christians. They went to lay their hands on those who likewise wanted to receive the Holy Spirit.

The laying on of hands is known to be one of the healing abilities of the Holy Spirit, as stated by Paul, of which this gift is given to <u>some</u> Apostles.

Reading how "Peter and John laid hands on them," it reminded me of the movie *The Resurrection*, starring Ellen Burstyn (1980). She was nominated for an Oscar for her performance in that movie, although few saw it in theaters then.

Epiphany Sermons: First Sunday after the Epiphany, Year C

In my research of that movie, I came across a short interview that Ellen Burstyn gave, about how she came to be in that movie. She said she was first contacted about reading for the lead role in a movie "about a woman dying and coming back as Jesus."

After some major revisions to the original script, the movie **changed** to a powerfully inspiring movie. The film showed how a woman was crippled in a car accident, in which her husband was killed, and in which she too had died. She visited the "afterlife" (a "near death experience"), before returning as a paraplegic.

The character's name is Edna, whose recovery had her moving back to live with her parents in rural Kansas; and, in her slow progress to managed health, she found out she an ability to heal others. That was a talent she had never had before.

She could lay her hands-on people with illnesses and heal them ... well, about seventy percent of them. Not all people were healed by her touch.

Being able to lay hands upon people became a forced religious side-show, and her inability to heal everyone caused her to be seen, by some, as a fake. Those pressures caused her to run away from her talent; but eventually, she realized it was more important to use her talent discretely. She had an epiphany that her abilities came from one more powerful than she, for more powerful purposeful than her "pay grade" was able to understand.

She began secretly touching the lives of others, so others would **feel** the power of God within themselves, giving them the courage to die forgiven, or have the strength to let God heal them for a higher goal to achieve.

It dawned on me that being washed of sin makes one so happy, one wants to go make others clean also. Unfortunately, the epiphany of cleansing does not make one yet ready to go out and "heal the world."

After all, you do have to die first … in ego … and be reborn as Jesus.

Trying to become a traveling medicine show, as Jesus, without a personal Lent first only brings failures that cause one to run and hide. After being Christened with the light of Christ, too often we hide it under a barrel.

Time spent reflecting on what God has in His plans for us is where we need to see how Jesus was **praying** after John baptized him. It is the aging process, the gaining of experience that brings wisdom, where we know it is **not** about us being healed, but about having others receive the Holy Spirit through us.

In the Olympics they call that "passing the torch." We are not the flame, but we bear it. Our touch allows another torch to be lit.

If having some person touch you is all it takes to stay filled with the Holy Spirit, then it is right to treat all Christians as babies. All anyone will ever need is to have someone lovingly hold them and gently pour warm water over their foreheads. It is just like bath time.

"Would you hand me one of my tub toys now … please?"

we ask the priest, pastor, minister or preacher, after we are Christened or baptized with water.

If the Samaritan converts to Christianity were so many that Philip needed help filling them with the Holy Spirit, then why didn't John the Baptizer just quit and say, "This is impossible. I've got no one else to help me here."?

Peter and James went to lay hands on people so the Holy Spirit would prove to them how important it is for **themselves** to desire it and for themselves to do **everything** possible to keep it after they got it.

Philip, Peter and John of Zebedee were not more powerful than John the Baptist and they were not more powerful than Jesus. They were torches needing to be lit. They were created with physical names, but they were formed as purposeful ... by God's fire.

The Apostles of Acts 8 went to do like Edna (the character in *The Resurrection*) did, after she realized the Holy Spirit does not come upon people to make them circus performers. It comes upon them so they can privately touch people with their hands AND open them up to receiving the Spirit. Then, one can only leave it up to the one who is truly more powerful than all – God - to take it from there.

The Holy Spirit is freely given, but only by God. To receive that gift, you must earn it. Then, it is wholly up to you to maintain it, by passing it on.

When you have been touched by one who is evidence that God does reside **with** His faithful, then you can be **with God** too. Once the Holy Spirit is strongly in control of one's being … then the real work begins.

Then, you **have** to share its presence; and you cannot do that by sitting on your hands.

Amen

Epiphany Sermons: First Sunday after the Epiphany, Year C

Second Sunday after the Epiphany

YEAR C

January 17, 2016

Relevant readings:
Isaiah 62:1-5
Psalm 36:5-10
1 Corinthians 12:1-11
John 2:1-11

The miracle of new wine in Cana

Not too long ago, my wife's daughter got married. It was my wife and her ex-husband who arranged the wedding dinner.

After the buffet food was quickly scooped up and taken back to a table seat, the younger guests soon found their way to the bar.

It seems a good wedding celebration requires that EVERYONE lose their inhibitions and have fun. Fun is easier to come by when one is drunk.

Now in that wedding I attended, the parents of the bride planned for wine and beer to be the alcoholic drinks that would be provided to the guests. However, the younger crowd wanted to show how well they could handle hard liquor, so they began running up a bar tab.

The daughter's father was quite surprised how much more the wedding dinner was going to cost, because of that allowance. It was a hard bullet to bite, but it is only money and everyone had fun.

When we read the stories in the Holy Bible, we often do not take the time to relate common events then with common events now. We tend to think we are different than those old dusty characters, so what we read can become a simplistic view of the past. We can think what was written captures all of what those ancient people did.

The wedding at Cana was more than we read. It was just like **all** wedding events throughout all time. Family and friends of the couple are invited to witness two lovers be joined in marriage, and then everyone sings, dances, and celebrates wildly.

All weddings are the same, regardless of how different they seem. Then, as now, it is a celebration where intended wildness is assisted by fermented drink.

This means my wife's daughter's wedding was (for all intent and purposes) EXACTLY like the wedding in Cana … except for the miracle.

It would have been a minor miracle if the young people had drunk the wine that had been planned for them to drink, rather than have them stampede like wildebeests to the watering hole, as if they had just survived a long drought. It would have been a miracle for skinny young boys and girls to eat lots of the buffet food, rather than leave most of it to be eaten by grandparents and parents. I guess they were saving room for booze.

Perhaps, my wife and her ex could have hired one of those stage hypnotists, who influence people to do crazy things. Maybe he could have convinced everyone that the table wine was shots of bourbon, or vodka, or gin? I imagine trying to make them think the water or iced tea was alcoholic would be impossible.

I know that I – for one – read about the miracle of Jesus changing the water into wine and see THAT as the totality of the miracle. Water, of no value (as far as getting one drunk is concerned), is changed into a beverage that makes one loosey-goosey (and costs anywhere from $6 to $20 a bottle at a shop selling spirits).

Think about it. The wedding party was going to come to a crashing halt if there was no more free wine to pass around. All the celebration over a marriage would be finished, if there were no more alcoholic beverage to be served.

Imagine someone announcing to the crowd, "Excuse me folk, but for the rest of the evening we will be serving well water, because we are out of wine. But, please, the band will play until midnight, so everyone HAVE FUN!"

Can you hear the moans and groans? Can you hear the whispers, "It's time to go"?

It was a miracle that Jesus saved the party.

But, is **that** truly the point of reading about the "first of his signs," as John put it?

Was it the miraculous transformation of water into wine that led John to write, "in Cana of Galilee … [was] (**his glory revealed**) … [so] his disciples believed in him"?

Personally, being one who prefers water or tea to alcoholic beverages, I might not have noticed the miracle had I been there.

Therefore, I think there is more to it than that. After all, John told us that the servants knew they were drawing a cup of river or well water for the chief steward to taste. The servants were not allowed to get drunk, so they were stone-cold sober when the steward announced, "Everyone serves the good wine first, and then the inferior wine after the guests have become drunk. But you have kept the good wine until now."

"Huh? Um, sir … that is freshly drawn water … no grapes have been added yet. Do you want to taste that again?" the servants must have thought.

The miracle was not about changing water into wine, but the effect that the water had on people: **believing** it was "good wine."

To me, good wine has a unpleasing taste, one which requires patience to drink. Only after I have consumed a couple of glasses of good wine, when the alcohol kicks in, does the unpleasing taste suddenly gets easier to handle. But that is me; and I was raised in a church that served Welch's grape juice for Communion. Talk about a thought that makes my cheeks draw in ....

To wine drinkers, there is still an expectation of an "alcohol taste," but not a vinegar-like taste. That is why the steward said standard practice was to serve the least unpleasing wine first, so after everyone is drunk you can open up the wines that are more sour and bitter. By then all the taste buds have given up on judging taste.

On the other hand, water is a drink that tastes sweet, even though it technically has no taste at all. Water is the most refreshing drink of all, but it is not alcoholic. Water meets all you need, but you have to provide your own entertainment. And, you never have to "acquire a taste" for water. Water **IS** the best drink, because water sustains life.

Now, think about this. At dinner functions it is common to find bottles of red and white wine on each table, so the diners can serve themselves. But, imagine you are Jewish and you know full well what large stone purification tubs are, and for what purpose they serve. Imagine you have to go to the outhouse to relive yourself after a few cups of wine and while on the way there you see servants filling up empty stone jars from a water-filled purification pot. You see the waiters filling containers that are then going to be set on the table for people to serve themselves.

Those water "pots" or "jars" were each capable of holding five to six gallons, so they were large and possibly ceremoniously marked.

You (being Jewish) know what the purification water is used for; but regardless of it being clean water, how would you feel after seeing that? It is not a place for aging fine wine.

It would be like using a bathtub to store wine.

Bathtubs often have rings around them because baths cause dirt and oil to come off our skin, in the process of bathing. If the water pots were "standing" in the proper place, then there would be a large tub to pour the water into, which a woman would ritually cleanse herself. Jewish purification tubs [*mikvah*] were mostly used by adult women, but also by men who developed skin lesions (leprosy).

In other words, a ritual cleansing tub has to be cleaned <u>well</u> after use, so it can be ready to be used again. While one would like to think the Cana wedding event had <u>clean</u> purification vessels ready, think about how drunk you would have to be to drink wine out of a vessel associated with the likes of that.

But the chief steward called that purification water "good wine."

If you remember last Sunday, when we saw John the Baptizer dip Jesus and others into the Jordan River, they were all baptized by water. The word "*baptizó*" means "to submerge, to immerse or dip under." John prophesied that one would come after him, who would baptize with the Holy Spirit. That means one who would submerge drunken egos, so the Mind of Christ could surface.

The fulfillment of that prophecy is the **true miracle** of the wedding of Cana. Everyone was baptized by water touched by the Holy Spirit. God was in the water the chief steward tasted, and he tasted how God is **always** "good wine." So, when the steward was **moved by the Holy Spirit** to explain, "Everyone serves the good wine first," this is saying how the Jews had been faithful servants of God … at first.

After they have become drunk with delusions about just how loosey-goosey they can get with their religion, they begin drinking the wine of inferior gods – those who say the bitterness of sin is now less distasteful, so drink all you want.

That statement by the chief steward acts as explaining why the same drunken party-goers would line up regularly at the Jordan River the next day (the morning after), to be baptized by John. Just as women regularly had to purify themselves prior to them being allowed back in the synagogue, the Jewish commitment to God was like eighteen days of being faithful, followed by twelve days of being repentant for having not really been faithful before.

BUT, the miracle of Cana was that Jesus waited until after all the wine had run out and everyone was reveling in the drunkenness of a marriage celebration BEFORE he served them the sweet taste of redemption. Redemption would be the "good wine" that Jesus would three years later tell his disciples, "This is my blood, the blood of a new covenant. Whenever you drink this do so in remembrance of me."

Now, if you see the wedding theme in both the readings from Isaiah and the psalm of David, as making good fits with the story of the wedding at Cana, you have to understand that is not co-inky-dink.

People filled with the Holy Spirit set these readings up long ago, for the purpose of us being able to connect the dots countless years later. The lectionary is put together with higher thought than casual choice. It does require faith and discipline to make all the connections come to life, but it can be done ... when one is willing to spend a good twelve hours devoted to one's religion ... on the day God set aside for BEING HOLY.

I have pointed this out before, as far as the sermons throughout Year B Pentecost went, as the lessons made it clear to me how we are all called to become <u>brides of Christ</u>. We are supposed to be <u>married to God</u>. We are supposed to give birth to a reborn <u>baby Jesus</u> ... **<u>AS US</u>** ... as a result of that union.

The same message applies today.

Isaiah wrote, "**You** shall be a crown of beauty in the hand of the LORD, and a royal diadem in the hand of **your** God. **You** shall no more be termed Forsaken, and your land shall no more be termed Desolate."

He continued his prophetic song singing, "For as a young man marries a young woman, so shall **your** builder **<u>marry you</u>**, and as the bridegroom rejoices over the bride, **so shall your God** rejoice over **you**."

YOU … regardless of you sex …shall **marry your builder** … God the Creator.

Thus, everyone sitting at this bus stop today and forever more is **like a woman**, in need of regular ritualistic cleansing; **BUT** …if **you** marry God all that ceases to be needed.

God – the "good wine" – rejoices over your marriage to Him. The purification pots are no longer needed! Fill them to the brim with GOOD WINE!!!

In David's song he sang, "They feast upon the abundance of your house; you give them drink from the river of your delights. For with you is the well of life, and in your light we see light. Continue your loving-kindness to those who know you, and your favor to those who are true of heart."

Praise the Lord! You married God!

This is just like the wedding celebration in Cana. The guests – all Jews – feasted on the abundance of God. They were given drink from the well by the Son of God. The water became the "good wine" of the LORD, as from the source of eternal life. The recognition of the best wine coming out last shows God's loving-kindness towards his faithful. His "favor to those who are true of heart" is God's gifts to His brides … those to be married to God.

That brings up the epistle of Paul to the Christians of Corinth. It is focused on the gifts of God, which is more of that "good wine."

One of the rituals of a wedding is the newlyweds opening the gifts that have been given to them. Gifts are a common element of a marriage and the celebration of a union.

The gifts of the Holy Spirit are given by God to all His new wives. Again, let me stress that "wife" does **not** mean only human females, but all who submit to God and all who commit to serve God and only God, now and forever.

The epiphany of today's readings is to get drunk with the Holy Spirit's love for God. We are **not** called to be guests at someone else's wedding party, where all we have to do is show up and get free food and booze.

That kind of lifestyle only leads to the morning after, when we line up at the river to be washed clean of our sins … once again. We get so used to needing regular purification that we build stone jars to immerse ourselves in. <u>We sit in one right now</u>.

The first miracle that showed **the glory of God in Jesus** was he baptized those at a wedding party in the Holy Spirit and they didn't even know it.

Just like the pilgrims who encountered Peter and the other Apostles on the Day of Pentecost, the chief steward thought the servants had brought **new wine** … not wine aged to perfection (the good stuff). The disciples who followed John the Baptist (who were at the wedding in Cana too) they saw this miracle of wine … it was wine so new it had never seen a grape … **as a baptism**. Instead of water poured over the skin of people, it was <u>new wine placed inside new skins</u>.

They believed in Jesus. Maybe they knew it then, or maybe they realized it later; but the **believed**.

It was then not yet <u>the hour</u> that Jesus was to begin his ministry and his legacy of miracles and healing. But it was time to clear the way towards that goal.

As part of that path, Jesus is calling now ... to be born within us, but at the <u>right hour</u>. Now, it is time for us to drink the good wine of God's redemption, to rejoice and celebrate in the baptism of our engagement. Soon we are to be God's newest wife.

We should long for the kiss between one true of heart and her lover ... a kiss as sweet as good wine.

You and that partridge sitting in a pear tree ...

K ... I ... S ... S ... I ... N ... G.

First comes **love**. Then comes **marriage**. Then comes baby Jesus in **us** ... his baby carriage.

Amen

Third Sunday after the Epiphany

YEAR C

January 24, 2016

Relevant readings:
Nehemiah 8:1-3, 5-6,
 and 8-10
Psalm 19
1 Corinthians 12:12-31a
Luke 4:14-21

Many members in the One Body of Christ

Recently, the Primates of the Anglican Communion voted to suspend the Episcopal Church U.S.A. from having any influence in rule changes and law restructuring for the global Church, for three years. After that period of suspension, a review and follow-up vote will determine if the two churches become permanently split.

At the core of this issue is the spread of influence that the Episcopal Church has allowed (if not supported and urged on), towards members seeking gay rights. This largely focuses on the blessing of same sex marriages, but that issue is a result of homosexuals having been elevated into positions of authority, leading the acceptance of changes to that end, with sights set on the global community being forced by ritual dogma being rewritten to bless the sin of adultery.

Adults commit sins of a sexual nature. Mosaic Law states:

> Do not have sexual relations with a man as one does with a woman; that is detestable. (Leviticus 18:22, NIV)

> If a man has sexual relations with a man as one does with a woman, both of them have done what is detestable. They are to be put to death; their blood will be on their own heads. (Leviticus 20:13, NIV)

To be "put to death" is open to interpretation, but it projects an outcome that is quite different than welcoming homosexuals to be the head of one's religious organization.

That becomes a perfect background for the readings today, in particular what Paul wrote in his first letter to the Christians of Corinth. While not overtly stated, it can be read as if Paul said, "This defines our Church!" A Christian Church is "one body" with members serving different roles, "**all** made to drink of one Spirit" and "**all** baptized into one body."

The "one body" that **IS** the Church **OF CHRIST** – and not any institution that serves any god other than Yahweh, **OUR LORD** – is not a <u>new religion</u>, replacing that first given by God to the Israelites, through Moses. It has **the SAME** laws, with the caveat being One Mind through which the laws are <u>understood</u>.

That One Mind comes from the wisdom of the Holy Spirit, as seen in the body of Jesus of Nazareth, who was the Christ, and the human Son of God. We must **ALL** share that One Mind and be reborn into that body ... all Christians in him and him in all Christians.

Many people think (so it seems) this is an easy transformation. However, it is not easy at all.

Since Moses first led the Israelites out of Egypt and into the Sinai wilderness – **NOTHING** has changed!

The modern Christian churches [all those that have come since the Church of Rome first took control] continually – just as the Tabernacle-Temple-led Israelites did continually – suffer through starts and sputters. One step forward, followed by two steps backwards.

Thus, we read throughout the Old Testament how there would be forty years of compliance to the laws, followed by forty years of straying. During the straying periods, things would get so bad – so many would be persecuted and killed – that someone would cry out to the LORD for Salvation – adding, "Please forgive us for thinking it was okay to do (<u>fill in the blank</u>)."

Epiphany Sermons: Third Sunday after the Epiphany, Year C

Sin ... Atone ... Sin again. (Repeat)

The people would place all their trust in one mortal leader, rather than each being a member of one Spiritual body, all controlled by the Mind of God. When the mortal leader dies, all hell breaks loose.

We are in one of those periods **NOW**, where we casually sit about thinking it is okay to do whatever makes us happy, expecting the Church to condone it, accept it, forgive it, and then bless all our sins away. Our faith is not in God, but in a surrogate of our choosing ... one who preaches in the little church down the lane.

Let me be the first to announce: The Church is **not** a social club that caters to the whims of the membership.

The ones who pay more to the Church are **not** owed special privilege by the Church.

The Church cannot pretend that it can step in for YOU, when YOU die and stand before God for judgment. The Church cannot play Jesus or God. The Church cannot act like a mother hen coddling a brood of sinners.

If and whenever that state of church sets in, such an organization ceases to be a Church **OF CHRIST**.

In the Old Testament reading from Nehemiah, we read: "Accordingly, the priest Ezra brought the law before the assembly, both men and women and all who could hear with understanding." It is important to realize how "all who could hear with understanding" means more than just a gathering of big brained people.

The "law of Moses, which the Lord had given to Israel" is **NOT** easily understood by atheists, agnostics, Communists, or members of religions serving other gods. If having the body part called a brain was all one needed to understand what the Covenant with God requires from one (in return for God's blessings), then the whole world could **WRONGLY** call itself Jews (or Christians).

If reading the books of the Holy Bible is all it takes to gain eternal life, then the promised rewards of God are easy to come by. However, reading and understanding are two different things.

Understanding the law of Moses, as well as ANYTHING written in the Sacred texts of the Holy Bible, requires a deep emotional commitment to God **AND** faith that understanding will come forth via divine inspiration. Understanding is necessary, in order to maintain one's trust in God's Word.

We read, "For all the people **wept** when they heard the words of the law." One does not weep from an intellectual ability to comprehend a written language. One weeps because one has been shown a deeper meaning, one that goes so far beyond the surface meaning of the written words. It is that **deep understanding** that becomes personal proof of the power of God. That depth, being heartfelt, is then enough for one to cry happy tears, for being allowed to see that meaning.

You will notice how Nehemiah does not write about how some of the assembly stood up and objected to the interpretation given by Ezra, Nehemiah and the Levites. No one complained about what was interpreted to the people, which gave them the sense to understand, saying that interpretation offended some of the people who were there. None tried to find a loophole in a law, because it was a law they knew they were breaking (along with others known). They made no attempt to pervert the understanding of the whole gathering.

The Jews of Nehemiah's Second Temple "revival" were those returned from exile, after Judah had lost everything their Covenant with God had provided their ancestors. They lost everything because of those who diluted the law of Moses, to the point of total disregard. They were attempting to regain an understanding like that held by the people in ancient days – before the corruption had set in.

Last week, in the Gospel story of the wedding in Cana, we heard how the chief steward told the bridegroom, "Everyone serves the good wine first, and when people have drunk freely, then the poor wine. But you have kept the good wine until now."

How many of you **understood** how to interpret that so it says, "The Israelites did good <u>to serve God at first</u>, but after they were <u>drunk with the sense of being special</u>, they began to settle for <u>lesser gods</u>"?

The arrival of Jesus has brought out the best wine – God's eternal Salvation for those who drink it. That meaning **IS** there, but it helps if someone with strong vision can assist your faith by exposing that truth to you.

The name Ezra means "Help" or "Strong Vision." Ezra

read the law **and** interpreted it for the people. He represented the body parts that pertained to divine insight, which goes beyond the scope of the organs called eyes.

Still, as we see today, there are those who cannot see that depth of meaning in the "water to wine" miracle. There are many who refuse to understand more than what suits their own needs.

In the psalm of David today, verse seven sings, "The law of the Lord is **perfect** and <u>revives the soul</u>; the testimony of the Lord is sure and <u>gives wisdom to the innocent</u>." When one realizes the Sacred texts are from the <u>perfection of God</u>, one needs to realize the equal need to have a higher MIND for understanding.

A human brain is too flawed to ever expect perfection to come from one ... without Spiritual assistance. This is such common knowledge we have an axiom that says, "The best-laid plans of mice and men often go awry." Mice have pea-sized brains, but size is not the problem.

In verse eight, David continued on singing: "The **statutes** of the Lord are **just** and <u>rejoice the heart</u>; the **commandment** of the Lord is <u>clear</u> and <u>gives light</u> to the eyes." This is the realization that brings tears to one's eyes. It is what makes the heart sing praises to the LORD.

That means, "If you do not like what the law says, then you do not appreciate perfection." If one does **not** seek perfect understanding of why there is One Religion that serves only the One God, then one needs to leave that assembly that is truly One Body in Christ, rather than expect that One Body to become subservient to any member's desires for special acceptance.

In Paul's analogy of a body with parts, it can be thought that all parts are equal, such that all parts have the right to freely express the qualities and characteristics of their part. However, that is far from what Paul is saying.

One Body **MUST** be controlled by One Mind, such that all of the parts are extensions of that Mind, for the purpose of extending that Mind beyond the body. In this way, "there is no dissension within the body," so "the members may have the same care for one another."

This means that when Paul said the "body of Christ" has been appointed by God, that includes all parts and elements: apostles, prophets, teachers, deeds of power, gifts of healing, forms of assistance, forms of leadership, and various kinds of tongues.

Where in that "body of Christ" are those that do nothing of value?

While Paul mentioned, "the members of the body that seem to be weaker are indispensable" and "our less respectable members are treated with greater respect," where did Paul say God appointed certain sinners as necessary parts of the "body of Christ"?

The term "weaker" should be read as "one who **only has one gift** of the Holy Spirit," not all seven.

Weaker does not simply mean those whose physical bodies feature blindness, deafness, lustfulness, selfishness, and diseases and imperfections. It is reference to the elders, whose time on earth is coming to a close; but they still serve God completely..

Who has the power of the Spirit because they love sex more than God?

Think about that ... without trying to play God.

Certainly, there are many bodies that need the light of truth shone upon them, so they can be healed; but healing comes with the demand to remain healed AND join the One Body of God, helping others to likewise be healed.

We read in the Gospels of Jesus's miraculous healing; but nowhere do we read, "And Jesus went up to the blind man and said, "Hey! Didn't I heal you already?"

Healing from the Holy Spirit means one stays healed AND one then becomes a healing member of the "one body of Christ."

The "one body of Christ" is not, will not, and cannot be focused on any one member of that body. **ALL** members follow the will of God, for the purpose of helping others find the light of truth.

Still, one has to understand there are many physical bodies in the world that are dead. They live mortal lives that lead to nothing more than their eventual deaths. The One Body of Christ is ALIVE by the Holy Spirit of God. The purpose of that One Body is to offer Salvation to a world of darkness and sin ... to shine a light by which the lost can be found, so the dead can be reborn.

Epiphany Sermons: Third Sunday after the Epiphany, Year C

No one can be reborn when all that one desires is <u>reinforcement</u> that death is a worthwhile option. Satan provides that support. Because death is a certainty in a mortal world, one that means an eternal soul is continually moved from one mortal prison to another - **Reincarnation**.

For the purpose of "one body in Christ" to be fulfilled, the dead and the living cannot be mixed together. You cannot sew <u>dead members</u> onto the One Living Body, or that One Body becomes less. The One Body reject that dead member.

Jesus said, "It is better for you to lose one part of your body than for your whole body to go into hell." (Matthew 5:30)

It is why Judas Iscariot never became an apostle. A dead member only betrays the one body.

In the Gospel story in Luke today, we read how Jesus was <u>filled with the power of the Spirit</u>. Jesus was like David, Ezra, Nehemiah, and Paul, in the sense that they **all** were capable of interpreting the scrolls, because they all had that power assisting them. That knowledge and wisdom did not come to them from self-generated intelligence.

Unlike the people who assembled at the Water Gate to the wall surrounding the City of David, to hear the law of Moses read to them and interpreted by rabbis; and, unlike the Christian apostles in Corinth, who were encouraged by Paul to understand the binding unity of the Church of Christ, the Jews in the synagogue of Nazareth were **not** "<u>living members</u> of the One Body" that had become known as Judaism.

Jesus entered as a rabbi, dressed in his ceremonial robe. He stood to read and he was handed the scroll that had chapter sixty-one of Isaiah written on it. Jesus read the first verse, and part of the second. Then, he sat down.

He read aloud (partially), "The Spirit of the Lord is on me … to bring good news to the poor. He has sent me to proclaim … the year of the Lord's favor."

The Jews who were gathered in attendance all leaned forward, waiting for the interpretation of the words of Isaiah, the revered prophet of Judah.

Then Jesus said, "Today this scripture has been fulfilled in your hearing."

The translation that says, "**in your hearing**," is better read as, "to your faculty of perception."

In other words, Jesus said, "If you are one gathered who can hear with understanding … if you do have an Israelite's faculty of perceiving interpreted scripture … then you may weep now, from an emotional release based on your faith that the Messiah would indeed be sent by God."

"I am he," is what Jesus said, in essence. "Praise the LORD!" That should be the response of one with true faith, who prays to God and expects divine revelations.

Alas …

What we do not read today is how the people in that synagogue began attacking Jesus, asking, "Is this not Joseph's son?" After an argument ensued, they would try to throw Jesus off a cliff; but Jesus disappeared. Jesus just passed right through them.

Those who have Jesus the Messiah in their midst but do not see HIM as fitting THEIR agenda and THEIR healing needs ... they lose the right to call themselves "Christians." They are better identified as "Christ killers."

The story of Jesus preaching in Nazareth is a reading that shows how the One Body in Christ goes into the midst of the dead. It shines light into darkness. It goes there <u>out of love</u>, **filled with the power of the Spirit**. Still, it shows how the darkness cannot comprehend the light.

Jesus will be seen next week saying, "No prophet is accepted in his hometown," which shows how the darkness ... the **DEAD** ... does not want to join with the living members and understand. It wants to kill the One Living Body.

Therefore, the message is for the light to pass through the darkness, in search of those who **seek the truth**, those who **do have faith**, and those who can **hear with understanding**.

For those who have understanding (after interpretation) and deeper faith in God from being able to hear, those are told, "Go your way, eat the fat and drink sweet wine and send portions of them to those for whom nothing is prepared."

Prepare a way for the dead to find the light, so that they have the opportunity to be reborn.

Amen

Fourth Sunday after the Epiphany

YEAR C

January 31, 2016

Relevant readings:
Jeremiah 1:4-10
Psalm 71:1-6
1 Corinthians 13:1-13
Luke 4:21-30

Hometown prophets and curing oneself

We are now at the fourth Sunday after the Epiphany. Remember what Epiphany means?

Epiphany Sermons: Fourth Sunday after the Epiphany, Year C

We are in our cycle of preparation, baptized by the Holy Spirit and readying our hearts to have our faith tested in the wilderness.

But it is more fun for many Christians to look at this period through the eyes of Carnival, where the fancy floats have all been prepped, decorated, stocked and loaded with people who will be throwing strings of red, yellow, green and purple beads to cheering crowds of people.

Some say the word "Carnival" comes from Late Latin, meaning, "farewell to meat," as a preparatory period before a fast.

"Carnival" brings to my mind a place of flashing lights, a Ferris wheel and cheap thrills, Kewpie dolls and stuffed animals for rings tossed and balls thrown at stacked cans. It means something only in town for a short time, before the big top tents are folded up and the show moves on to another town.

Still, most Christians see Epiphany as a one-day event, with no connection to a season that ends on "Fat Tuesday" … "*Mardi Gras*" … also called "Shrove Tuesday," "Pancake Tuesday," or "Pancake Day." We associate that as the end of an unknown period of time (longer than forty days), when we are allowed to do anything we want (if not expected to test the limits of sins), before we boldly sacrifice **one** vice.

Ten days from now is all the time we have left to act like bears planning for hibernation. We see Carnival as a time to rush to get full of berries, leftover salmon, wayward hikers and/or any and all park pick-a-nick baskets left unattended. In other words, we think surviving Lent is all about over-eating now … satiating all our sinful lusts … ahead of forty days of forcing ourselves to do without.

Doing without **one sin** ... for a whole month and a half! (Praise be to God that February only has 28 days!)

The problem with that view of this time of year is it completely misses the point of Epiphany and the true meaning of the Lenten period.

If you miss those points, then you set yourself up to be just like one of the Jews of Nazareth that tried to throw Jesus over the cliff.

Last week we read that Jesus was filled with the power of the Spirit when he went to Nazareth. Last week and today we recall Jesus reading from the book of the prophet Isaiah and saying, "Today this scripture has been fulfilled in your hearing."

That part, "in your hearing," actually means, "those who also are full of the power of the Spirit, so they can understand."

Jesus had just read Isaiah saying that the promised Messiah would come demonstrating signs: of good news to the poor; proclaiming the release of bondage to worldly sins; to give foresight to those who were blind; and to free those oppressed by dogmatic leaders.

All of that was in the report that preceded Jesus's arrival in Nazareth. For those who were enabled by the power of the Holy Spirit to understand an interpretation of holy scripture

Epiphany Sermons: Fourth Sunday after the Epiphany, Year C

… (according to last week's reading from Nehemiah) … by Jesus's saying, "That's me," that should have led to tears of joy from an assembly of those who could understand.

Instead, the hackles of their necks got stiff.

None of them were filled with the power of understanding. They were the same ole "stiff-necked" bunch that God often sighed over.

The Jews of Nazareth reacted about the same way a Christian congregation (of the Catholic-Episcopal-Methodist persuasion) would react to someone standing in the pulpit saying, "Epiphany is not about partying hardy, free days of debauchery, or eating pancakes until you pop a button. Epiphany is about being filled with the Holy Spirit so you can understand what it is you believe in."

I know some Episcopalians who would have stood up and cheered Jesus's homily, simply because they would have only heard it as short in length. But, to tell an Episcopalian he or she is misunderstanding the purpose of one's religion, then it is when they start asking, "Where's the torch and pitchfork?"

When the argument between Jesus and the Nazarenes had Jesus tell them about how little Elijah had done for the Israelites (of the Northern Kingdom), they became livid.

"How dare you say something negative about the greatest prophet of the ancient days!" they must have shouted.

The scrolls they kept safely in protective racks were, to them, **all** that was holy about Judaism. Because Isaiah had scrolls there, **he** was holy. Because the scrolls (what we know as the books of Kings) told of Elijah, then **Elijah** was holy. **BUT**, there certainly were no scrolls about Joseph of Nazareth and his impish son, who the Jews of Nazareth watched grow up … Jesus.

Jesus said the sixty-first chapter of Isaiah's book told of him and his public record.

Imagine how that would sound TODAY, if someone was to come and sit on this bus stop bench and proclaim, "I am the fulfillment of a Biblical prophecy!"

Would you say, "Alleluia!" Or, would you gather together in small groups and begin a whisper campaign of destruction?

What if God spoke to you and said that EVERY book in the Holy Bible was about YOU? Would you believe God?

Could you become brave enough to walk up to a stranger and say, "I am the Son of Adam"?

Could you proclaim, "I am the one who the prophets Jeremiah and Isaiah foretold"?

Could you say with conviction, "I am the resurrection of Jesus Christ"?

To be able to say such things, they would ALL have to be statements of **truth** and not simply thoughts of possibility; because God **only** speaks truth.

To be able to say such things, YOU would have to be filled

with the power of the Spirit, such that none of the words you uttered were formulated from self-generated thoughts in your brain, willfully spit out of your lips.

You would have to be well aware of the dangers that would rise up, but you would have no concern over what others might try to do to you for speaking the **truth**.

When Jesus told the Jews of Nazareth that he was the Messiah prophesied by Isaiah and that he had already done greater things that the most renown of Israel's prophets had done, Jesus was speaking as a child would speak.

Have you ever watched a child speak before a large audience … when the father has to prompt the child by whispering what to say … then the child obediently says that ... loudly?

Jesus spoke what the Father whispered. Jesus was not the son of Joseph, with Joseph whispering to Jesus. Jesus was the Son of God; and, as Jeremiah wrote in song, "The Lord said to me, "Do not say, "I am only a boy"; for you shall go to all to whom I send you, and you shall speak whatever I command you."

God instructed His Son, "Do not be afraid of them, for I am with you to deliver you." Jeremiah then continued, saying "Now I have put my words in your mouth."

In David's song of praise, he began by stating the essence of being with the power of the Spirit. He sang, "In you, O Lord, have I taken refuge; let me never be ashamed." Thus, when filled with the Holy Spirit you have no fears to keep your mouth quiet.

David then sang, "I have been sustained by you ever since I was born; from my mother's womb you have been my strength; my praise shall be <u>always</u> with you."

David did not write that song as a baby. He wrote it as an adult, one who had come to that dawning, after having been filled with the Holy Spirit.

When Paul wrote in his epistle to the Christians of Corinth, he mentioned his childhood as well. He wrote, "When I was a child, I spoke like a child, I thought like a child, I reasoned like a child; when I became an adult, I put an end to childish ways."

Adulthood does have a way of slapping the child out of us. What was once cute becomes nothing more than a **sign** of immaturity and foolishness, after a certain point in physical development has been reached.

Paul said he put an end to childish ways, but he did not put an end to the core being of a child, which is **love**. Instead, he wrote, "**If** I have prophetic powers, and understand all mysteries and all knowledge, and **if** I have all faith, so as to remove mountains, **but** do <u>not have love</u>, I am **nothing**."

Paul then defined "**love**" as, "Love **is** <u>patient</u>; love **is** <u>kind</u>; love is **not** <u>envious</u> or <u>boastful</u> or <u>arrogant</u> or <u>rude</u>. It does **not** <u>insist</u> on its <u>own way</u>; it is **not** <u>irritable</u> or <u>resentful</u>; it does **not** <u>rejoice in wrongdoing</u>, **but** <u>rejoices in the truth</u>. It <u>bears all things</u>, <u>believes all things</u>, <u>hopes all things</u>, <u>endures all things</u>. **Love never ends**."

This means **love IS God**. Therefore, **if** one can do amazing

Epiphany Sermons: Fourth Sunday after the Epiphany, Year C

things, **but** one is without God, then one is nothing.

Paul wrote, "Faith, hope, and love abide, these three," which means they all patiently wait together in expectation. Paul then said, "The greatest of these is love."

When you realize "love" means God, and God is the most important element in that spiritual compound, then "faith" is the repentance of sins from understanding one's childish wrongs, and "hope" is the promise of redemption from those sins ... as an adult. But, without God, faith and hope are <u>nothing</u>.

Jesus witnessed that <u>lack</u> in the synagogue in Nazareth.

The same condition of lack is present in Christian churches all around the world (certainly in all other denominations). Christianity has become a replication of that failed state of Judaism that Jesus knew.

Therefore, as Paul wrote, "Now we see in the mirror, dimly, but then we will see face to face." We either learn from our past ... or we are doomed to repeat past mistakes.

Jesus has become like Elijah. Both were prophets that ascended into heaven as living human beings. The Jews still expect Elijah will return again, <u>before</u> their Messiah comes. Christians expect Jesus will return again too.

But, wasn't Jesus like Elijah returned ... unrecognized?

Hasn't Jesus since returned countless times after he ascended ... in the Apostles, in Paul, in all who are and have been filled with the power of the Spirit ... those who have been appointed over nations and kingdoms – those of Christendom?

Was Jesus not recognizable in all of those bodies AND was he not unrecognizable when he appeared as the gardener at the tomb ... on the road to Emmaus ... and by the shores of the sea?

Why do we continue to look for external salvation coming from the sky, as if faith and hope is everything ... when without God in our hearts, giving us the power of the Holy Spirit within, making us Jesus reborn to fearlessly speak God's will ... we are nothing?

The season of Epiphany is time to grow up, stand up tall, see how ALL the holy scriptures were written for YOU <u>to understand</u> AND for YOU to go forth and explain and interpret <u>so other will understand</u>.

You must be empowered with **truth** so you can say, "This scripture has been fulfilled in your hearing."

> "Deliver me, my God, from the hand of the wicked, from the clutches of the evildoers and the oppressor. For you are my hope, O Lord God, my confidence since I was young." (Psalm 71:4-5)

> "Fear not, little flock, for it is your Father's good pleasure to give you the kingdom." (Luke 12:32)

Amen

Epiphany Sermons: Fourth Sunday after the Epiphany, Year C

Last Sunday after the Epiphany

YEAR C

February 7, 2016

Relevant readings:
Exodus 34:29-35
Psalm 99
2 Corinthians 3:12-4:2
Luke 9:28-43

Preparing for a forty-day camping trip ... or ... How to put on a glow

We are on the verge of Lent … about to spend forty days of having our faith tested.

Epiphany Sermons: Last Sunday after the Epiphany, Year C

Well, I say that, but often our faith is tested about like Moses' was, when he came down with the original set of tablets, after having spent forty days on top of Mount Horeb (aka Mt. Sinai, but "*horeb*" means "glowing / heat").

All the people Moses thought were holding down the fort at the foot of the mountain, being good Israelites, were dancing and carrying away around an idol of a golden calf they had erected.

So much for the agreement they had with Moses.

Everyone had told Moses, "Sure, go ahead. We will spend forty days here, honoring God and his prophet Moses by not worrying about anything. We fully <u>believe</u> we are in good hands and protected."

A guy named Art Linkletter made famous the phrase, "Kids say the darndest things." Alter that as now so the saying is, "Israelites say the darndest things." Heck, go ahead and amend it to say, "Christians say the darndest things."

Moses was so mad at what he saw that he slammed that first set of tablets down on a rock and broke them into pieces.

Moses' face was not shining bright white like God was with him then, after forty days. Instead, his face was glowing red with anger.

Sometimes we forget, but Moses ordered the Levites to kill all the pretend priests for God who had suggested building that idol of worship. They killed three thousand Israelites that day … because they really did not have what it took to serve God.

One way to look at it is as this: The three thousand Israelites would have died slow deaths from heat, thirst, famine, snake and scorpion bites, if they had just been banished and not allowed to follow Moses and his gang. So, killing them saved them all the pain of slow, sure death.

Perhaps, it was because of Moses having been filled with the Holy Spirit, from spending forty days with God, that **God** caused Moses to break the tablets and kill the unworthy?

<pause>

It might be that this version is a prophetic vision about the future, when the Israelites would themselves be the ones who shattered the tablets. It might be that Moses only spent forty days with God and then delivered the Law whole, unharmed.

I will leave that seed for thought to grow within you. Just let it find a fertile lobe to settle in and leave it alone ... for now.

<pause>

What we read today is after Moses had gone back up the mountain and spent another forty days with God, reproducing the agreement.

The first Covenant was etched by the finger of God and was written on both front and back of the tablets. The second was chiseled by Moses as God dictated, and it was only on

Epiphany Sermons: Last Sunday after the Epiphany, Year C

one side of each tablet.

Ever think that the golden calf caused God to hold back on a few graces and rewards God had written before, the second time? Ever think God determined, "They had a wonderful agreement with the first set of tablets, but they blew it. Now I really need to lay down the law?"

<pause>

When Moses finally got the Israelites to agree to God's terms, they had to tell Moses he was scaring them with his glowing face. They feared, after having seen wrong-doers executed, that at the first mistake they too might be killed by Moses, because Moses' glow was like God watching them.

They made Moses wear a veil so they would not be afraid. They liked **not** being so close to God.

It seems that Moses made a compromise, just to keep from killing most of those would-be priests for God, leaving few remaining at the end of the journey (forty years) to divide and conquer the Promised Land.

Maybe Moses took forty years getting to the Promised Land because he felt like he was Sergeant Carter leading a group of Private Gomer Pyles in that new army of priests for God?

<pause>

When you read what Paul wrote to the Corinthians, you would think he heard the sound of cymbals and tambourines around a golden calf in the background, trying the patience of the new Apostles he had left behind in Corinth.

He wrote, "We act with great boldness, not like Moses, who put a veil over his face to keep the people of Israel gazing at the end of the glory that was being set aside."

Isn't it just like most people, to see the goal as being in hand, well before having done what is necessary to actually achieve that goal? The Israelites loved being chosen by God, but they really didn't care too much about having to do priestly work.

Paul surmised about those people, "Their minds were hardened. Indeed, to this very day, when they hear the reading of the old covenant, that same veil is still there, since only in Christ is it set aside."

Golly gee willikers, can you believe that? There were Israelites whose hearts could not see why they had made an agreement with God, just like there were Jews who could not understand what it was for?

Could that veil thing be why so many Christians have hardened minds about Bible Studies?

That is almost like calling some Christians, those who worshiper **things** of value, **things** that could symbolically be melted down and shaped into a golden calf, people who wear the veils of ignorance.

Some quite proudly, I might add.

Veil wearers don't understand how Moses giving them the

Epiphany Sermons: Last Sunday after the Epiphany, Year C

Law, in exchange for eternal happiness in heaven with God, was a good thing. Many figured all it meant was having to memorize all those laws.

Not just ten commandments, but six hundred thirteen laws. You knew that, right? You could pass a test on listing the first two hundred, right?

<pause>

Memorizing laws is the **simple part**, because one doesn't have to understand why a law exists. People put more effort into devising tricks of memory than they do into understanding **why** they need to remember things in the first place.

However, Paul set the Corinthians straight about what Christians do: "Since it is by God's mercy that we are **engaged in** this ministry, we do not lose **heart**."

Christians are ministers, not royalty inheriting special recognition. Christians are voluntarily Christian, because they love God.

Paul went on, saying "We have renounced the shameful things that one hides; we refuse to practice cunning or to falsify God's word."

Nope. Not us.

We think Christians are allowed to wear our skeletons proudly, while using cunning to get perverseness accepted as a character trait worthy of becoming a high religious leader. We gladly welcome false shepherds to come and make Scripture seem to be approving all lifestyles, saying, "Jesus would forgive skeletons."

Hmmmmmmm

And Jesus told us how to melt our religion down and form idols of Mammon, because Jesus wants all Christians to be rich, is that it?

<pause>

Now in the Gospel setting, Jesus was in the northern city of Caesarea Philippi. There he left all his followers except Peter, James and John (of Zebedee), with the four of them hiking up the tallest mountain in Israel, Mount Hermon.

By that time in Jesus's ministry the disciples were showing flashes of the Holy Spirit. They could do some things. They could preach and heal a little. Peter had even blurted out that he knew Jesus was the Messiah, the Son of the living God.

Of course, I am sure that revelation surprised Peter when he said that; but when the Holy Spirit takes over one's body, one just sits back and watches … with the experience leaving a lasting impression.

Peter believed what he said, after he said it.

So, Peter was on this trip with Jesus; and, hiking up a real high mountain can be exhausting. The oxygen gets thinner at high altitudes. For that reason, Jesus took three disciples with him because they were needed to carry supplies for camping, and maybe ever carry ropes to make sure if anyone fell off a ledge, that disciple could be rescued.

It gets cold at night in the high mountains, even in the summer time. There is a snow pack at some elevations year-round. So, they would be carrying some stuff to pitch tents for a place to sleep overnight.

We read, "Now Peter and his companions were weighed down with sleep," so the story is focused on a time that was after a long hard day of hiking, when it was time to sleep.

Jesus was off alone, praying. The disciples did not want to go to sleep without Jesus in their tent (or in his own tent), so they waited on him to finish his prayers.

Then they saw him begin to glow. Jesus was talking to God, and just like Moses would glow after coming out of the tent of meeting, after talking with God … low and behold there was Moses with Jesus … and Elijah too! All three were glowing brightly in the dim lighting. God must have been nearby!

Peter got so excited, he offered to pitch some more tents so everyone could have a warm place to stay the night; but then a cloud overshadowed him and James and John.

All three disciples were suddenly in the dark and that "terrified" them.

The darkness is when there is no glow, no light, no truth, no God assisting one. But God then spoke, saying, "This is my son, my Chosen: Listen to him!"

<pause>

You have to see the parallel to a golden calf and a tabernacle for a dead prophet as being what Peter had just proposed. Building a tabernacle to a patriarch was idolatry! That was a written Commandment, where a recommendation to sin then led to such a terrifying response by God.

What is in the past will **not** save you, so worshiping anything or anyone other than God will always leave you in the dark and terrified.

Don't do it!

Listen to what Jesus Christ preaches. **Be Jesus** by putting him in your heart.

<pause>

Now after this camping trip was over, the four returned to Caesarea Philippi. There a crowd had gathered to get the disciples who had been left behind to heal them. There was a clamor about a man's son having a demon in him. The disciples did not have that power of healing yet.

Jesus greeted that crowd by saying, "You faithless and perverse generation, how much longer must I be with you and bear with you?"

Does that sound like a little anger … kinda like how Moses might have greeted the crowd of Israelites dancing around the golden calf they had erected?

The people in that crowd all wanted something for nothing. Maybe they called themselves Jews, but they all had on thick veils that blinded them from becoming like the disciples. Their woeful existence was their <u>excuse</u> for not themselves being healed AND them then out healing others. They even had the gall to complain about the disciples not being as good as Jesus.

Jesus then cured a boy of a demon; but what you have to be able to see – by removing the veil from **your** eyes, like Paul said Christians do – is see how the boy was punished by an evil spirit from his past.

Evil spirits from the past are like the karma of a past life still haunting one's soul. The demons Jesus cast out (which the disciples could not do) were done so by him commanding them to **die** … to return to the past, which no longer exists.

Jesus, in essence, forgave a boy in a present life for the sins his soul's body had committed in a past life. The boy was healed through <u>forgiveness</u>. Jesus rebuked the demon for not having sought forgiveness when repentance was first due God.

When Jesus was seen with Elijah and Moses, those were spirits from his past lives. Those spirits were far from evil, just as Jesus was not haunted by past demons. Good spirits accompanied Jesus and encouraged him in his prayers. Jesus had the spirit of the Law and the fulfillment of the spirit of prophecy within him.

Jesus's words still ring true today, however. We **are** a faithless and perverse generation. All generations are and always have been, which is why God chose a lineage that would become His priests who would instill faith and prevent perverted natures.

But we drag our sins around with us like the chains that surrounded the ghost of Marley, when he appeared to warn Ebenezer Scrooge to change or suffer eternally. Like Paul said, our minds are hardened, with veils over our minds when we read these holy passages each Sunday.

We cannot see ourselves as the ones Jesus scolds. We no longer try to go through the motions of renouncing the shameful things that used to be hidden in our closets. Instead, we bring them out and flaunt them!

Televangelists falsify God's word to make a buck. People find it easier to believe in falsified commandments, when lies promise the world to come. People dance and sing around the television (or radio), giving away their cash (gold rings) to worship television idols. All the time their eyes are covered by self-inflicted veils that prevent them from seeing their own sins.

It is just like what Moses saw when he came down from spending forty days in the presence of God, so God could put down in writing everything that a holy person **must do** in order to be considered one of God's chosen.

Jesus was Chosen! We **must** be like Jesus. Nothing else will satisfy God.

<pause>

Those who were deemed unworthy by Moses were eliminated from consideration as Israelites. The three thousand pretenders became like the Egyptian chariot men … all spirits of the past.

Jesus has asked, "How much longer must I be with you and bear with you?" That asks, "When will the Jesus hammer come down on the sinners of the world?"

I imagine more than three thousand will be judged unworthy on that day.

<pause>

This Wednesday is when Lent begins. We have forty days to get our glow on.

Let that time be when we start "proclaiming the greatness of the Lord our God and worship him upon his holy hill; for the Lord our God is the Holy One."

Moses and Elijah were God's holy guides for Jesus.

Jesus is God's true Chosen Son, who will attend to your needs in the wilderness and in ministry.

Listen to him!

Amen

www.ingramcontent.com/pod-product-compliance
Lightning Source LLC
Chambersburg PA
CBHW071950110526
44592CB00012B/1043